D1546892

DUCKWORTH EGYPTOLOGY

Performance and Drama
in
Ancient Egypt

Robyn Gillam

Duckworth

First published in 2005 by
Gerald Duckworth & Co. Ltd.
90-93 Cowcross Street, London EC1M 6BF
Tel: 020 7490 7300
Fax: 020 7490 0080
inquiries@duckworth-publishers.co.uk
www.ducknet.co.uk

A catalogue record for this book is available
from the British Library

ISBN 0 7156 3404 6

Typset by Ray Davies
Printed and bound in Great Britain by
Biddles Ltd, King's Lynn Norfolk

Contents

Preface

This book is intended as an intervention in an ongoing discussion on the relationship of archaeology to performance and seeks to extend this discussion to the arena of Egyptology. In contrast to other contributions to the subject of performance archaeology, this study makes use of texts as well as other materials. It does not, however, examine these texts and materials in detail. Neither does it study specific activities indicated by performance, such as music, dance or ritual gesture. These subjects, as they relate to Egypt, have been exhaustively dealt with elsewhere. The purpose of this work is to suggest a framework in which to talk about performance in ancient Egyptian culture through re-examination and reinterpretation of known materials, many of them already familiar, and to initiate a discussion in this area. It seeks to locate current interest in performance within its own context and also contains a plea for the use of controlled re-enactment, not only as a pedagogical tool but also as an aid to scholarly research.

Acknowledgements

Among the many people who have contributed to the making of this book, I would like to thank the following in particular: Nicholas Reeves and Deborah Blake at Duckworth, for their interest in and encouragement of this project; Stuart Tyson Smith, who facilitated my contact with Julia Sanchez and her symposium 'Creating an Archaeology of Performance', which took place at SAA in Denver of 2002; Julia Sanchez for the invitation to participate in this symposium; Ian Hodder for his support and encouragement of my work and Alessandra Lopez y Royo for the invitation to participate in her session 'Archaeology and Performance' at TAG 2002 in Manchester.

This project would not have been possible but for the efforts of all my Toronto students on the Egypt in the Greek and Roman Mediterranean course in the Humanities Department at York University, from 1998 to the present, and especially my colleague and co-teacher in this course, Paul Swarney, with whom I initially devised the performance assignments and without whose boundless enthusiasm and encouragement they would not have achieved their successful outcomes.

I would like to thank Susan Conolly for permission to use the image of the colonnade at Philae in Chapter 5 and Ania Pienio for permission to reproduce the storyboard in Chapter 6. I owe a particular debt of gratitude to Lynn Holden, who has provided all the line drawings, maps and tables for this book. I would also like to thank my father, Thomas Gillam, for his ongoing and enthusiastic support, as well as the Streetcar Foundation.

Illustrations

Chronological Table with the Names of Kings

All dates are BCE unless otherwise stated.

Dynasty 0, before 3100
    Scorpion
    Narmer (Menes)
Dynasty 1, *c.* 3100-2900
    Den
Dynasty 2, *c.* 2900-2675
    Khasekhemwy

OLD KINGDOM
Dynasty 3, *c.* 2675-2625
    Djoser (Netcherikhet), 2656-2637
Dynasty 4, *c.* 2625-2500
Dynasty 5, *c.* 2500-2350
    Neferirkare, 2581-2561
    Neuserre, 2551-2527
Dynasty 6, *c.* 2350-2170
    Pepy II (Neferkare), 2273-2179
Dynasties 7-10, *c.* 2170-2000

MIDDLE KINGDOM
Dynasty 11, *c.* 2000-1938
    Mentuhotep Nebhepetre
Dynasty 12, *c.* 1938-1759
    Senwosret I (Kheperkare), 1918-1873
    Senwosret III (Khakaure), 1825-1788
Dynasties 13-17, *c.* 1759-1539

NEW KINGDOM
Dynasty 18, 1539-1292
    Amenhotep I, 1514-1493
    Thutmose III, 1479-1425
    Hatshepsut, 1472-1458
    Amenhotep III, 1390-1353
    Akhenaten, 1353-1336
    Tutankhamen, 1332-1322
    Horemheb, 1319-1292

Dynasties 19-20, 1292-1075
  Sety I, 1290-1279
  Ramesses II, 1279-1213
  Ramesses III, 1182-1151
  Ramesses IV, 1151-1145
  Ramesses IX, 1126-1108
Third Intermediate Period, 1075-712
Dynasties 21-22, 1075-717
  Osorkon II, 924-909
Dynasties 23-25, 825-664
  Piye, 750-712
  Shabaka, 712-698
  Taharqa, 690-664
Dynasties 26-29, 664-380
Dynasty 30, 380-343
  Nectanebo I, 380-362
  Nectanebo II, 360-343
Second Persian Period, 343-332
  Alexander, 332-323
  Philip Arrhidaeus, 323-316
  Alexander son of Alexander, 316-304
Ptolemaic Period, 304-30
  Ptolemy I Soter, 304-285
  Ptolemy II Philadelpus, 282-246
  Ptolemy III Euergetes I, 246-222
  Ptolemy IV Philopator, 222-204
  Ptolemy V Epiphanes, 205-180
  Ptolemy VI Philometer, 180-164; 163-45
  Ptolemy VII Neos Philopator, 145
  Ptolemy VIII Euergetes II, 170-163; 145-116
  Cleopatra III & Ptolemy IX Soter II, 116-107; 88-80
  Cleopatra III & Ptolemy X Alexander I, 107-88
  Cleopatra Berenice, 81-80
  Ptolemy XI Alexander II, 80
  Ptolemy XII Neos Dionysos (Auletes), 80-58; 55-51
  Berenice IV, 58-55
  Cleopatra VII Philopator, 57-30
Roman Period, 30 BCE – 313 CE
  Caesar (Augustus), 30 BCE – 14 CE
  Domitian, 81-96 CE
  Hadrian, 117-138 CE
  Antoninus Pius, 138-161 CE
Coptic Period, 313-642 CE

Introduction

Of Archaeologies and Performances

In the opening episode of his TV series *The History of Britain*, Simon Schama takes viewers on a tour of the Neolithic sites of Orkney. As he approaches the great tumulus at Maes Howe and penetrates its interior, Schama describes how the ancient people crawled through the long dark entrance passage before entering the lofty burial chamber each time they made a new interment. He even suggests what their feelings might have been on these occasions and how their emotions were affected by the spaces of the structure that they had created for the burials.

While Schama's interpretation of this monument can be seen as part of a well-established tradition of imaginative (some might say over-imaginative) presentation in historical documentaries, as well as feeding a perceived desire for historical re-enactment on the part of the general public, it also reflects recent trends in the scholarship surrounding British prehistory that have been gathered under the heading of performance archaeology.

To those unfamilar with it, the juxtaposition of archaeology with performance may seem bizarre, even nonsensical. After all, archaeology is a scholarly, scientific pursuit that provides us with hard facts (i.e. material remains) from the past, while performance is, well, just putting on a show. Although theatre, whether live or mass-mediated, is (sometimes) an art form and there exist intermediate categories of performance or performance art, there is nothing scientific about it. The performative and the theatrical are invariably trying to pass themselves off as something they are not, although we are, for the most part, complicit in their deception. All this is just 'common sense', what everybody knows. However, 'common sense' assumptions, the unexamined expectations that structure the day-to-day world, are not always the same as those utilized in the 'discourses' generated by the specialized professions and institutions that dominate our highly structured, bureaucratized world – discourses such as history, economics, archaeology, psychology, art history, ethnology and so on. To make matters even more complicated, this discursive world is in a state of flux; different areas of specialization borrow from each other, professional boundaries shift and genres of thought and writing become blurred.

Scholarly discourses even study and borrow from commonsense notions about the world. Look what happens to our word 'performance'.

Simon Schama is himself performing, performing for the camera and, hopefully, for a huge audience on network and cable television. Is Schama performing himself, is he putting it on, is he putting one across, is he pretending to be an expert on what he is talking about? (To some degree, yes; Schama is an early modern historian, but not a prehistorian/archaeologist.) The very existence of educational television calls into question our assumption that TV and film are fictional categories like theatre. What about other documentaries? What about the news? Aren't they all true? Well, not really. Reporters and camera operators select their subject and they present it in conformance with the same conventions as fictional narratives, because these conventions are common to all language-based communication, even if they are also subject to cultural variations. Non-fiction and documentary works, like their fictional counterparts, have an audience that is separated from its subject, to which it must be presented in a comprehensible and engaging way.

So we begin to see how performance is not so separate from real life after all. And it gets more complicated. Books, films, television, websites and so on are remote forms of communication that are derived from face-to-face interactions between people. While bodily gestures play an important role in these interactions, spoken language, an apparently unique attribute of the human species, is of primary importance. Language, a mental construct conveyed through physical modifications producing sounds, describes and produces effects on the physical world, which it represents through a series of abstract equivalences, the 'turns' or figures of speech such as analogy, metaphor, simile and so on. And so we can see that although human communication can effect change in the physical environment, it can do so only by a process that represents that which it is not. Every speech act is a performance, a pretence of something that it is not, because it cannot be any other way, and the mental activity that precedes speech is no different. Every night as the mind spools through its routines and reviews input data while we sleep, it presents it in the form of scenarios with stories and actors. These are our dreams, the ongoing performance of our mental states. But while language and pictures can represent or show us something about an event, person or thing, a performance has the unique ability to not only represent or show it but to *re-present* it, to *make it happen again*. Not all performances aspire to do this, but those that are more ritualized are more likely to do so than ones intended primarily for entertainment.

If the visualization of actions in which the subject may or may not take part is essential to the function of language in the mind, it suggests that a 'dramatic' narrative is a basic form of the presentation of data and its understanding. It may that such 'phatic' presentation is vital to the link between language and the body, in which its abstract content is concre-

2

tized. It may also explain why things are more easily understood by 'acting them out' even more than just imagining them to happen. Such may explain the presence of highly conventional or ritual activity in all human societies, as well as the apparent ubiquity of dramatic presentation, whether or not it is connected with ritual. As regards history and archaeology, it may explain the tremendous popularity of historical re-enactment and impersonation among the general public in the developed world.

The first use of this technique in an antiquarian setting in modern times was in 1891 when Artur Hazelius moved his Museum of Scandinavian Folklore in Stockholm outside, re-erecting large rural buildings and peopling them with costumed interpreters. He called this *ersatz* community Skansen, and addressed this idealized representation of rural Swedish life to the working class rather than to the bourgeoisie who had been the target audience of the nineteenth-century museum (Bennett 1988). Hazelius' idea has proved extraordinarily popular in every sense of the word. The idea was enthusiastically taken up by almost every European government with populist pretensions throughout the twentieth century as well as by private museums and theme parks across North America, from which it has penetrated most mainstream heritage institutions other than art galleries. Costumed interpreters are to be found everywhere, from Colonial Williamsburg to the Canadian Museum of Civilization (Gillam 1994).

Fig. 1. Visitor and actor/interpreter at the Canadian Museum of Civilization.

Parallel to this development and in some cases even surpassing it in popularity is the practice of historical re-enactment by societies of enthusiastic amateurs. While an early and enduring facet of such activities is military re-enactment (to kill or be killed is still the way that most people get to enter history), they can also grow to encompass other aspects of past societies, especially those relating to daily life, such as food, clothing and craft activities. Popular participation in such creative anachronism can intersect with history, but especially with archaeology, leading not so much to contestation as to some equally creative collaborations. The pressure of popular culture on archaeology and history can be seen in the importance of military re-enactments in productions as diverse as the Canadian Broadcasting Corporation's series *Canada: A People's History* (2000) or Ridley Scott's *Gladiator* (1999), where amateur historical re-enactors played a key role, even if they did not always feel that it was appreciated. Almost every documentary on ancient Egypt that now appears on the specialty channels of cable and satellite TV now includes some historical enactment. Even if most academics continue to refuse to consider the legitimacy of such activities on screen or off, it may be that scholars and amateur re-enactors have been able to coexist and might even learn something from each other, as a paper presented by a re-enactor at the 2002 Theoretical Archaeology Group conference suggests (Appleby 2002).

So while it seems obvious that there is pressure from popular culture on archaeology and history to 'perform', so there is also pressure from other academic disciplines and from within archaeology, not only for 'action', but also for its examination.

What distinguishes specialized academic discourses from 'common sense' or vernacular understanding of the world is that they are formed in detachment from it, that they are *theorized*. The English word 'theory' comes from the Greek *theoria*, meaning contemplation, speculation or sight. It is related to *theatron*, or viewing place, the theatre. So what theorists do is observe the world around them in the splendid isolation recommended by Plato and Socrates (Bourdieu 1990, 27-8), preferably from the great height of an exalted social position. While such a state of affairs was unlikely to trouble any would-be theorists in the past, during the past two hundred years demands from members of the non-elite classes for inclusion in culturally and socially important institutions have placed pressure on academic disciplines other than archaeology. While more radical cultural theorists have called for the demolition of scholarly detachment as a classist fossil (Ross 1989), such demands have had little impact in the humanities and social sciences, let alone the sciences. Political concerns have to some degree shaped the objects of enquiry, if not the methods by which they are studied. Theory is more overt than it ever was. Let us see how this has played out in relation to the question of performance and archaeology.

Introduction

By the mid-twentieth century, archaeology had come to depend heavily on all kinds of scientific and technical operations, from surveying techniques to radiocarbon dating. As ever more sophisticated techniques for the recording and preservation of artefacts and sites developed, the discipline took on the identity of a social science, leaning more and more heavily towards the scientific. Processual archaeology sought to understand the past as a series of abstract routines or 'processes' which focussed on systems rather than on individual actors (Hodder 1992, 83-121). However, the increasing mass and complexity of archaeological data challenged even a scientific approach to the material. Increasingly close relationships between archaeology and ethnography/anthropology also drew attention to the subjects who created the archaeological record, if only to their absence. It was largely through exposure to anthropological theory, both structuralist and poststructuralist (Hodder 1991, 4-19), that post-processual archaeology began to develop in the late 1970s.

Post-structuralism led archaeologists to question not only how they used the data but the point of view from which they did it. The relationship of field workers from the developed world to the post-colonial societies in which they worked was examined, as was the consciousness of sex and gender within the profession and in what it studied (Shanks and Tilley 1987). Archaeologists began to make increasing use of conceptual models developed by anthropologists, especially as they related to small-scale societies and how these might be related to the material remains of past non-literate cultures or non-elite groups in literate societies. They also began to give thought to the relationship of the material world to the subject, especially how it interacted with space and time. In the absence of a speaking subject, its manufactured products could be made to speak for it in any number of ways. In part because of their relationship to ethnology, archaeologists made extensive use of the figure of analogy, comparing one thing to another as parallel causes. A speaking subject is also a sentient and feeling one. The experiential dimension of material existence has also given rise to a phenomenological side to archaeology as well as an objective one (Hamiliakis, Pluciennik and Tarlow 2002, 8-13).

Although the post-processual moment in archaeology may or may not have passed, its effects and approaches are many and complex (Thomas 2000a). Performance archaeology is just one of its varied effects. Let us now examine some ideas about performance that have influenced its development and the subject that will be explored in this book.

Long ago, in 1983, Clifford Geertz noted a blurring of genres in the humanities and the social sciences, where disciplines on either side of the fence had begun to borrow from each other. He noted a tendency among social scientists, humanists and philosophers to construct models of social behaviour on analogies to what may be described as performative activities. Wittgenstein and Goffman used games and Turner talked about 'social dramas', while Geertz himself described traditional Balinese society as a 'theater state'. He also noted the interest of scholars as different as Durkheim, Frye and Foucault in social acts of a ritual, specular character (Geertz 1983).

While Geertz's overview concentrated on the social sciences and humanities, we might also note the rise of psychodrama, a branch of psychotherapy devised and popularized by J.L. Moreno, a colleague and rival of Freud's. Moreno set out to challenge the notion 'in the beginning was the word' as foundational to psychology, replacing it with the act (Moreno 1963). He argued that psychological constructs and neuroses originated in infancy before the acquisition of language and therefore were better accessed by acting rather than talking them out. To this end Moreno devised a performance structure and even a special kind of theatre where this therapy could take place. The protagonists played 'roles', a term which Moreno took from classical Greek theatre, from which he took the form of his performances. The 'role' derived from the roll or scroll from which the ancient actors read their lines. While psychodrama enjoyed great success first in Europe and then in the United States in the 1950s and 60s, it has now been largely discredited as a medical therapy (D'Amato, Carl and Raymond 1988). However, its wider influence is disproportionate to its apparent status as a footnote to the history of psychology. Moreno's techniques have been widely adapted and applied as an educational tool. They play an important role in many forms of critical pedagogy from preschool to university teaching, in vocational and management training, and in crime prevention and rehabilitation (Duplessis and Lochner 1981; Caso and Finkelberg 1999). Indeed, 'role playing' has migrated from specialized discourse to the vernacular world of 'common sense'. We all do it.

A similar intention to Moreno's can be discerned in Antonin Artaud's project for a theatre of cruelty, in which gesture and sound replaced words and players acted without social restraints to shock the audience into seeing the brutality of human life (Artaud 1958). While Artaud spent the latter part of his life in a mental institution, his ideas were adopted by a number of mid-twentieth-century playwrights and can be argued to have influenced the rise of not only performance art, but a number of popular genres such as horror films and 'reality' TV.

Performance art, which originated in the USA in the 1950s in collective events described as 'happenings', involves the deliberately dissonant use of various media in a way that imitates collage, and it must be performed live. Well-known exponents of performance art include Claes Oldenberg, John Cage, Nam June Paik and Joseph Bueys. Performance pieces have tended to become simpler over time and have also influenced and been influenced by other categories of performance.

Psychodrama, the theatre of cruelty and performance art, all 'blurred genres', have in common that they problematize the relationship between speech and physical action. This uncertainty can also be discerned in the work of two social theorists whose work is important for anthropology and archaeology, Pierre Bourdieu and Michel de Certeau.

Bourdieu, a sociologist, explained social formation using the analogy of market economies. Although preoccupied with cultural relations between different social classes in contemporary France, Bourdieu also studied French rural society as well as that of the Berbers of North Africa, or 'Kabylia' (Robbins 1991, 10-46). He concluded that mythopoeic thought patterns commonly found in traditional societies were the product of everyday practices and the logic that determined them. Bourdieu even formulated a basic law of the economy of logic – that only so much logic (that is, 'rationality') is used as is required in a given situation. He termed the way of thinking and operating generated by such practical logic as the *habitus*, from the Latin, where it means condition of the body, character, style, attire, disposition, state of feeling or habit. While we may understand *habitus* simply as social conditioning, Bourdieu had much higher aspirations for his neologism, seeing it as an underlying organising principle for not only social structures but also the minds of the people who inhabit them. He was at pains to emphasize that although execution of the routines of the *habitus* was in conformance with the social conditions of the actors, it was not, strictly speaking, done of their conscious volition. The *habitus* was inculcated in early childhood through physical rather than verbal cues (e.g. 'Sit up straight', 'Don't play with your food') rather than verbal, conceptual ones (Bourdieu 1990, 66-9, 71-7). Indeed, Bourdieu's set-piece analysis of the layout of the Kabyle house where everything in the outside world is reversed (Bourdieu 1970) is explained by him through the simple physical trope or 'turn' of turning around and going inside the house (Bourdieu 1990, 93). Indeed, he saw an unbridgeable divide between the traditional 'common sense' of the *habitus* and the institutionalized world of modernity with its validating educational, disciplinary and economic institutions. The former was based on semi-autonomic bodily gestures and expediency, the latter on concepts formulated in writing in a detached 'habit' of mind derived from the practice of Greek philosophy, the product of an elite social class. The specular nature of 'theory' is what sets abstract thought apart from practical thought and makes all our science, social science and other intellectual institutions possible (Bourdieu 1990, 27-8). Although Bourdieu was at pains to show that institutions like the academic one of which he was a part operated in conformity with their own *habitus*, he seemed to be defeated by his own methods of research, which were of course grounded in the specular qualities of scholarly detachment (Robbins 1991, 147-50).

Criticism along these lines was levelled at Bourdieu by Michel de Certeau in *Arts de faire* (translated as *The Practice of Everyday Life*, 1984). De Certeau suggested that, like many an academic, Bourdieu could see only in the primitive 'other' what was in reality right under his own nose.

What the Kabyle house reversed was not the world, but the French school system. The political unconscious of the professorial class had its reified image in the unconscious habituation of the peasant to his structurally produced world view. Not only is this apparently inadvertent, it is also deeply insulting to the social actors it describes (de Certeau 1984, 50-60). De Certeau was much less interested in the practical logic of small-scale, underdeveloped societies than in that of his own. He detected much the same practices in the everyday life of the subjects of modernity, where this traditional practical 'know-how' was ever more on the defensive against the institutionalized laws, culture and economy of global capitalism. It survived in household arrangements, patterns of walking in the city and other uses or – more likely – misuses of aspects of the hegemonic environment. And far from being a semi-conscious reflex, the practice of everyday life drew on reserves of cunning and memory deployed in the face of spatial insecurity and diminishing time. De Certeau's hero was not Socrates, but Odysseus, prized for his *metis*, his native wit, by all Greeks, not just the elite (de Certeau 1984, 77-90). But despite their cleverness, de Certeau's everyday subjects are always fighting a losing battle against the hegemonic forces that constrain their lives through law, education, time management and relentless commodification. Induction into literate education initiates the subject into the hegemonic capitalist system, strategically institutionalized in written data and abstract thought in contrast with the tactical, oral world of practical everyday life (de Certeau 1984, 136).

Like Bourdieu, de Certeau creates an unbridgeable divide between word and text and, to a lesser degree, between word and act. Both of them appear to be under the influence of Saussure's original structural analysis of language, where *parole* is overdetermined by *langue*, even though they are critical of it (Bourdieu 1990, 30-3). Just as Moreno believed that psychological complexes must be formed before speech is 'acquired', so do Bourdieu and de Certeau, along with other social scientists and philosophers, see language as part of a programme of forced acculturation, if not exactly a virus invading the pristine primate body. If we accept, like Chomsky (1968), that the human mind (a physical entity) may be 'hardwired' for language, which by its very nature operates in an abstract, analogical manner, then we may suspect that the dichotomy between speech and action, between mind and body, or between theory and practice is not so hard and fast as it seems.

The existence of such links was made even clearer by J.L. Austin, a philosopher of 'ordinary language'. In *How to Do Things with Words* (1962) Austin distinguished two types of speech: constative, or descriptive, and performative. Performative speech acts were distinguished by their ability to accomplish, in whole or in part, an *action*. Such utterances were often of a formulaic or ritual character, like the words uttered by the officiant of a marriage ceremony, or the naming of a ship, or somebody drafting a will or making a bet. For the performative to be effective, there must be consensus among those involved in the act it verbalizes that it is part of a recognized procedure, that the persons and circumstances are appropriate, that the procedure has been executed correctly and completely, that the persons speaking these utterances mean what they say and that they conduct themselves accordingly (Austin 1962, 14-24). Therefore, although performatives, unlike statements, could not be true or false, they could be subject to infelicity. Austin distinguished between locutionary acts that have a meaning, illocutionary acts that have a force, and perlocutionary acts which achieve certain effects by saying something (Austin 1962, 120-31).

Austin's text gave rise to speech-act theory, which is used by philosophers and literary critics to show that language is use oriented and context dependent. It privileges the intention of the speaker over the interpretation of the hearer, in clear contrast to structuralist interpretations of language. From the point of view of archaeology and of performance, one of Austin's most important successors is Judith Butler. Butler's most well-known and influential use of the idea of the performative utterance is to be found in *Gender Trouble* (1991), where she explores how the gender identity of a subject is created by the normative pronouncements of others. Butler, whose philosophical background is in investigations of subject formation in the works of Hegel and those influenced by him, has based her position on a statement made by Nietzsche in the *Genealogy of Morals*, that there is no subject behind the doing except in as far as it is necessary to assign blame for a prior act (Butler 1997, 45). In other words, the act produces the subject and not the other way around. By the same token social identities, like those of gender, are the product of performative utterances like 'It's a girl!' or, to follow a similar speech-act model, that of interpellation, suggested by Louis Althusser, of being hailed by a figure in authority such as a policeman (Butler 1993, 7-8; 1997, 24-6; Althusser 1971, 161-2). Subjects thereafter constitute their own identity by acting it out. Although these formations produce identification on the surface of the body, these identifications are fantasies that are unmasked in the infelicities that performative utterances are more often plagued by than not. That social roles such as that of gender are imitative and performative is innately revealed when they are parodied in activities where their components are improperly deployed, as in drag (Butler 1991, 134-41) or, to use Austin's example, when a man marries a monkey (Austin 1962, 24).

There are important implications for archaeology in Butler's theories. That subjects act out their identity through speech-related acts, in the material world in space and time, means it is possible to interpret their traces on site in ways other than those dependent on an ethnographic analogy, which becomes extremely problematic when there are no subjects to interview or watch. Speech-act theory also privileges the experience, i.e.

the acts of the subject, allowing the phenomenological study of the past in addition to its objectivity.

This brings us back to the idea of performance archaeology, an approach developed by British prehistorians and explored most extensively to date by Michael Shanks and Mike Pearson in *Theatre/Archaeology* (2001). This unique work brings together Shanks, a classicist and archaeological theorist, with Pearson, a practitioner of theatre and performance, its more public and less formal equivalent. Apart from investigating archaeology itself as a performance, Pearson and Shanks also query the rising popularity of enactment on historic sites, noted above, and suggest more creative, self-conscious strategies for its use. They explore not only the relationship of space to the body but how made objects can extend it both physically and temporally. Pearson presents a definition of performance as any organized activity presented to witnesses, and the relationship of object to memory is explored. *Theatre/Archaeology* is presented not as a conventional academic text, but as a collage of different images, voices and typefaces. But while such forms of presentation remain controversial, the approaches to the past laid out therein have wide currency in archaeological circles. Beating a path through the changing landscape (Ingold 1993) and exploring the production of ceremonial space (Parker Pearson and Ramilisonina 1998) or its experiential dimension (Richards 1993) not only give archaeologists new tools for understanding their materials, but assist in its interpretation for the general public. Colin Richards' explication of the Neolithic monuments of Orkney (1993) provided the basis for Simon Schama's script and even, perhaps, his performance, described at the beginning of this chapter.

The concept of performance archaeology is hopefully now not as strange as it first appeared. Theories about the relationship of performance, language and space have clearly added much to our understanding of the monuments of prehistoric Britain, or even later traces left by the lives of people of the non-elite classes. The production of ideas and material objects does not take place in a vacuum. The two are obviously related human activities, activities that like all such acts are to some degree staged. While some of these staged activities are more diagnostic than others, we must make some effort to distinguish the more meaningful performances. More to the point, how can we apply these theories to the material and textual remains of ancient Egyptian culture? Let us try to find out.

Materials for a History of Performance in Ancient Egypt

The survey of current theories about performance and performativity used in current archaeological discourse in the Introduction suggests that, so defined, it encompasses much of human activity, including speech acts. Obviously, attempting to describe all such activity taking place in a culture such as Egypt, one that vanished over a thousand years ago and endured over three millennia, is a daunting, if not impossible, task. Add to this that much of what we know of this vanished culture comes to us through written texts, a problematic medium for many archaeologists, and our difficulties multiply.

Phenomenological and experiential aspects of human culture such as performance can be understood from a number of approaches used by contemporary archaeological theory. Sites are located in landscapes, with all their ecological and economic implications. The structures found in the sites themselves can be seen as overdetermined by both the landscape they are in as well as the human subjects who constructed them in terms of spatial, environmental and social relations. The human subjects leave their own traces in physical remains, giving clues to how bodies interacted with the sites and the landscape, as do the objects of their material culture that function as physical prostheses (McLuhan 1966; Pearson and Shanks 2001) in their interaction with their surroundings. The basic components of these – scenario, landscape, figure and ground – provide the form of the picture; content or meaning is often provided by analogy with present-day small-scale societies such as the Kabyle whom Bourdieu used as the basis of many of his theories. While the assumption that these analogies are valid for vanished, past societies is sometimes questioned. (Wobst 1978), it is generally assumed that they function in much the way that ethnographers and sociologists have described, if only because these existing small-scale societies are the only empirical link that the developed world has to 'other' cultures.

Indeed, it can be argued that the relation of our own culture to that of others forms the basis of a system of binary oppositions, discernable particularly in the thought of Bourdieu and de Certeau, but also in other theories of society and culture used in interpretive archaeology. Not only is there an absolute separation between oral and written culture, but other, related oppositions are also generated, such as traditional/modern, hegemonic/non-hegemonic, institutional/non-institutional, economic/social, elite/non-elite, strategic/tactical and conceptual/practical. These dichotomies reflect not only the perceived absolute difference between modern and 'traditional' societies, but also suggest conflicts within modernity itself.

What these oppositions reflect are the class struggles of modernity, taken up by many twentieth-century intellectuals who have been influential in the development of social and cultural theory, especially in sociology and cultural studies. Cultural studies, a field whose agendas and approaches have been particularly influential in the formation of archaeological theory, has taken as its field the study of popular/mass culture, and as its project, for the most part, its valorization. This project has involved the championing of the tactical, stolen and reactive interventions of 'ordinary people' in the hegemonic, obtuse and jejune products of hegemonic culture. From the aspirations of the Paris communards to destroy Notre-Dame cathedral to the disruption of a night at the opera by the Marx Brothers and the re-attribution of the *Odyssey* to Homer Simpson, high culture has been seen as an alien body to be destroyed, poached from or ridiculed, but not something that has any meaningful connection to the lives of regular people.

According to Althusser (1971), all cultural and educational institutions are to be classified as ideological state apparatuses, designed to create a false consciousness about real social and economic relations. Paramount among these hegemonic acts must be the inculcation of writing, an act that according to de Certeau initiates the subject into a capitalist and conquering society (1984, 131-53). But while this subject might be party to neo-colonial adventures abroad, at home he continues to fight a losing battle against these dominating cultural and economic structures, armed only with his wits, a good pair of shoes and ever-diminishing amounts of time. Despite the obvious fact that all of these thinkers are members of the elite they so heartily despise, and that they are clearly aware that there is in reality a great deal of overlap between 'practical' and hegemonic social formations, and that some non-hegemonic ones can be every bit as oppressive as their opposite number, these binary, polemical habits of thinking die hard. The deep-seated motifs of binary opposition found in the work of such social theorists reflect, perhaps, not just class relations in Modernity, but also the fact that we have almost reached the point where our culture has no 'outside', nothing that can convincingly play the role of 'other', resulting in an imaginative and theoretical block to trying to re-envisage a past with multiple 'others' and no obvious centre.

The consequences of this way of thinking may be seen in John Baines' and Christopher Eyre's theories about literacy in ancient Egyptian society (Baines 1983). Starting from the assumption that no more than one to five per cent of the population were ever literate (Baines and Eyre 1983), Baines and Eyre explain Egyptian elite culture as a small and irrelevant outgrowth on a traditional non-literate society of the type recognizable to most anthropologists. While the elite created self-perpetuating institutions for its own benefit, these were rudimentary, and the material culture created was mostly for the purposes of social and ceremonial display of the type found in small-scale societies such as the Kabyle described by Bourdieu. Even the writing system was fraudulent, as it did not really attempt to represent spoken language (Baines 1989, 473).

Baines and Eyre's approach can be related to a process of theoretical formation described by de Certeau as 'cut-out and turn over' (1984, 62-4). In this process a scholar isolates a part of the data, which becomes a metonymic figure for the whole, and then inverts it so that it becomes comprehensible and illuminates his whole discourse. Not only have Baines and Eyre isolated Egyptian elite culture from its whole social context, but they reversed its apparent importance into something wholly insignificant. The insignificance of elite culture reveals that Egypt was after all a traditional non-literate society that can be easily interpreted using models like Jack Goody's concept of non-scriptural literacy (1975). This remarkable theoretical 'turn' may also be linked to the binary framework of thinking that we have noted above. If the culture of modernity presupposes universal literacy, then the culture of the other must entail its opposite. If modernity has produced hegemonic legal, economic and cultural institutions, they cannot possibly exist elsewhere.

While neither of these scholars have come to these conclusions in so many words, it should be pointed out that current studies of pre-modern societies tend to focus on their provisional, 'practical' character. Even Foucault's researches on hegemonic structures such as the prison and the mental institution revealed practices that tended to undermine their functioning. It appears that even the most institutionalized, structured and automated of social formations is subject to 'practical' interventions, as de Certeau (1984, 45-9) took pains to demonstrate. Almost any social formation can have both an institutional and a provisional character, depending on time, development, intention and the kind of people involved. Modern institutionalized society clearly originated somewhere and is the product of a long development, as well as periods of growth and retrenchment. The bureaucratic government structures of Egypt and Mesopotamia provided a model that has been followed and developed intermittently for millennia. To create an intelligentsia requires not necessarily big houses or large computers, but the leisure time to develop books and literacy. Furthermore, the very existence of our own culture and its prehistory presuppose an intermediate formation between it and the non-literate traditional society. Although literacy is certainly related to class, it also a matter of degree, with differing levels of literacy appropriated to the 'practical' needs of many different social actors. While there was certainly pressure from non-elite formations on Egyptian high culture, as there was in the other direction (and not just at tax time, when scribes showed up on a peasant's land with a troop of soldiers to collect), we may assume that these were not separate worlds but part of a community that shared a common culture.

While I freely acknowledge that Egyptian high culture was an elite formation intended to demonstrate the 'naturalness' of the social relations it perpetuated and presented, thereby serving the interests of the dominant class, it must be pointed out that it was made possible by wealth created by the surplus value generated by goods and services provided by the rest of society. Not only that, its own products were the result, whether directly or indirectly, of non-elite skilled and unskilled labour. While some forms of cultural production were the work of the elite themselves, most were generated by others who, although they might thereby achieve social mobility, for the most part remained outside the ruling class. Thus we may discern even more possibilities for social and cultural interactions between classes.

It must also be remembered that the society developed over time. Just as developed modern societies evolved out of complex pre-modern formations, so the complex societies of the ancient Near East in Egypt and Mesopotamia originated in small-scale societies. State formation, which took place in the late fourth millennium, was preceded by the development of a hierarchical, class-based society that served to concentrate material wealth in the hands of an elite (Bard 1994) and facilitated the development of an ideological apparatus that provided the rationale for this operation (Kemp 1989). At the other end of this process, in the third to fifth centuries of the Common Era we see these ideological state apparatuses gradually devolve into locally based institutions kept up in an *ad hoc* 'practical' fashion, like the social structures of Kabylia, Bali or their own Predynastic prototypes (Frankfurter 1997). Likewise, the location in the class hierarchy will dictate the form that social expression takes. As de Certeau has noted, practical routines and oral cultures still survive in developed modern society, so we should certainly expect to find them among the non-elite classes of Pharaonic Egypt, even if they are not socially or culturally self-sufficient, as I have argued above.

Now that we have attempted a definition of Pharaonic Egyptian society that places it somewhere between a non-literate small-scale society and full-blown institutionalized modernity, that has identified its elite culture as a product of both the base and the superstructure, we are now in a position to decide what materials a history of performance or performativity in this culture would consist of. Obviously the full range of activities encompassed by the definitions of these terms that have been examined in the Introduction cannot be covered in this brief study. Furthermore, the inclusion of every action or speech-act that can be construed as an organized activity taking place before witnesses is really too wide a definition of an activity that means something much more specific to most readers and researchers. When anthropologists speak of performances they generally mean organized routines of a conventional nature with social and/or religious meanings, such as weddings, funerals or harvest festivals. Such routines may be presented before the community and possibly require some level of their participation, or they may take place in a more private venue with just a few actors, as in the case of story-telling sessions, initiations or cultic acts. When social historians speak of performance they may be thinking of dramatic performance of the type seen in classical Greek theatre, medieval mystery plays or Elizabethan dramas, of court masques, of coronation rituals, royal progresses, carnivals, riots, graduation ceremonies, courts and legislatures, in addition to celebrations of the weddings-and-funerals type mentioned above. These scholarly interests in turn reflect ideas about performance in contemporary culture, which are generally based on the idea of professional (or at least designated) performers going through a routine in front of an audience that has often paid for the privilege of being entertained. While such expectations do not really coincide with the activities that went on in past societies, they may serve as a guideline for what kinds of activities we decide to study.

In this book we shall be looking at community ceremonies such as funerals (much better documented than weddings in the archaeological record), at political pageants such as coronations and jubilees, at religious events such as cultic performances and other 'secret' acts, and at evidence for smaller-scale events like informal magical ceremonies, musical concerts and exhibitions of dance, as well as the possible existence of oral storytelling and similar kinds of textually based performances. And although some of this evidence does come from the archaeological record of material culture, much of it is to be found in texts and representations coming from documents and monuments at elite sites.

The inspiration for this investigation was provided by a very particular group of texts found in Graeco-Roman period temples and by some papyrus books. These sources, which will be described in more detail below, provide a unique insight into the different kinds of performances that took place at or near temples in this period. Either by implication or quite specifically, they describe how a particular operation may be performed. At Esna is found the liturgy of certain festivals and the texts that were recited at them; at Edfu long inscriptions accompanied by representations present a dramatization of the triumph of Horus, the god of kingship, over his enemies and his enthronement; at Dendara texts and pictures give detailed instructions on how to re-present the resurrection of his father, Osiris, through the medium of two small figures of the god (Derchain 1981). A papyrus now in Vienna which gives the procedure for mummifying the divine Apis bull of Memphis may be compared to these inscriptions, as can two copies of another book that gives the recitations appropriate to various junctures in the standard mummification ritual (Gillam 2002a). The extreme specificity of these texts makes it entirely possible to perform them, on or off site. Between 1998 and the present, routines based on these

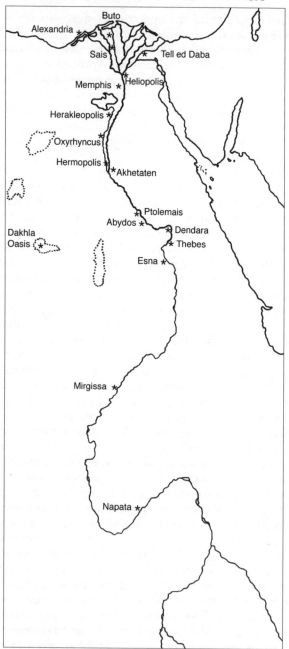

Fig. 2. Map of Egypt and Nubia.

sources have been performed by my undergraduate students in the Programme in Classical and Religious Studies at York University. The experience gained in performing these activities, while of great pedagogical value, is also of interest from a scholarly perspective. It not only throws some light on the logistics of mounting these operations, but also raises wider issues about the role of performance in Egyptian cult worship and society at this period, as well as earlier in its history. In order to understand these texts better it is necessary to attempt to identify written documents and other materials that attest to these activities throughout the life of Egyptian culture.

Each historical period will be examined in turn for evidence of performance-based activities and all pertinent sources will be dealt with strictly within the time frame in which they are attested. Although there is a strong diachronic tendency in the study of Egyptian cultural and especially religious documents, in which texts or representations are apt to be retrojected backwards in time, I will try to refrain from this practice. Although religious and especially cultic acts tend to be of a highly conservative nature in all cultures, they are capable of sudden and innovative development, as happened at the period of Egyptian state formation as well as in the late 18th Dynasty under the auspices of the heterodox ruler Akhenaten (Kemp 1989, 276-87). We may be sure that not only were there other such episodes of which we remain ignorant, but that even the most conservative of these procedures was subject to incremental development. For example, even if the activity described in the Ramesseum Dramatic Papyrus (Sethe 1928) likely originates in the Old Kingdom, it was found in the context of the late Middle Kingdom, a period that differed considerably from the earlier one in regard to social and economic conditions. Let us now attempt to frame our material with the aid of a brief historical overview.

The prehistoric period in Egypt (before 3100 BCE) provides an increasing but still limited corpus of material that can be used as evidence for performance-based practices. Since no texts were created before the very end of this time, this particular avenue of investigation remains closed, leaving only human and material remains as well as a number of sites relating to settlement and other activities. In this period the physical environment differed considerably from that of the present (Wendorf and Schild 1980, 236-41, 345-51). Much of the Sahara region was covered with grasslands, and people inhabiting the region led a transhumant existence (Wendorf and Schild 1980, 264-72), later moving between moister areas, such as the coast and the Nile Valley, and the uplands, depending on the time of the year or larger climatic patterns. At first hunter-gatherers, the inhabitants of this region later adopted agriculture and animal husbandry, which gradually led to the differentiation between settled farmers and nomadic herder populations that we see by historic times. From about 5000 BCE small settlements are found in the valley, while traces of campsites, watering holes and flint-working sites are found outside it (Wendorf and Schild 1980). The presence of burials in the vicinity of the valley from this time onwards implies beliefs about the afterlife and presumably ceremonies to mark the death of individuals. Numerous petro-glyphs found in what are now desert areas show figures of humans and animals in relationship to each other, which include hunting scenes as well as boats. Similar representations are found on pottery made in the valley. It has been suggested that these figures represent the king and the gods as known from sources of the historic period (Wilkinson 2002), and some of these scenes may have mythological and/or ceremonial significance.

Towards the end of the Predynastic Period, *c.* 3200 BCE), graves in cemeteries adjacent to the valley begin to exhibit differences in the quantity and richness of grave goods, pointing to the development of social hierarchies based on differences in wealth (Bard 1994), quickly leading to formation of a number of city-states in the southern part of present-day Egypt and infiltration of northern cultures by the southern in the northern valley and delta (Wilkinson 1996, 94-5). At centres such as Naqada and Hierokonpolis can be seen not only elaborate burials in chambered tombs (Bard 1994, 77-81) but also fortified enclosures with temples and large houses (Adams 1987, 176-202). Royal tombs at Abydos, dating from the transitional period between the late prehistoric and the beginning of the 1st Dynasty (Dreyer 1998), show characteristics similar to those of the later royal graves, which added sacrificial burials and ceremonial enclosures at the edge of the cultivated area, suggesting the existence of elaborate funeral ceremonies (O'Connor 1989).

Evidence from the Archaic period, comprising the 1st and 2nd dynasties suggests a high degree of social and cultural continuity from the period of state formation that preceded it. The royal tombs at Abydos expand on the earlier models, with extensive burial structures, large numbers of sacrificial burials (Hoffman 1979, 275-9) and larger and more elaborate ceremonial centres at the edge of the valley (O'Connor 1989; 1995). Although sacrificial burials were discontinued after the mid-1st Dynasty, non-royal persons continued to be buried in the vicinity of royal tombs and other elite cemeteries show a high degree of material affluence as well as elaboration of beliefs and, no doubt, ceremonies around death and the afterlife (Wilkinson 1996, 86-8). Short inscriptions which now occur in royal and elite tombs indicate the existence of religious and state festivals (Serrano 2002), many of which are attested in later Egyptian history, as well as an elaborately structured royal household that was also the centre of government (Helck 1954, 9-28).

By the 3rd Dynasty (*c.* 2700 BCE), the royal tomb had become a huge, even more elaborate structure centred on a pyramid and consisting of a complex of passageways, courtyards and shrines, suggesting ever more highly developed ceremonial procedures. Subsequent to this, in the later 3rd and early 4th Dynasty, the layout of the royal tombs changed from a rectangular enclosure to a series of structures on a longitudinal axis with a gigantic pyramid at the western end and a small temple at the eastern one, on the edge of the valley, connected by a long stone causeway. While the pyramids eventually became smaller and the temples more elaborate, this pattern of the royal tomb endured until the end of the Old Kingdom (*c.* 2150 BCE) (Kemp 1989, 53-63). The royal tombs were always surrounded by an elite cemetery whose tombs were equipped with chapels for the celebration of the cult of the deceased person and used for family gatherings at special holidays. The more ostentatious ones were decorated with texts and representations which depict the statue cult, the funerary ceremonies and preparation of the tomb, display autobiographies of the deceased, and give much other, incidental information about life at this time (if only we can interpret it) (Harpur 1987; Lichtheim 1990). Towards the end of the Old Kingdom, elites outside the capital became more economically independent and made their own elaborate tombs, which were decorated in much the same way (Harpur 1987, 10; Kanawati 1973). Apart from depicting the cult of the deceased, where offerings of food and drink were presented to a statue, these tomb chapels show the funeral procession, making of goods for the tomb, the typical occupations and life achievements of the deceased and the festivals celebrated by the family in memory of the departed and other ancestors (Harpur 1987, 59-84, 113-15, 136-69).

It is not until the end of the 5th Dynasty (*c.* 2350 BCE) that texts appear in the burial chamber inside the pyramids that relate to the resurrection of the king as a divine being. While it has been argued that they may represent in whole or in part a 'script' for the funeral ceremony, this cannot be proven. However, they do suggest the way this space may have been conceptualized, if not how it was used (Barta 1981; Allen 1994).

Although it is obvious that the people of Old Kingdom Egypt must have had many different kinds of ceremonies and performances in their lives apart from funerals and days of the dead, we know little about them. Some incidental evidence of work songs, games, music and dance performances and circumcision ceremonies can be found in the private tomb chapels. Settlement archaeology has not revealed much to help us. Non-royal temples had irregular ground plans (Kemp 1989, 65-83) and non-elite burials are more similar to those of their prehistoric ancestors than of their upper-class contemporaries, suggesting a considerable cultural as well as economic divide between them (Baines 1989).

Egyptian elite burial practices of later periods retained many similarities to those of the Old Kingdom, and the tomb chapels contained comparable material, even if it was subject to variation over time. Burial equipment tended to become more elaborate and extensive, and by 2000 BCE well-to-do private burials were provided with collections of texts similar to those earlier inscribed in the royal pyramids (Hayes 1953, 303-30; Lesko 1991, 101-3). Partly because of the preferences of earlier archaeologists and explorers and partly through accidents of survival, a great deal of our knowledge of Egyptian culture comes from funerary deposits and sites. Although this serves to conceal much of Egyptian life from us, it also suggests that funerals and mortuary monuments were an important occasion for social display and conspicuous expenditure, as they are in some cultures today, such as Bali.

Around 2150 BCE the Old Kingdom came to an end and the ruling elite lost its grip on power. Large-scale royal tomb building ceased and the sophistication and wealth of material culture temporarily declined. By 2000 BCE the country was reunited under rulers from the south, who attempted to recreate the Old Kingdom world through the construction of administrative, cultic and mortuary spaces and the revival of earlier styles in the visual and textual arts of the elite.

The preservation of literary texts on papyrus from the Middle Kingdom provides another source for learning about ceremonial and performance-based acts in Egyptian life These works, written in a 'realistic' style, describe interactions between members of different classes, social and judicial routines, funeral and court ceremonies and entertainments for members of the elite (Parkinson 2002).

A well-preserved planned settlement intended to service the royal pyramid complexes (which were always important economic multipliers), sited at Gurob in the Faiyum, provides us with the opportunity to link a body of texts with actual living spaces. Although the site provides us with few documentary sources, it provides a wealth of literary, technical and religious material, pointing to occupational and perhaps even social diversity in this community (Kemp, 1989, 149-57). That community celebrations existed is suggested by the development of a public commemorative area at Abydos, the site of the tombs of the earliest kings, now identified with Osiris, god of the dead and resurrection.

State execration rituals like those of the Old Kingdom are also attested at this period, with a particularly elaborate example being excavated at the frontier fort of Mirgissa in Nubia from the mid-12th Dynasty (Vila, 1963). However, the most striking evidence for performative activity from the Middle Kingdom period is a papyrus book, the so-called Ramesseum Dramatic Papyrus, a work unique in the Egyptian textual corpus. It combines text with vignettes in a way similar to wall decoration found in temples and tombs. Its content, which relates the succession of Horus as the king of Egypt, appears to take the form of a dramatic 'script' like those from the Ptolemaic period (Sethe, 1928).

The Middle Kingdom ended sometime after 1750 BCE with political fragmentation of the country and domination of its northern part by foreigners known as *heqau khasut* ('rulers of foreign countries') in Egyptian and later in Greek as Hyksos. These people, who originated in Canaan, dominated the whole Levant between the seventeenth and fifteenth centuries BCE (Redford 1992, 98-122).

1. Materials for a History of Performance in Ancient Egypt

By 1550 BCE the native rulers of southern Egypt had driven the Hyksos out of the country and embarked on a policy of aggressive military and political expansion into the Levant and Nubia. This had a number of important social and economic effects. First and foremost was a great influx in material wealth, initially through plunder, later through trade and diplomatic gifting. Although this wealth initially found its way into temple and state treasuries, its economic effects seemed to have gradually 'trickled down' to the lower levels of society over the next hundred and fifty years. Secondly, Egyptians were exposed to foreigners and their culture at a higher level of intensity than ever before. Whether they were prisoners of war, foreign dignitaries, hostages, traders or craft experts or just friends, these people affected language, arts and crafts, modes of dress, religious observances and even architecture (Redford 1992, 192-237).

The acquisition of a foreign 'empire' on one hand and an enormous influx of people and goods on the other required a far more sophisticated administrative structure than had been required previously. Thus, from the early 18th Dynasty onwards, there seems to have been a deliberate government policy to train and deploy a greatly expanded scribal class. The ruling house of the 18th Dynasty sought to emphasize its unprecedented wealth and political influence with extensive renovations to existing temples and much new building at sacred sites. The small, frequently irregular buildings of the past were replaced with symmetrical stone structures, often on a large scale. The temple of the rulers' city god, Amun at Thebes (Luxor), shows the growth of not only a gigantic complex of stone buildings but also of a growing network of gateways, colossal pillared halls, courtyards and processional avenues. Texts and representations in the temples document the development of a public life for the god inextricably linked to that of the king. The Egyptian monarchy is clearly evolving into a public, specular institution. This trend reached its peak in the reign of Amenhotep III's son Amenhotep IV, who repudiated the gods of Egypt and replaced them with an abstract sun deity to whom he had exclusive and direct access. While Akhenaten's social experiment was a failure, it allows us to see how the development of the specular monarchy and its state cult was a function of having an educated, urbanized population as an audience (Kemp 1989, 183-231, 263-79).

Although Akhenaten's successors reverted to a more traditional ideology and state cult, they did however retain the public spectacle developed by the 18th Dynasty kings (Kemp, loc. cit.). Although almost all the New Kingdom rulers were buried in tombs concealed in the western hills of Luxor, they constructed large temples in the valley before the hills that were important centres of ceremonial and economic life, being used during the lifetime of the ruler as well as after his death. The need for workers on site to construct these tombs has also helped provide us with one of the most well-documented communities of the ancient world.

The necropolis workers' village at Deir el-Medina, west of Luxor, was occupied from the reign of Thutmose I to the end of the 20th Dynasty, a period of over four hundred years. The village was located in the desert, isolated from the valley and other settlements apparently to preserve the secret of the location of the royal tombs. Its inhabitants were supplied with food and water by the central administration of the cemetery as part of their remuneration. By the Ramesside Period (thirteenth to twelfth centuries BCE) many community members enjoyed a considerable level of affluence, with decorated houses, elaborate family tombs and a high level of literacy. We see them taking part in community activities such as religious festivals like the appearance of the oracular image of the local god, similar to those at the great temples across the river, or engaged in political activities such as the organization of strikes and demonstrations triggered by disruptions in the food supply. Life in this village came to an end in the latter part of the twelfth century BCE, when parties of raiding Libyans made it unsafe to live there (McDowell 1999).

The so-called Third Intermediate Period (1100-712 BCE) that followed the New Kingdom was characterized by political fragmentation, internecine violence and foreign invasion. It was not, however, a period of cultural stagnation. Visual art flourished; new technologies, such as in metalworking, were introduced; and a new, more user-friendly form of cursive writing (Demotic) was introduced. The high priests of the temple of Amun at Thebes, who took control of Upper Egypt after the end of the New Kingdom, appear to have continued the traditions of cultic spectacle established in the 18th Dynasty (Myśliwiec 2000, 17-67).

Around 730 BCE Egypt was invaded by the Nubian Piye, ruler of the kingdom of Kush and a devotee of Amun. He defeated its northern rulers, whom he considered to be unclean foreigners, and he purified and celebrated the cult in all the major temples, especially that of Amun at Thebes, where he stayed for the great processional festival of Opet. Piye and his successors had sufficient control of resources and labour to undertake large-scale construction projects on a number of sacred sites, something which had not been done in over four hundred years. The architecture of the Kushite period is notable for the innovation of the open colonnade found in courtyards or along ceremonial avenues, as well as large gateways, suggesting the continuing importance of the processions found in the New Kingdom and hinted at an expanded role for them (Morkot 1999, 167-250).

Following the Assyrian invasion in 674 BCE, the Kushites left Egypt, which came to be controlled by kings from the northern city of Sais. These rulers followed the example of the Kushites in that they rebuilt extensively at sacred sites and promoted a cultural style that harked back to the Old Kingdom, 'the time of the ancestors', a perceived golden age. Foremost among their projects was refurbishment of the cultic and funerary installations of the divine Apis bull, an animal cult of Memphis that originated at the beginning of the 1st Dynasty (Myśliwiec 2000, 105-34).

1. Materials for a History of Performance in Ancient Egypt

With the Persian conquest of 525 BCE Egyptian political independence came to an end, apart from a seventy-five-year period of revolt during the fifth and fourth centuries BCE (28th to 30th Dynasties). However, the power and prestige of the temples continued, making them the centres of cultural life, and the animal cults in particular gained in popularity (Myśliwiec 2000, 135-76).

After the defeat of the Persians by Alexander, his Macedonian and Greek followers took over Egypt after 334 BCE. By 300 BCE Ptolemy, satrap of Egypt, felt safe enough to declare himself king, and his descendants ruled the country until 30 BCE. The Ptolemies apparently made use of the existing administrative framework and they exploited their role as semi-divine traditional rulers, some more adeptly than others. A serious revolt in the south of the country during the second century, led by the priests of Amun at Thebes, was put down but elicited from the Greek rulers economic and social concessions to the other major religious centres. The native temples remained custodians of the royal cult outside Alexandria and may even have exerted considerable influence inside it (Bowman 1986, 167-70). In exchange for aggressively exploiting the agricultural and other natural resources of the country, the Ptolemaic regime encouraged a huge flowering of religious art, literature, spectacle and performance, which was documented in the temples in ever more ingenious and esoteric pictures and hieroglyphic texts. These are the source of the most well-documented ritual routines and performances (Derchain 1981), but they may show Hellenistic and other Near Eastern influences as well as echoing earlier native practices.

When Egypt become a Roman province in 30 BCE the administrative and financial structure was changed and temple revenues were scaled back, but building activity and artistic production in this sector continued on a somewhat diminished scale (Bowman 1986, 65ff.; Bagnall 1993, 261-73). Apart from the temples and monumental works of art in this period, there is also an unprecedented quantity of papyrus documents, archaeological sites and material culture. We know that Egyptian literary production continued. Documentary sources show us that even if the great temples were in decline, religious observances continued on a smaller scale at more humble sanctuaries or even in people's homes (Frankfurter 1997, 37-144, 238-64).

Funerals are also well documented in Graeco-Roman times. Not only was the process of mummification and the provision of Osirian burial equipment accessible for a greater portion of the population than ever before, we have evidence for not only how these services were costed and paid for but also how they were carried out (Ikram and Dodson 1998, 49-52, 104-5, 129-31). The embalming ritual, found on papyri dating from the mid-first century CE (Sauneron 1952; Goyon 1972), shows us, as does the Apis embalming ritual (Vos 1993), that mummification was as much a performance as a technical process. While it is clear that performance-based activities developed in Egypt with the help of royal and, later, clerical patronage and that their growth was apparently spurred by the development of an urbanized, educated audience, how this development continued and concluded requires careful and synchronic study rather than diachronic generalization.

Performances from Prehistoric Times
to the End of the Old Kingdom

Performance is, by its very nature, ephemeral. Trying to find evidence for it in the remote prehistory of Egypt going back beyond the fourth millennium BCE and in the formative period of the historic state is a challenging, perhaps futile, exercise. However, investigation of this period reveals some interesting continuities as well as ruptures with later 'classic' periods of Egyptian civilization.

Although the indigenous Predynastic Neolithic culture of Lower Egypt (the Delta and lower river valley of the Nile) and the earliest phase of the Upper Egyptian (upper, southern river valley) suggest an egalitarian society, the later phases of Upper Egyptian Predynastic, or Naqada, culture give unequivocal evidence of increasing social stratification (Bard 1994, Wilkinson 1996). Many of the products of this culture, including painted pottery, flint, bone and ivory work, painted linens, stone sculpture and rock engraving have all been identified as luxury products made for an elite class. Not surprisingly, much of the figurative decoration of these objects has been linked to the later texts and representations of mature Egyptian civilization.

The Naqada painted pottery shows a limited number of motifs, including long, many-oared boats with cabins, female figures with upraised arms, animals such as large birds, and male figures, sometimes shown on the boats or with weapons. There are also landscape elements such as trees and crenellated friezes that probably represent the hills bordering the Nile Valley. Thus the pot decorations can be read as landscapes with figures where oared ships peopled with armed men ply the river, on whose banks are shown women with upraised arms among birds and trees. These motifs are also found in other media, either singly or together – in sculpture, petroglyphs in the desert, carvings in bone and ivory and even wall and fabric paintings. The figures with upraised arms have also been the subject of vigorous debate: are they figures of dancing women or representations of goddesses, whose arms suggest the horns of the cattle in which form they were later thought to appear (Garfinkel 2001)?

Materials for the formation of a state

The end of the Predynastic Period, Naqada III and Dynasty '0', is distinguished by extremely rapid development of the 'high' forms of elite culture: brick architecture; visual arts – drawing and painting, freestanding and relief sculpture; stone and metal working; and, closely related to drawing, the hieroglyphic script which begins to develop even before this period. Dockets, or 'labels', originally attached to various commodities placed in elite and royal tombs of Dynasty 0 and 1, have survived where little else remains. Their historical value lies in that, along with the quantity of the material documented, they date them by the year of their manufacture or collection. Years were not numbered but were named after important events that happened in them. Obviously, for practical purposes, a year would not be named for a unique or extraordinary event, but for an important but regularly occurring happening, allowing it to be designated in advance and not after the fact. In the period of state formation, the king and his economic and ideological state apparatuses, which sought to dominate the entire country, provided the obvious source for such events. Thus the events recorded on the labels are of a ceremonial or official nature. Although sometime in the 3rd Dynasty the system of named years was discarded in favour of numbered regnal years of a particular king, the earlier dating method apparently provided the basis of annalistic records, fragments of which form a document known as the 'Palermo Stone'. Although none of the fragments of these annals have a properly documented source, the entries are sufficiently similar to the earlier labels to suggest an authentic origin, perhaps in the 5th Dynasty. While the events chronicled in these annals, as well as the labels and other documents of the late Predynastic and Archaic Periods, are not terribly informative from the perspective of a modern historian, they offer the possibility of understanding something about the regular ceremonial events of the early Egyptian state.

The Palermo Stone (Schäfer, 1902) is expertly carved in the classic style of an Old Kingdom hieroglyphic inscription. It is much easier to read than the labels and other early documents, which are often crudely drawn and date from a period before many of the signs had achieved their final form. Scholars have often used it as a guide for interpreting them. Only a few different kinds of activities are attested in the parts of this document covering the Archaic Period: defeat of enemies (both internal and external), founding of buildings and canals, manufacture and dedication of statues of gods and kings, and celebration of royal and divine ceremonies and festivals. Happenings connected with the king tend to predominate and only a few occur with any regularity. The most commonly occurring events are the Following of Horus (*shemsu Hor*), the Festival of Sokar (*heb Sokar*), the Uniting of the Two Lands (*sema tawy*), the Circuit of the Walls (*peher inbu*), and the Appearance of the King of Upper and Lower Egypt, together or separately (*kha nesu bity*). The Sed Festival (*heb Sed*) and the Running of the Apis Bull (*pecherer Hapy*) are also attested, but not with the same frequency.

With the exception of the Following of Horus, all the items on the list are well documented in later periods. The Uniting of the Two Lands, the Circuit of the Walls and the Appearance of the King of Upper and Lower Egypt tend to occur at the beginning of a reign and may refer to the coronation of the king or his accession to power (Wilkinson 1999, 208-11). The Circuit of the Walls is later documented as a race or walk performed by the king around the walls of Memphis, the new capital of early dynastic Egypt. The Appearance of the King of Upper and Lower Egypt and the Uniting of the Two Lands refer to the concept of the dual monarchy that apparently took its final form in the mid-1st Dynasty, in the reign of Den, when the Upper Egyptian rulers had finally attained total control of the northern part of the country (Wilkinson 1999, 75-6). While the 'appearance' of the king becomes a conventional way of describing his accession, the Uniting of the Two Lands may have never actually taken place, but it is a conventional figure in art and hieroglyphic script, with two heraldic plants wrapped around the sign for union. Historically the most significant union may be that between the principal kingdoms of Upper Egypt, located at Nubet (Naqada), Thinis and Hierakonpolis, not the later conquest of the north.

The Sed Festival and the Running of the Apis Bull are both well-attested activities throughout the whole of Egyptian history. The Running of the Apis Bull, which also took place around the walls of Memphis, was clearly connected with the founding of this city by the victorious Upper Egyptian rulers of Dynasty 0, and referred to the importance of cattle in the economy of Chalcolithic Egypt (Wilkinson 2003). While Apis became an oracular animal and an important deity in his own right in the later period, for a long time he was closely associated with the king and appeared as a token of his wealth and mastery of the land. The Sed Festival, or festival of royal renewal, was an important event also celebrated throughout Egyptian history, although not with such frequency as others. Although it is not completely understood or documented and obviously changed over time, it is mentioned on both the Palermo Stone and in the earlier Archaic documents. Before turning to what scholars have to say about its celebration at this early period, let us examine what we can learn of its general characteristics.

The Sed Festival

The Sed Festival is attested in all periods of Egyptian history, but only four detailed representations of it exist, accompanied by short labelling texts. No extended 'script' for this activity has yet been positively identified (but see below, on the Ramesseum Dramatic Papyrus). The earliest detailed representation dates from the reign of King Ne-user-re of the 5th Dynasty; there are two from the 18th Dynasty of Amenhotep III and his son Akhenaten and a fourth from the 22nd Dynasty, from the reign of Osorkon II. In the bilingual Ptolemaic decree of Memphis (the so-called 'Rosetta Stone'), the Sed Festival is referred to in Greek as 'the thirty-year festival', or *triakontaeteridon* (Budge 1929, 66). At later periods kings did indeed celebrate the festivals after reigning thirty years and at intervals of three years thereafter, but they could also be celebrated at irregular intervals, perhaps at important or dangerous junctures (Frankfort 1948, 80). The word 'Sed' is not well understood – it could be the word for tail (the king at times wears a bull's tail), the name of the jackal god whose standard ('the opener of the ways') precedes the king on this and other occasions, or perhaps the word for the distinctive long cloak that the king wears for part of the proceedings (Martin 1984). While details of the Sed remain obscure, it is clear that its main import was the rejuvenation of the king. Therefore some aspects of his accession were repeated, such as enthronement in both the Upper and Lower Egyptian crown and homage offered by the elite. However, until later periods the Sed Festival is much better documented than the accession. Perhaps this is a matter of decorum and ideology: the king must always be perceived to be always already there; that way his authority is much harder to challenge.

There is considerable variation in what happened in the Sed over the life of Egyptian culture, but certain elements are invariable. They are a booth with a double throne (the basis of the hieroglyph *sd*), a long, enveloping cloak worn by the king, a staircase (often associated with the booth) and a run or walk by the king between crescent-shaped markers (Serrano 2002, 47-9). The Neuserre reliefs are over five hundred years later than the late Predynastic and early Archaic material, but are part of the same direct tradition, with no obvious social or cultural break. The basic sequence of events has been studied by Werner Kaiser (1971) and is as follows.

Foundation rites are performed for a building called the palace (*ah*) in which the king changes his costume for various parts of the activity. There is an inspection and census of cattle, followed by a procession in which the king walks with members of the elite who play various roles in the Sed (Helck 1987, 11-12). On two occasions the king receives homage of the elite and then runs a course between two crescent-shaped markers, 'taking possession of the field', i.e. his domain. The king is preceded in his run by a standard topped by the jackal Sed, the opener of the way. Cattle are allotted to other participants in the festival. After this the king's feet are washed and he returns to the palace. The festival concludes when the king is carried in a palanquin as ruler of Upper and Lower Egypt. During the course of the Sed the king also visited shrines of all the principal gods of Egypt and distributed many gifts to those who participated in it, as can be seen from labels and other finds surviving from Archaic and Old Kingdom tombs (Serrano 2002, 58-65, 68-70).

The Narmer Macehead from Hierakonpolis is one a series of votive ceremonial objects found in a deposit at the main temple in this town (Quibell 1900, pl. 26b; Adams 1995, 4). The relief decoration with which it is carved shows a number of elements common to all Sed Festivals: the king is seated in a booth at the top of a stairway, he is wearing a long cloak and crescent-shaped markers are present. Livestock are depicted in pens. However, there are six markers rather than four, and three men are running between them who appear to have their hands bound. There are also persons attending on the king who carry his sandals and fan him, a detail found in other royal scenes as well as in the Sed Festival. They also carry a number of standards, including that of Sed. A figure in a palanquin is placed in front of the king's throne. Although other interpretations can be offered (Serrano 2002, 53), this figure appears in other Sed depictions, where it can be designated as a royal child or a divine image (Kemp 1989, 92-3; Gohary 1992, 11).

The festival is more clearly shown in two labels from Abydos, one carved, the other painted (Serrano 2002, 68). The top register behind the year sign shows the king in the double crown running between two groups of three markers like those found on the Narmer Macehead. Behind this, afterwards, he sits in a stepped booth, wearing the long cloak and the double crown. The lowest register of the painted label is well preserved enough to show the king harpooning a hippopotamus.

A seal impression from the tomb of the high official Hemaka dates from this reign and shows two scenes, the king in a red crown running behind a bull and in the white crown running, with the Sed standard in front of him, towards a baboon who is holding out a bowl. There is considerable controversy about this image. Does it represent one subject or two (Serrano 2002, 69-70)? As they have baselines underneath them, do the figures of the king represent statues (Eaton-Krauß 1984, 90-2)? The letter *p* is all that survives of an inscription on the left-hand side, suggesting it should be read *pecherer Hapy* or 'running of the Apis bull', an event attested for this reign on the Palermo Stone (Schäfer 1902, 21). The presence of a baboon at the Sed Festival is attested in the later reliefs of Netcherikhet. Helck (1950; 1987, 9-10) has argued that the baboon represents the royal predecessor or ancestors, 'the white one of the great' into whose shrine the king runs at the end of his race to receive a drink of wine.

A fuller and more canonical representation of the Sed can be found in reliefs carved in the underground galleries of the Step Pyramid complex of Netcherikhet at Saqqara. The first panel shows the king 'standing (in) (the shrine of) Horus of Behdet' the place of enthronement (Friedman 1995, 20).

In the second scene, the king runs from between two sets of three markers into the 'white palace'. This building is shown twice, first with its name and second with a baboon sitting on top of it. This is no doubt a way of showing the creature inside the building. The baboon, who wears a double sash like that worn by the lector priest or reader in cultic performances, is apparently about to offer the bowl to the king, as seen on the sealing of Den discussed above. The king is dressed in a brief loincloth. He carries the container with his certificate of rulership, which according to Helck (1987, 10) he will present to the baboon. In the third panel he continues the race, even more scantily clad in only a penis sheath. The caption on this scene has been interpreted by Friedman (1995, 14, 29) to suggest that the king runs not only between the markers, but out of a gateway on the south-west side of the enclosure and around its walls. This run recapitulated the 'circuit of the walls' associated with the king's accession in the early documents.

The fourth panel shows a very similar scene, except that one of the animated hieroglyphs which are found in these scenes is shown in a gesture of rejoicing, suggesting that the course has been successfully completed. The last two pictures show the king attired as in the first scene standing in the shrines of Horus of Letopolis or Shmin (a place just to the north of Memphis) and finally, the *per wer*, or great house, the national shrine of Upper Egypt. There is no representation of the king sitting in the booth in his long robe, because there is a three-dimensional version of this in his *serdab*, or statue chamber, on the northern side of the pyramid (Smith 1981, 53).

Furthermore, there is an actual booth, complete with two sets of stairs, in a courtyard on the east side of the pyramid, containing life-sized representations of the shrines of the gods of the two lands. To the south of the pyramid we find a great courtyard, complete with a dais on the north side and two sets of markers in its centre. The funerary enclosure of Netcherikhet is both a multimedia artwork and a representation of a Sed Festival installation. The purpose of this ensemble has been hotly debated – was the festival actually celebrated here or was it intended to magically reproduce itself for the king in eternity (Strudwick 1985; Smith 1981, 57)? Friedman (1995, 32) has argued that the representations of the king in the reliefs show statues of him performing the festival, which have parallels elsewhere and suggest that actual rites were commemorated or performed magically with images.

Can we understand the Sed Festival as a performance or as theatre? Richard Schechner (1988) defines a performance as a whole event including audience, actors and technical support, and theatre as a specific set of gestures done by performers in such a context. Theatre is a visible or audible set of events of well-known components or a score invented during rehearsal. The score or script is not necessarily a text, but something that pre-exists any given enactment and which takes a persistent shape and is known by performers and spectators. Certainly the Sed was embedded in a holistic kind of event. The Egyptian word *heb*, 'festival', has a meaning close to that of holiday, in its original sense of a religious celebration (Erman and Grapow 1955, III, 57-8; Bleeker 1967, 27-8) with all that entails, including communal celebration with merrymaking, feasting and gift giving. Depictions of cattle and their enumeration suggest high-protein feasting, the evidence of Archaic Period labels and later custom-made objects points to large-scale gift giving (Serrano 2002, 49, 53-4, 65ff.), and the contents of the magazines of the Archaic tombs, especially that of Netcherikhet, point to the consumption of large quantities of wine, some of it imported, at least by the elite (Helck 1987, 10; Wilkinson 1999, 41-2, 119).

There is certainly no doubt that the main events of the Sed Festival were well known among the elite class and others, if only through texts, representations or hearsay. Although the festival was clearly subject to variation, especially during the Archaic Period, its basic shape was universally recognizable and its representations consistent enough over a 3,000-year period for us to recognize them. However, the Sed clearly resides nearer the ritual end of the continuum between ritual and theatre in that it is effective rather than entertaining (Schechner 1988, 120ff.). The whole operation is designed to get results, that is, the rejuvenation of the king. The elite audience also participates in the festival, and belief as opposed to appreciation or criticism is encouraged. On the other hand, the large expenditure, especially the gift giving, entailed in this activity seems to have been designed to impress the audience as favourably as possible.

Schechner states that a performance creates its own space (1988, 60). The existence of the Netcherikhet complex, with its re-presentation of the Sed installation, allows us to explore this idea with reference not only to the 3rd Dynasty and later festivals but also to their Archaic and Predynastic forerunners. Kaiser (1969) has drawn attention to the fact that the so-called funerary enclosures of the 1st and later 2nd Dynasty at Abydos closely resemble the Neterikhet enclosure in that they are all rectangular, are surrounded by a niched wall and have a gateway in either the north-east or south-west corner (O'Connor 1989, 78-80). In most cases these entrances open into small chambers or buildings (O'Connor 1989, 76-9) which give the whole ensemble a close resemblance to the common hiero-glyphic sign *hut*, 'house', 'establishment' or 'temple'. They suggest a walled brick enclosure with a guardhouse to restrict access to the interior (Spencer 1984, 22-3).

Although many types of installation might require restricted access, Schechner (1988, 59-60) cites ethnographic material that is particularly interesting in this regard. During the Nanda initiation ceremony of Fiji, a rectangular stone enclosure measuring 100 feet x 50 feet is constructed, surrounded by a three-foot wall. This conceals the nature of the ordeal both from the initiates prior to entering the enclosure and from the audience, as well as providing an encompassing, self-contained space for the experience. In another example, although women are excluded from the ceremonial house of the Iatmul of Niugini, ceremonies are staged so they may be partially visible to them, and the music is performed with them in mind (Schechner 1988, 60-1).

Although we see the elite participating in and watching the Sed Festival on the Narmer Macehead and the Neuserre reliefs, it is likely that another audience was to be found outside the enclosure, even if the walls were high enough to prevent them from seeing inside. This would have been the rest of the population, known as *rekhyt*, written with a lapwing or plover (Gardiner 1947, I, *15-17; II, *447-8; 1957, 470, 472). Avian life was extremely plentiful and important to the early Egyptians, which explains why many common signs in the hieroglyphic script represent it. Plovers were small and very plentiful birds, like pigeons. As early as Dynasty 0 the Scorpion macehead shows bedraggled plovers hanging from the royal standards, a vivid reminder of the class warfare behind an ideology that pitted the king against external enemies and vaguely defined forces of chaos (Wilkinson 1999, 248). Although the king and the elite may have despised the other classes, their acquiescence to his rule was essential and was likely solicited through limited participation or witnessing of performances and ceremonies such as the Sed Festival. The act of making a circuit of the walls, whether of the palace during the accession, of the city of Memphis with the Apis bull, or of a special ceremonial enclosure in the case of the Sed, allowed the ruler to be visible to an audience that was not permitted inside the restricted space of the enclosure, even if they could hear what was going on inside. The pattern of exclusion and revelation in early Egyptian cultures seems to be at the heart of such performances.

The interior of the Netcherikhet enclosure allows us to see how the performance ordered the space inside the enclosure. Inside the single actual entrance, a passage leads north to the Sed Festival court, while straight ahead is an entrance colonnade. On its southern side, to the left, is a small shrine that has been identified with the 'white palace' where the ancestor baboon receives the king's credentials (Wilkinson 1999, 248). The entrance hall gives on to the southern half of the enclosure where the run between the markers was performed, and there stood an altar adjacent to the pyramid (Lauer 1999, 16). Next to this is the court where the shrines of the gods of Upper and Lower Egypt are located, with the base of the double booth preserved at its southern end. Behind these shrines is the so-called Temple T, a building that most probably represents the place where the king changed his costume (Ricke 1944, 89-96; Lauer 1999, 16). To the north of this courtyard are two further courtyards with adjacent buildings known as the north and south house because they are decorated with the sedge and the papyrus, the heraldic plants of Upper and Lower Egypt. Lauer (1962, 165; 1999, 18-19) believes that these structures represent the places where the king received the homage of his elite subjects at the end of the festival.

Fig. 3. Step Pyramid complex showing the southern end of the festival court
with the platform for the king's throne and a chapel in the background.

The Netcherikhet complex combined the functions of a ceremonial and
a funerary installation, which had been kept separate in earlier royal
structures. The position of the earlier mastaba and later pyramid mirrors
not only a similar structure in the enclosure of Khasekhemwy at Abydos,
but also the position of a purpose-built mound of sand in the early temple
at Hierakonpolis. A similar installation that may also have existed in the
early temple at Heliopolis, opposite Memphis (where Netcherikhet also
erected stone structures [Wilkinson 1999, 91]), was later known as 'the
high sand' (Petrie 1915, 3-4, pl. 1; Ricke 1935), the site of the sanctuary,
which according to later Egyptian lore stood on the primeval mound which
arose out of chaos as the site of the creation of the world (Frankfort 1948,
152). The funerary enclosure not only represented the royal palace and
ceremonial enclosure, but also the temple and the beginnings of universal
history.

In Schechner's terminology (1988, 7), event time (a sequence that must
be completed) and set time (the period in which the sequence is to be
fulfilled) are replaced by symbolic conflated time, as is the norm for ritual
events. The traditional, primeval character of the Sed is guaranteed by the
simple primitive architecture that is reproduced in stone in the design of
the divine and national shrines, which conform to a type consisting of a
structure with a light wooden frame, curved roof and matting and woven
grass screens (Smith 1981, 57-8; Kemp 1989, 95-7). We have already seen
such buildings depicted in Predynastic and Archaic art and their imitation

continues for the duration of Egyptian culture (Kemp 1989, 95-101), but a recent discovery has provided an actual example as part of a similar installation.

In 1985-6 Michael Hoffman discovered an extensive structure in area HK29A at Hierakonpolis, which consisted of an extensive parabola-shaped mud-plastered floor measuring about 32 x 13 metres. It was originally bounded by a mud-covered fence which was later replaced by a mud-brick wall. On its north side were the remains of several rectangular buildings and a gateway, and on the south side was a large structure with four very large post-holes. A huge post at the end of the courtyard probably supported a totemic figure. This building, which has a convex roof and was built of wood and reeds, has been identified by Renée Friedman (1996, 30-4) with the *per wer*, the national shrine of Upper Egypt, a building of a type frequently depicted on late Predynastic and Archaic artefacts and at the Netcherikhet complex. The site also yielded evidence of pottery and the remains of cattle and large aquatic fauna such as Nile perch, crocodiles and turtles. Three different periods of occupation can be discerned: Naqada IIc-d, Naqada III to 1st Dynasty, and early 1st Dynasty, with the reigns of Aha and Djer attested. At the end of this time the buildings were carefully dismantled and the pottery vessels and incense burners were buried in a pit. Friedman thinks that the old building materials were transferred to the new temple in the centre of the town (1996, 30). Thus we are likely dealing with a prototype of the ceremonial enclosure where performances like the Sed Festival were enacted.

There were other actors in this performance besides the king. Although they are only sporadically documented in the Archaic Period (Kaplony 1963, 1201-18), the Neuserre reliefs show us that the Sed called for specialized roles. These included the friends (*semeru*); chamberlains (*imy khent*) who assisted the king by carrying his palanquin, washing his feet, changing his costume etc.; the servant of the souls of Nekhen and Pe (*hem bau Nekhen Pe*), who carried the Sed standard in front of the king; the masters of ceremonies (*iry ta*); the man from Heliopolis (*Iwnw*); and the servants of the throne (*hemu sut*) (Von Bissing 1923; Frankfort 1948, 81). While this list presents us with a mixture of dramatic parts and technical support roles, it suggests a performance characterized by physical and aural interaction between persons playing a variety of roles. The Neuserre reliefs show dialogue as well as action (Frankfort 1948, 83-5): the attending men have replaced the baboon as the recipient of the king's credentials, crying 'Come, bring (it)!' Elsewhere they are replaced by a pair of women representing Meret, the double goddess of Upper and Lower Egypt (Berlandini 1980, 82). Such variations suggest that the festival was subject to continual reworking around its basic script; things could be added, subtracted and reinstated according to the taste, ideological needs and resources of the celebrants.

However, the existence of the Netcherikhet and earlier funerary enclosures raises the question of whether the festival was performed at the king's funeral or if he used the enclosure for this purpose during his lifetime. Much later, rulers such as Ramesses III did perform the Sed Festival at their own funerary temple, and from the 4th Dynasty onwards the royal residence and the funerary complex where adjacent to each other (Lehner 1997, 231).

Other Archaic ceremonies

The other periodic or ceremonial activities attested in the Archaic Period and on the Palermo Stone have also have been incorporated into the Sed, especially the Circuit of the Walls and the Appearance of the King of Upper and Lower Egypt. The Running of the Apis Bull is also thought by some to have been included (Helck 1987, 11, 14). The Festival of Sokar, a chthonic god connected with the Memphite necropolis who was carried in procession in a distinctively decorated boat (Gaballa and Kitchen 1969), is attested in a number of archaic sources (Serrano 2002, 92-8). Documents that survive from the 6th Dynasty archive of priests in the temple of King Neferirkare show that a number of sacred emblems were carried in this procession (Posener-Kriéger 1976, 59-70, 549-52), but unfortunately most of our knowledge of this festival comes from a much later period (see below, Chapter 4).

Our examination of the Sed Festival and these other performances shows apparent overlapping of activities such as circumambulation, running, enthronement, processions and interactions with animals. It is more likely that such activities functioned as basic units of performance rather than as acts unique to a particular ceremony or ritual. Figures like the lector priest and the servant of the god found in the Sed Festival performed many other kinds of ceremonial activities. The performances of early Egypt were a form of recombinant culture just as they were in later periods.

Helck (1987, 5-48), Wilkinson (1999, 208-23) and Serrano (2002) identify the Hippopotamus hunt as a standard ceremony or performance. Wilkinson (1999, 216-17) and Serrano (2002, 79-80) describe it as a festival of victory, like the despatching of prisoners. While there are quite a few prehistoric depictions of hippopotami from prehistoric times and of kings and other figures hunting them from the late Predynastic and early Archaic Period (Decker and Harb 1994, 353-7), the interpretation of Helck, Wilkinson and Serrano depends on the Ptolemaic 'dramatic' text known as the Triumph of Horus, which was part of a festival of victory celebrated at the temple of Edfu in the second century BCE (see Chapter 5). Apart from the 3,000-year gap that separates these sources, it should be noted that almost no evidence for a royal hunt exists in the intervening period. The motif is found almost only in mortuary texts and related material (Decker and Harb 1994, 276-7). The purely symbolic nature of this act may be explained by the extreme danger of hunting real hippos. The animal used in the Edfu pageant was surely a small model (Fairman 1973, 48-9). The notation occurs only once on the Palermo Stone (Schäfer 1902, 20) because killing a hippopotamus is not a repeatable action that can be controlled, but a dangerous exploit. The cachet of the early rulers of Egypt may have been founded on such acts, but they probably did not care to repeat them on a regular basis. There are good reasons why Old Kingdom tomb reliefs show members of the elite watching lesser mortals carrying out this activity (Decker and Harb 1994, 359-70). In other words, identification of performances also depends on assessment of their feasibility.

The Rite of the Opening of the Mouth, a central ritual of Egyptian cult worship that called down spirits of gods or other beings into images or objects, is referred to in Old Kingdom funerary inscriptions but is not completely documented until the New Kingdom. It is discussed below in Chapter 4.

Funerary ceremonies

For reasons of decorum there are virtually no depictions of a royal funeral at any time in Egyptian history apart from the Amarna Period. It has been suggested that a papyrus from a Middle Kingdom tomb at the Ramesseum contains a text that relates to the performance of the ceremonies (Gardiner 1955), and this will be examined in the next chapter. A number of attempts have been made to relate the Pyramid Texts from late Old Kingdom royal tombs to the actual obsequies of the king (e.g. Spiegel 1960; Altemüller 1972; Barta 1981; Allen 1994) and the locations inside the pyramid and funerary complex where they occurred. The task of reconstructing a royal funeral after the 3rd Dynasty is made much more difficult by a complete change in plan of the funerary complexes. The rectangular enclosure with large empty spaces for performances is replaced by a plan on a longitudinal east-west axis in which the pyramid and its temple are placed on the high desert, far from the temple at the edge of valley, to which it is joined by a stone or brick causeway (Kemp 1989, 62-3). Although the causeway suggests a processional axis, the entrances to it are very narrow and the rooms and courtyards inside the buildings, which are largely of solid masonry, are not at all spacious. This has led Dieter Arnold (1979) to suggest that the funeral took place outside the complex in temporary structures on the desert plateau. However, Rainer Stadelmann (1997, 10-11) has pointed out that causeways had on occasion been blocked with masonry, suggesting that this had been done after the funeral. A similar phenomenon has been noted at Abydos, where the entrances of some of the early dynastic enclosures have been bricked up (O'Connor 1989, 76-7).

If this king's temples were staffed by priests who performed his cult for centuries, as shown by the existence of an archive (Posener-Kriéger 1969), and others like those of Menkaure were long in use and even modified by their staff (Kemp 1989, 145-9), why is not possible that funeral ceremonies could be performed in them? Only the inner coffin or even the mummy of the king may have travelled up the causeway, with much of the other funerary equipment either disassembled, as in the case of Khufu's mother, Hetepheres (Lehner 1985, 17-35), or, like the stone sarcophagus, placed inside the pyramid while it was under construction. The royal funerary complexes can be decorated with reliefs but, as noted in Chapter 1, these are not informative about funeral ceremonies. Depictions of the Sed Festival must be commemorative or magical, since there is no large space within the complexes to perform its activities.

We are much better informed about private funerary ceremonies, which are depicted in tomb chapel reliefs of the 5th and 6th Dynasties. There are two types of funeral scenes. First, the better-known ones from the 6th Dynasty, of which those from the tombs of Qar and Idu at Giza and the tomb of Pepy-ᶜankh Heny Kem at Meir are the most complete (Simpson 1976, figs 24, 35; Blackman and Apted 1953, pls 42-3), present a detailed depiction of transport of the body to the embalming house and its subsequent journey to the cemetery. The second group, found in a number of 5th Dynasty tombs in the Memphite necropolis, present a more aphoristic, even 'symbolic' representation. They concentrate on the manufacture and transport of the statue(s) of the deceased to the cemetery. While the statue was vital to the deceased's spiritual return to this world, as achieved through the Rite of the Opening of the Mouth, it may also be argued that the statue represents the body in its coffin, which for reasons of decorum was not shown, although these strictures where later relaxed (Settgast 1963, 18-20).

The more mimetic character of the 6th Dynasty funeral depictions provide a convenient starting point for reconstructing these performances. In the tomb of Idu we see the friends and family of the deceased, both men and women, weeping, tearing their hair and throwing themselves on the ground (Simpson 1976, fig. 35). This is when, immediately following death, the deceased's body is taken to 'the beautiful west'. Sometimes it is said to be resting in the *per djet,* or pious foundation (Settgast 1963, 7). These institutions became very important during the Old Kingdom and were made up of the family, associates and dependents of prominent members of the social elite who performed obligations and derived income from their funerary cults. These institutions no doubt indicate larger networks of social relations between members of the elite social class and their dependents. It was the members of the *djet,* as well as immediate family members, who were responsible for performing the funerary ceremony.

After being removed from the family home or the *per djet,* the body was taken to the beautiful west, a cemetery that generally lay on the edge of the western desert. As in many other cultures, beliefs about the afterlife and ceremonies around them were closely tied to the natural world and the landscape, with the setting sun providing a powerful metaphor for

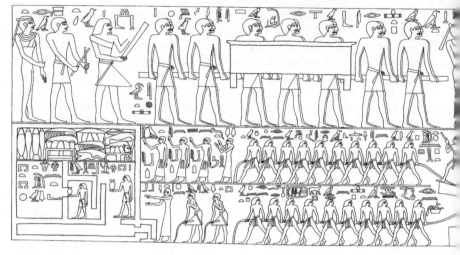

Fig. 4. Funeral procession from the tomb chapel of Qar, Giza (6th Dynasty).
Redrawn from the original publication by Lynn Holden.

death from at least the late prehistoric period, as the Dynasty 0 cemetery
at Abydos shows (Richards 1999, 85-7). This journey took place by boat,
either across the river or via a network of canals or irrigation basins, to
the immediate destination, the *ibu*, or tent of purification, an installation
that had to be located next to running water. The tent was rectangular in
shape, with three entrances and no roof. One entrance, equipped with a
ramp, abutted directly on to the water and was located in the centre of one
of the long sides. The other two were at either end of the structure
(Grdseloff 1941, 10-12). On its journey to the *ibu* the corpse was accompanied by two embalmers, two female mourners and a lector priest. In the tomb
of Qar (Simpson 1976, fig. 35) the embalmers are shown walking in front of
and behind the coffin, beating sticks together. A woman mourner follows each
embalmer. The women are identified as 'kites', carrion birds whose calls
sound like people crying (Frankfort 1948, 41). The kites also represent Isis
and her sister Nepthys, as the mourners of their brother Osiris.

Two lector priests are shown, one at the head of the procession and the
other directly behind the coffin, reading 'beatifications' or 'glorifications'
from scrolls for the spirit of the deceased. '*Sakh*', the word that yields this
translation, means literally 'make effective'. This means that the priests'
recitations, intended to make the mummy and statues of Qar into a
functioning entity in the next world, will accomplish exactly what they say
if recited correctly by the right person and with the proper actions. In other
words, not only are they performative in the Austinian or Butlerian sense,
but these utterances are effective by virtue of having the property of
'magic' (*heka*). The effective utterance and the spell are one and the same
(Ritner 1993, 30-5).

38

The coffin is carried by 'venerable worthies', a role that can also be filled by the members of the *djet* or the friends of the deceased (who might be the same people). The performative speeches of the priests continue in the *ibu* and are accompanied by food offerings, for which cattle are slaughtered. A number of special objects are required for what goes on there, including a tub, different kinds of pottery vessels, an ankh sign, a pair of sandals, special baskets and a chest containing 'the necessities' (Grdseloff 1941, 25-31; Settgast 1963, 9-14). One of the embalmers and a kite are shown reciting words while leaning over a food offering, but the speech is not recorded. After the necessary acts of the *ibu* were performed, the body was taken to the *wabet*, a building known from later sources to be the place where the body was embalmed. The coffin is shown being either carried or ferried there on a boat and is once again accompanied by a lector priest, two embalmers and the kites.

In the tomb of Qar a most interesting depiction of this building shows it in plan with screen doorways, nested rooms and blind corridors reminiscent of both the building plans found in 3rd Dynasty private tombs and at the Step Pyramid of Netcherikhet. The building is labelled '*wabet* of attendance' and depicts the lector priest entering and inside the building holding a jar. As in the *ibu*, there is a magazine filled with food offerings. The *wabet* in the tomb of Pepy-ankh is indicated only as a doorway with a torus moulding, flanked by two columns with palm capitals (like those found in royal mortuary temples). The lector priest, two embalmers, a male mourner and the kites are shown inside with the food offerings. Outside the *wabet* we see a group of women performing a dance, clothed in long skirts decorated with ribbons and moving their hands in an apparently restrained fashion, while another claps in accompaniment. This whole scene is labelled 'mourning by the two acacias' and in the register below we see another woman clad in a long dress labelled as the leader of the acacia house, and two men with whips who are friends of the acacia house. The acacia house was the place where offerings were prepared and effective utterances recited for the deceased (Edel 1970).

There is considerable discussion as to what exactly went on in the tent of purification and the *wabet* (Grdseloff 1941, 5-14, 31-9; Lehner 1997, 28; Settgast 1963, 15). The proximity of the tent to running water suggests that it was used for washing the body and perhaps for its evisceration. The large tub, baskets and chests are reminiscent of the kind of equipment used to eviscerate the Apis bull in the Ptolemaic document P. Vindob. 3873 (see below, Chapter 5). However, not only is the document over 2,000 years later than these Old Kingdom representations, but the process of mummification differed considerably at this early period (Ikram and Dodson 1998, 109-13). While it is likely that the body was wrapped in the *wabet*, it is uncertain where desiccation took place. Many of the perceived problems in understanding the Old Kingdom funeral arise when attempts are made to equate part of the royal mortuary complex with these structures (Lehner 1997, 27). If we concentrate on private funerals, most of these difficulties disappear, although it is unclear whether the Rite of the Opening of the Mouth was performed in the tent or in the *wabet* (Grdseloff 1941, 36-9; Settgast 1963, 14). However, we can still make the general observation that the funeral as a whole, including the embalming, was a performance-based activity. As in the Sed and other royal ceremonies, there are a number of actors, a script and different costumes and props, with the action taking place at different sites. Although both the tent and the *wabet* are designed to exclude outsiders and prevent them from seeing inside, the presence of the dancers outside the *wabet* suggests that mourners were allowed in its immediate proximity, interacting in some way with those inside, as in the examples from Melanesian culture noted by Schechner, discussed above. Although preparation of the body was the preserve of the embalmer and the lector priest, close family members who played the parts of the kites and the male mourner were permitted in these restricted areas.

The next important part of the ceremony was the procession to the tomb. It must be remembered that a period of over two months (Lehner 1997, 26) separated this event from the initial removal of the body from the family. So perhaps the performances shown outside the *wabet* took place over an extended period of time. The body in its coffin was placed on a sledge with a canopy over it and dragged to the burial place by a pair of oxen. The coffin was accompanied by the lector priest as well as the family, friends and associates of the deceased. For example, Djau, a provincial governor in Upper Egypt in the late 6th Dynasty, is shown in his tomb chapel accompanied by the band of the *djet* and members of his administrative staff (Davies 1902, 7; Settgast 1963, 21). The procession was headed by a group of men carrying staffs, including the embalmers as well as the friends and chamberlains (*imy-khent*) that we have already encountered at the Sed Festival.

The kites were prominent in this procession, either in front of and behind the coffin or near the head of the procession, where the *iba* dancers were also to be found. Although they were sometimes attired in long dresses and made graceful gestures with their arms, the *iba* dancers more typically wore very brief skirts and kicked their legs high in the air, as we see in the tomb of Djau. They also wore their hair in long plaits with weights on the ends that whirled around with the violent movements of their heads. The weights, the *ibau*, were made of pottery or bone and were named after the pieces used in *senet*, a board game of chance that had associations with death and the afterlife (Pusch 1984, 851-5), as chess does in our culture. The young girls who performed this dance were perhaps intended to sexually stimulate the spirit of the deceased, who was thought to re-engender himself into another existence (Altenmüller 1978), a belief that assumes that male is the default gender. As the sledge moved across the desert sands to the tomb, a man walked in front of it, pouring water from a jar under the runners to facilitate its movement. This act may also have had symbolic significance, for later mortuary texts emphasize the importance of fresh water for the soul (Settgast 1963, 22). The procession also included the statue of the deceased made for the mortuary cult, as well as the canopic jars which contained the internal organs that had been removed from the body (Settgast 1963, pl. 1).

No Old Kingdom texts or representations indicate what ceremonies took place at the tomb on the day of burial. They may have included the Rite of the Opening of the Mouth being performed on the statue, although according to the text this took place in the sculptors' workshop. On the royal mastabas of the 1st Dynasty the cult place was in the centre of the eastern side, where two large stele engraved with the king's name were set up (Kemp 1989; Wilkinson 1999, 234). The eastward orientation reflected the hope that he would be reborn like the sun, and the siting of a *serdab*, on the south-western side of the mastaba of Den, towards the entry of the great wadi of Abydos, was perhaps equated with the entrance to the next world (Wilkinson 1999, 236; Richards 1999, 92).

Cult places are also found in the central niche of the recessed facades of non-royal 1st Dynasty elite tombs. Smaller tombs of the late Predynastic and early Archaic Period at Tarkhan, adjacent to the Faiyum, south of Memphis, show the cult niche protected by a surrounding wall that forms a small enclosure or courtyard with a screened, indirect entrance, like that found in contemporary temples at Elephantine and Abydos and closely resembling the Egyptian letter *h* (also the writing of 'courtyard') (Vandier 1952, 693-4). The desire for concealment, or at least discretion, suggested by this kind of plan is greatly elaborated in elite tombs of the 2nd and 3rd Dynasty, where plans featuring many-branching corridors and dead ends show a close similarity to the ground plans of the buildings and substructure of the Step Pyramid complex (Vandier 1952, 709-10, 889-901, 904-5, 914-16; Roth 1993, 40-3). Alongside the development of these labyrinthine plans there appears a more symmetrical cult emplacement focussed on the central niche, with two side niches forming a cruciform plan (Vandier 1952, 705-9). This so-called cruciform chapel becomes standard at the beginning of the 4th Dynasty, at the same time that the royal funerary complex abandons its form as a rectangular enclosure, filled with asymmetrically planned and sited structures, for a longitudinally oriented installation consisting of valley temple, causeway, mortuary temple and (initially) a very large pyramid.

Ann Roth (1993, 51-5) has suggested that these changes reflect a different kind of relationship between the king and members of the elite, one of perceived benevolence to much lesser subjects, based on a divinity shared with the sun god. This resulted in more large, open spaces in the buildings and a less indirect approach to the cult place. However, it is also possible that these changes reflect different performance styles used in the celebration of the burial. Perhaps these more open and spacious chapels mark the point at which the Rite of the Opening of the Mouth was transferred here from the sculptors' workshop. Roth also points out the appearance at this period of more elaborate relief and painted decoration which often features the family of the deceased, as well as the innovation of multiple burial shafts in the superstructure for family members (1993, 42). Probably related to this is the appearance of the standard offering formula describing the tomb and burial service as a gift of the king and the siting of elite private burials close to the royal tomb; before this they had occupied different cemeteries. The standard offering formula also mentions for the first time a series of festivals where offerings and prayers are made to the deceased (Spalinger 1996, 1-24). For example, we read in the tomb of Idu,

> May he be glorified very greatly by lector priests and embalmers, at the New Year's festival, at the Thoth festival, at the first of the year, at the Wag-feast, at the feast of Sokar, at the great festival, at the festival of lights, at the Sadj festival, at the coming forth of Min, at the half month (and) month festivals, at all the seasonal feasts, at the beginning of every week, at all great festivals and throughout the course of every day ... (after Simpson 1976, 21).

We are already familiar with some of these festivals from the Archaic Period and most of them are also attested in the archives of the temple of King Neferirkare, where they were the occasion for substantial offerings of food and drink, which then reverted to the priesthood (Posener-Kriéger 1968, 315, 535-63, 637-41) and possibly to the tombs of select individuals in the surrounding cemetery. Since Idu was a functionary in the mortuary establishment of Khufu, near whose great pyramid he is buried (Simpson 1968, vii), it is possible that he expected to receive offerings at his tomb

that originated at his former place of employment. With how much ceremony such redistributions were carried out we do not know, but it is
noteworthy that the lector priests and embalmers, the same persons who
officiated at the funeral, were expected to continue to recite spells to make
the spirit 'effective' on these occasions as well. We can also be sure that
the family of the deceased took part in these festivals, as we know they did
in later times (Schott 1952). The provision of the more spacious, decorated
chapels may be primarily to accommodate their visits on these holidays.

One of the celebratory performances depicted in the tomb of Idu and
other old Kingdom tomb chapels is the *sen netcheru,* or 'meeting the gods',
which features scantily clad *iba* dancers performing to the accompaniment
of harp, flute and handclapping, with songs about the epiphany of Hathor,
the goddess of sexual love and regeneration. The dancers and handclapping women wear a special collar called the *menat,* also connected with
this goddess. Below the musicians we see men playing *senet* and other
board games, and above them children – naked girls and boys – play in
mock conflict. Among the dancers and musicians are two of Idu's daughters, and one of the playing children is his son. Hartwig Altenmüller (1978)
has linked these performances with later festivals for the dead and suggests that the dancing and games are intended to sexually arouse the
departed spirit for its own self-regeneration (as during the funeral procession) and to help it overcome obstacles encountered on the way to the next
world (as represented in the *senet* game and the children's mock battles).

It is also possible that the autobiographical statements and appeals to
passers-by to recite the offering ritual have a performative intent, but
whether or not they were intended to be part of an actual performance is
unclear. Ann Roth has suggested that the men who served as funerary
priests may have celebrated rite-of-passage ceremonies which were paid
for by their patron, and this explains why activities like circumcision are
depicted in some chapels (Roth 1991, 62-72). Although we know that
circumcision was performed on Egyptian adolescent boys, these scenes do
not provide any information about the nature or location of any initiation
ceremony or other performance such as the Australian bora ceremony
described by Schechner (1988, 44).

Conclusion

To summarize, the late Predynastic to Old Kingdom Periods provide
rather limited evidence for many of the festivals and ceremonies attested
in later Egyptian culture. Most of this takes the form of pictures and brief
textual explanations. The early annals found on the Palermo Stone and
archaic labels provide little other information except to show that certain
festivals were regularly celebrated and that many of them were under
direct royal patronage. The existence of large enclosures and later pyramid complexes suggests places where activities like the Sed Festival or the

royal funeral could have been celebrated. Although the Netcherikhet complex provides us with some evidence for the spatial organization of the Sed performance, it must be remembered that it is almost certainly a representation and not a real performance site. Actual traces of its celebration are limited almost entirely to the gifts (or the labels from them) given to members of the elite who participated, as well as to the fact that its highest-ranking members generally hold titles that point to roles played in the performance. The Pyramid Texts provide no real clue as to how the royal funeral was celebrated in the buildings connected with the royal tomb. However, that they were so used seems to be suggested not only by the bricking up of royal causeways after the funeral but also by the continued statue cult documented in the archive of the Neferirkare temple, as well as evidence of ongoing use and occupation at other sites. The divine statue cult and the festivals celebrated in the temples are alluded to in these documents only through inventories of cult objects, offerings and personnel. The animation of the cult statue which took place by means of the Rite of the Opening of the Mouth is attested in the Pyramid Texts and inscriptions and representations in the tombs of private individuals, although detailed scripts are much later. Apart from periodic festivals celebrated at the tomb, the early Egyptians had many other celebrations and performances that cannot be described here in detail.

However, we can make some general observations about these early performances. First, most of those that we know about were under the direct patronage of the king. This is not surprising, since the ruler was the main source of power, prestige and wealth at this time. In the period of state formation we find the first canonical depictions of the king celebrating the gods or triumphing over his enemies, and the formation of hieroglyphic writing. Such works of art, along with brick architecture with recessed panelling, are the earliest surviving elements of the ideology of rulership. However, slate palettes, statues, paintings and reliefs and architecture have a limited circulation. The non-elite classes might see the king emerge from the ceremonial enclosure and run around the walls. They would no doubt be aware of the human sacrifices that took place at the royal funeral. The appearance of the king in his great boat on the river was like that of a god. The early ceremonial enclosures imply restricted access but also suggest a wider audience outside it. The same principle can be seen in private funeral ceremonies where mourners sing and dance outside the tent of purification or the *wabet*. The opening up of the space of royal funerary temples and chapels implies more elaborate but less restricted ritual performances.

Schechner (1988) has noted that performances form a continuum that moves between the poles of ritual and entertainment. While all the activities described in this chapter have a ritual character, they are also part of that continuum. The games and musical performances at the *sen netcheru* probably had the object of enjoyment as well as being an exercise in ritual re-presentation. The fact that some of the singers and dancers are labelled as 'stars' (meaning in Egyptian roughly what it does in English) suggests a level of proficiency, if not professionalism, that entertained as well as made ritual effective. Near the great pyramid is a tomb of a woman who was the director of royal entertainment, and a number of elite males hold similar titles (Manniche 1991, 121-2). A later folktale tells of how King Sneferu of the 4th Dynasty liked to be amused by scantily clad girls (Lichtheim 1975, 216-17). Performances must have existed in Old Kingdom Egypt that were closer to entertainment than ritual, but unfortunately we have little or no evidence for them.

Performances in the Middle Kingdom

The centralized hegemony of the Old Kingdom ended sometime after 2150 BCE; its passing may be marked on one hand by the disappearance of the large-scale royal pyramid complexes that had once dominated the landscape and the economy, or in the textual record, by the marking in the 19th Dynasty (thirteenth-century BCE) king list known as the Turin Canon of 955 years and ten days from the beginning of the united kingdom to what is conventionally known as the 8th Dynasty (Redford 1986, 11-12). The appearance of this rubric in the document suggests that an important dividing line in the Egyptians' self-perception of their historical development had been reached. Thereafter, all that happened before was of a piece with the time of the gods, the period of the ancestors, or *pauty*, whose golden age the ruling elite would forever be trying to reprise.

Attempts at reprisal and re-invention started early, barely more than a century after the demise of the last great Memphite ruler, Pepi II. In southern Egypt, in the hitherto unremarkable city of Waset, or Thebes, Mentuhotep Nebhepetre successfully completed a three-generation struggle to control the entire land, and in the process began to appropriate and revive the style of its former rulers. Mentuhotep made many additions to important temples and built himself an unusual burial complex (Lehner 1997, 266-7) that may help throw some light on court ceremonial of this period, but there is little other evidence for royal pageantry before the end of the 11th Dynasty. While his family imitated and successfully revived the canons of the official visual arts of the Old Kingdom (Fischer 1959), it was left to another Theban family, who deposed them, to move the centre of government back to Memphis and to recreate the classic Old Kingdom pyramid complex as a focus for the royal mortuary cult (Lehner 1997, 168-83).

The house of Senwosret, better known as the 12th Dynasty, initially went to great lengths to show its rulers as closely conforming to the style of representation of the 4th and 5th dynasties. Although their pyramids were much smaller and mostly built of brick, the temples themselves became increasingly elaborate and the residences and settlement cities attached to them were greatly expanded (Lehner 1997, 168-83). Furthermore, the lands supporting these royal establishments underwent an unprecedented expansion, leading to the opening up of the Faiyum, a formerly marshy area to the south-west of Memphis, significantly increasing available arable land for the whole country (Kemp 1989, 149-57; Butzer 1976, 36-7, 92-3). The early 12th Dynasty kings seem to have added another weapon to their ideological arsenal as well – the political-literary tract, a genre that owes its survival as much to literary excellence as to political effectiveness (Posener 1956). However, despite their economic and cultural innovations, these rulers still craved the legitimacy conferred by traditional-seeming pageants. While some fragmentary depictions of the Sed Festival survive (Martin 1984, 785), it is this period that provides us with our first obvious performance text.

The Ramesseum Dramatic Papyrus

The Ramesseum Dramatic Papyrus, now in Berlin, was discovered in a re-used Middle Kingdom tomb beneath the funerary temple complex of Ramesses II by J.E. Quibell in 1895-6, but its contents were studied and published quite some time after that, as its fragile state required extensive conservation (Sethe 1928, 83). As the contents of this document are so important for our study, we shall focus on it first before placing it in a wider context.

The papyrus in its present state consists of fragments which can be fitted together to complete 139 vertical columns of text, although some fragments cannot be placed in the existing scheme and the beginning and end are missing. While vertical columns are commonly found in many early papyrus documents and religious texts, this document is unusual in that the columns are separated by ruled vertical lines and are further divided by horizontal lines. The bottom quarter of the document has been reserved for labelled vignettes illustrating the text. The text is retrograde, meaning that the signs face away from the beginning of the text rather than towards it, as is customary; this is characteristic of conservative religious compositions like the later *Book of the Dead*. However, some signs break the general direction rule; these are found in the names of personages to whom, according to the text, words are spoken. The script, although identifiable as late Middle Kingdom hieratic or cursive, is written in a deliberately old-fashioned manner and the language is filled with archaic usages and words (Sethe 1928, 86-9).

This unusual layout is found in only one other text, the so-called Shabaka Stone, a badly damaged 25th Dynasty (eighth century BCE) inscription which contains a variety of material intended to validate Memphis as the capital of Egypt and its god Ptah as the creator of the universe (Sethe 1928; Frankfort 1948, 24-35). Like the papyrus, it displays carefully laid out vertical columns and archaic language and orthography, although it lacks vignettes. The section most closely resembling the Ramesseum Papyrus describes the conflict waged by Horus and his uncle Seth for control of Egypt, and has long been agreed to portray dramatic action; it will be discussed more fully in Chapter 5. The similarities of

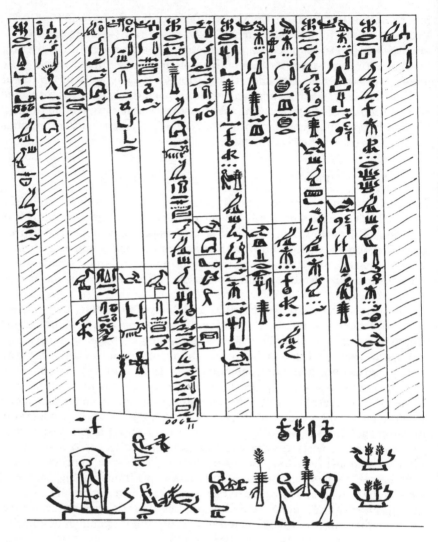

Fig. 5. Ramesseum Dramatic Papyrus, Columns 41-54 (12th Dynasty). Redrawn from the original publication by Lynn Holden.

these texts led Kurt Sethe, who was studying the papyrus, to publish them together in 1928. In naming the earlier of these documents the Ramesseum Dramatic Papyrus, Sethe accomplished his own perfomative act, setting the agenda for the discussion of this text.

In his publication Sethe established that the text may be divided into forty-six scenes, each of which can be divided into five basic components.

3. Performances in the Middle Kingdom

The first element is the narrative which describes the action, beginning with the phrase 'it happened that ...' (Sethe 1928, 89), to be understood as an unmarked tense (Drioton 1957, 263-4), and followed by a gloss explaining the mythological significance of the action and who the actors carrying it out represent (Sethe 1928, 90-1; Frankfort 1948, 123-6). The next element, usually in the following column, is the dialogue, presented graphically with the names of the speaker and the interlocutor facing each other, introduced by the phrase 'words spoken'. The horizontal lines dividing the columns create boxes listing props, actors or location required for the scene. Beneath this the vignette portion of the scroll functions as 'scenic notes' that more graphically show how it is to be staged. Schematic drawings show actors performing with the props, with labels identifying them and briefly noting the actions described in more detail above (Sethe 1928, 91-2). Once the observer gets used to the layout, it becomes evident that it is an extremely clear method of showing all the elements required for each scene, as well as allowing the reader to isolate things required for all the scenes, such as props or location, simply by running their eye along the boxes midway down the columns. Such a document would seem to be designed for use by the person in overall control of this activity, or, as we would say, the director (Drioton 1956, 226; Goyon 1972, 92).

The layout of the Ramesseum Dramatic Papyrus also suggests something about the concepts of performance behind it. Most obvious is the importance of role-playing. The author(s) of this work are scrupulous in distinguishing between the actors and the parts they play. As noted above, every action is glossed to explain that the actors are re-presenting divine characters and events; even the props often stand for something other than themselves (Frankfort 1948, 124-5, 132-5). The symbolic character of the action places it closer to ritual than to a realistic theatrical performance, as does the insertion of 'real' events like the threshing of corn and the consumption of a meal. The actors are specified by occupational titles, emphasizing their social position and relevance. However, the sketches suggest that attention was paid to the configuration of actors and props – the 'blocking' – implying that how these acts looked was important for reasons other than ritual effectiveness. Was there an audience for this dramatic presentation, and who was in it? In order to try to answer this question, it is necessary to look at the subject matter of the script.

Although Sethe's reconstruction of the text can be improved upon, his narrative reconstruction will be followed here for the sake of simplicity. The first seven scenes describe the preparation of equipment such as boats, as well as sacrifices to statues of the king on the boats. Royal insignia are brought out in scene 8 and, according to the text, there is a march through the mountains. Next, in scene 9, corn is threshed by male donkeys (Sethe 1928, 103-38; Frankfort 1948, 126-7). Throughout the play an ongoing dialogue takes place between Thoth, the god of wisdom and writing, and Horus, that explains the mythological significance of the actions. These characters also speak with the children of Horus, Isis, Seth and other figures associated with the Osiris cycle. The corn represents Osiris and the jackasses are Seth and his followers. Horus appeals to them: 'Don't beat my father.' As the asses carry away the grain, so does Osiris ascend into heaven. The ships are decorated with tree boughs; a calf and a goose are sacrificed and decapitated and their heads are displayed (scenes 9 to 13) (Sethe 1928, 139-56; Frankfort 1948, 126). The heads are presented as a gift, along with a Djed pillar, an object known from protodynastic times which was later said to represent the spinal column of Osiris or a dead tree (Altenmüller 1972). Its erection in scene 14 is interpreted to signify the apotheosis of Osiris and triumph over his brother Seth, who is pinned to the ground underneath it, so Seth may take Osiris up to heaven. A loaf and a beer jug are presented to the king as a symbolic meal and stick-fighting refers to the conflict between Osiris and Seth and its resolution (Sethe 1928, 156-67; Frankfort 1948, 126-7).

The produce of the land, as well as its producers, symbolized by two pairs of carpenters and milkmaids, is offered to the king (scenes 19 to 25) (Sethe 1928, 167-92; Frankfort 1948, 129). In scene 26 members of the royal court circumambulate two standards topped by falcons, and in scenes 27 and 29 the king is presented with insignia of rule, sceptres, two feathers and a gold ring, as well as food. The Great Ones of Upper and Lower Egypt are summoned before the king, cosmetics are offered to him and bread halves are given to them (Sethe 1928, 195-201, 201-11; Frankfort 1948, 127). These bread halves are explained as their heads being returned to them (scenes 30 to 32) (Sethe 1928, 213-27; Frankfort 1948, 130-3). The lector priest brings the *qeni* vest (see Chapter 4) and makes offerings of food and cloth, and officials called *sekhenu ankh* ('spirit seekers') bring in a statue of the king's father. Two female singing musicians are chosen to play Isis and Nepthys, Osiris' sisters, who mourn his passing (scenes 33 to 39) (Sethe 1928, 213-27; Frankfort 1948, 130-3). After offerings of meat and linen are made, food is brought for the induction of the spirit seekers into the palace, and the provincial governors of the east and west are invited to share in the meal. They are anointed with oil and offerings of natron and water are made at the palace (scenes 40 to 46) (Sethe 1928, 227-43).

Noting that some of the figures of the kings in the boat are labelled with the throne name of Senwosret I, Sethe assumed that the document provided a script for his coronation, which took place after his assumption to power following the assassination of his father, Amenemhet I (Sethe 1928, 98-9, 246-7), an event also celebrated in the political romance of Sinuhe. The insertion into the royal ceremony of the myth of how Horus succeeds his father, Osiris, and overcomes his enemies is particularly appropriate under the circumstances but, by this point, probably traditional. Scholars focussed on the archaic nature of the text, noting that the title 'spirit seeker' and locations such as 'the hall of eating and standing' mentioned in this text are otherwise attested only in the 1st and 2nd Dynasties (Frankfort 1948, 129). Hermann Junker suggested that the references to an unspecified 'town god', found in many of the scenes that suggested enactments in different geographical locations, referred to the Following of Horus mentioned in Archaic Period documents and on the Palermo Stone (Junker 1949). However, later researchers focussed on similarities with the Sed Festival (Barta 1976), including use of the same personnel, such as the children of the king and the Great Ones of Upper and Lower Egypt; acts like kissing the ground; and circumambulation. While some connections can be made with earlier representations in the temple of Neuserre and in the Archaic material, more significant parallels can be made with later depictions of the Sed Festival from the reign of Amenhotep III (see below), which show the raising of the Djed pillar, an event not attested in earlier Sed depictions. That scholars might confuse an account of the Sed Festival with that of the coronation is not unexpected, as the one is actually a representation of the other. However, the probable identification of the Ramesseum Dramatic Papyrus as a script for the Sed Festival raises the same questions we have asked about its celebration in the Old Kingdom: who was the audience, where was it celebrated and who was responsible for its execution?

These questions cannot be any more easily answered for the Middle Kingdom. Although we have a substantially complete script, we lack a detailed depiction like that of Neuserre, documentation in the form of notices and gifts, and possible performance sites like HK29a or the Step Pyramid complex. The typical Middle Kingdom royal funerary complex, like its earlier Old Kingdom model, offers no obvious space for such an activity. No other likely sites such as the Archaic ceremonial enclosures have been discovered. The text of the papyrus suggests that, like its earlier incarnation, the Middle Kingdom Sed was acted out by members of the royal court and ancillary personnel, and that it had musical accompaniment in the form of singing and percussion. The main difference is what the papyrus and its location tell us about who might direct such an activity.

We have already suggested that the layout of this document suggests that it was drawn up by or designed for the use of the person in charge of the overall direction of the activity. Such a person would be by definition literate and highly knowledgeable about ritual and mythological matters. Little remained of the robbed-out burial in which the papyrus was found, save for the box that contained it. There survived no indication of who the tomb's occupant was or what titles he (most likely) held. However, the box and its contents speak volumes. The box itself was covered with white plaster on which was painted the image of a jackal (Quibell 1898, 3). This immediately suggests the hieroglyphic rebus *hery seshta*, a cryptographic writing of the title signifying 'one who is over the secrets', a designation with a whole range of meanings from private secretary to one in charge of religious arcana (Erman and Grapow 1955, 299.2; Ritner 1993, 232). In this playful writing, first attested during the Middle Kingdom, the latter end of the spectrum is emphasized. Anubis, the god of cemeteries and helper of Osiris, embodied in a jackal, is also a figure who epitomizes the mystery implicit in fundamental transformations, such as that between life and death (DuQuesne 1995). Such secrets include writings as well as acts, suggested by the onomatopoeia between sesh, 'writing', and seshta, 'secrets'. While writing was itself a technology accessible to the few rather than the many, its use also encompassed the recording of magic spells and effective rituals whose form and content often remained hidden (Ritner 1993, 202-4).

The contents of the box included twenty-three papyri. Apart from the Ramesseum Dramatic Papyrus and two literary works, 'The Eloquent Peasant' and 'The Story of Sinuhe', there were a series of despatches from the fortresses of Semna and Kuban in Nubia, an onomasticon, or list of words arranged in categories, two texts consisting of wise sayings, hymns, an embalming diary, a number of magical and medical texts, and accounts (Reeves 2000, 96). One extremely fragmentary work, Papyrus E, appears to be a funerary liturgy (Gardiner 1955). Like the Dramatic Papyrus, it is written in an archaizing hand in vertical columns with a retrograde orientation. Although it lacks the ruled columns, boxes and vignettes found in the former document, Papyrus E has a number of similarities. As well as the name of Senwosret I written on the back of the document, it also mentions a number of the same royal functionaries, like the Great Ones and the king's children, as well as some of the same locations, such as the *per wer* we have already encountered in the Archaic Period.

Although the document is only partially preserved, it is possible to see that it refers to the established funerary ritual of the breaking of the red pots (Gardiner 1955, 16; Ritner 1993, 144-7) and the repeated circumambulation of a tomb. The deceased is mentioned only as Osiris MN ('the late so-and-so'), showing that this is a template for an activity, not a description of one. As in the Dramatic Papyrus there are numerous sacrifices of animals and presentations of offerings, as well as the craftspeople responsible for their manufacture. There also seem to be a long procession and indications of utterances by the principal functionaries, as well as responses ('wailing') by a group called 'the crowd' or 'the rest'. It is not possible to tell if this group can be said to constitute the 'audience' of non-elite spectators, as suggested by Gardiner (1955, 12), but it is a tempting hypothesis. The presence of an audience would also support Schechner's dictum that performances of a more ritual cast consist of holistic events in which spectators are all to some degree participants (1988, 86). However, there are some important differences between the Dramatic Papyrus and Papyrus E. The latter lacks the elaborate layout of the former and there is no trace of special format for the dialogue. This suggests that the event it is intended to choreograph, while on a large scale, is not so much a complex dramatic performance with role-playing actors speaking dialogue as a procession supplemented by a presentation and ceremony.

The presence of these two unique documents, Papyrus E and the Dramatic Papyrus, suggests that they belonged to someone with an interest, if not expertise, in staging such events. It may also be possible that these documents, marked as they are with the name of Senwosret I, were preserved out of antiquarian and learned interest. However, the presence of so many magical papyri in this collection, as well as a large collection of magical instruments ranging from statuettes to wands (Quibell 1898, 3) suggests that they were not so much the property of a 'magician' (Ritner 1993, 223-32) as of a civil servant, learned scholar and ritual expert whose speciality was not only performative utterance but also performative activity. The 'secret' of his magic chest was not just the key to suspending the usual natural operations of the world in which he lived, but also how to 're-present' its definitive religious and mythological moments in a way that was both magically and socially effective.

The Story of Sinuhe and the Ceremonies of Hathor

The subject of the contents of this box brings us back to the Story of Sinuhe, a great propagandistic romance written on behalf of Senwosret I and, for over a thousand years after, a favourite literary classic of the Egyptians. This story, which chronicled the flight, exile and subsequent return of a prominent courtier following the murder of Amenemhet I, has also long held the interest of scholars, who have disagreed over its message, its grammar and syntax and even its literary form (Simpson 1984). Of late it is the epic, performative quality of this work that has drawn attention, involving even public recitations (Parkinson 2000; 2003). However, whatever the form of the text, its intention or the conditions of its reception, it clearly depicts a society almost as interested in performance and spectacle as our own. The death of the old king is vividly evoked in the image of a falcon flying up to heaven. Sinuhe is dramatically rescued from death by exposure when he hears the lowing of cattle and the sounds of voices. While in exile in the land of Yaa in the Levant, he must fight a challenger to his land in single combat. Not only is the rival a formidable warrior, but the combat takes place in front of the entire community, who have gathered from first light in eager anticipation of an engaging spectacle.

When Sinuhe finally decides to leave Yaa to return to Egypt, he is persuaded by a letter from Senwosret containing a detailed description of a lavish Egyptian funeral (see further below). Sinuhe returns to Egypt escorted by foreigners until he arrives at the border, where he is met by a great fleet which takes him back in a triumphant progress to the royal residence. Next day he is escorted into the palace by twenty men and kisses the earth between the pair of great sphinxes that flank the gateway. Sinuhe is welcomed by the royal children and the companions – persons already familiar to us – and taken through a courtyard and into an audience chamber, where the king sits on the throne under a canopy of electrum. Overcome by this sight, in what may be fittingly described as a dramatic moment, Sinuhe swoons in terror. However, the king takes pity on him and ushers in his wife and children to perform what appears to be a ceremony of supplication to the king. It consists of a song of praise that closely links the ruler to the goddess Hathor, especially in her incarnation as the royal cobra on his brow, accompanied by the shaking of necklaces and rattles sacred to Hathor. Although it is possible that in the context of the story this performance is inserted for comic relief, since Sinuhe was long ago forgiven, it may be closely related to well-attested ritual acts as well as suggestive textual and archaeological evidence.

In later periods the king offers Hathor her sacred rattle, the sistrum, to calm her anger, or alternatively the goddess is shown holding it to the ruler's nose in order to transmit the breath of life and the power of rulership (Roberts 1995, 57-8). However, although the sistrum rattle and the necklace are attested in the Old Kingdom at feasts of the dead (see above, Chapter 2), where they are thought to play some role in their resurrection, no images of their use as by the king and goddess are to be found. However, female musicians using the *menat* and the sistrum began to be connected with her cult from the late 5th Dynasty onwards, and these objects are increasingly seen as attributes of her cult priestesses from this time on. During the Old Kingdom and First Intermediate Period, the title of Priestess of Hathor was quite common among the female elite, with the exception of the king's wives (Galvin 1984; Gillam 1995, 223-30). However, in the 11th Dynasty, under Mentuhotep Nebhepetre, this situation changes. Early in his career this king built a chapel near her temple at Dendara in Upper Egypt, which shows him symbolically uniting the heraldic plants of Upper and Lower Egypt before the goddess. In return she offers him her sistrum and *menat* necklace as well as the milk of her sacred cows (Habachi 1963, 19-28).

Around this time Mentuhotep also began work on an ambitious funerary complex in his home town of Thebes, which, after a number of changes in plan, took the form of a terraced structure surrounded by colonnades and perhaps topped by a pyramid (Arnold 1974, 63-7, 84-9; 1979, 34-8). It was built at the foot of a mountain which contained a grotto sacred to the goddess (Arnold 1971, 83-4; Pinch 1993, 4). Throughout his long reign Mentuhotep both married and closely associated himself with priestesses of Hathor. When these women died they were buried under the colonnades or somewhere else in the grounds of the complex (Arnold 1981, 64-6). The remains of their chapels and burial equipment showed them being fed milk of the sacred cows and associating with their royal spouse in the manner of private people, displaying affection and even sitting on a bed together. One of the these women, who was probably not married to the king, had tattoos on her arms and legs (Ikram and Dodson 1997, 115), which in other Egyptian contexts is associated with dancers and musicians (Manniche 1991, 110, 116).

Under the subsequent 12th Dynasty, while the title of cult priestess of Hathor becomes scarce and almost disappears, a new type of jewellery with a strong Hathoric theme appears in the burial of female royalty (Gillam 1995, 211-14, 233-4). Wives and daughters were decked out in the cobra, sacred plumes and lioness manifestations of Hathor and their toilet articles were decorated with her cow-eared face. Their girdles of golden cowry shells were made so that they jingled like the sistrum. Even their names, Sat-Hathor ('daughter of Hathor'), Sat-Hathor-Iunet ('Daughter of Hathor of Dendara') and Khenmet-nefer-Hedjet ('the one who bears the beautiful White Crown'), testify to their close involvement in the theology of rulership (Scandone-Matthiae 1985). It has been argued that these costumes were used in ceremonies like that described in the Story of Sinuhe, which in themselves foreshadow increasingly elaborate state-ments of royal propagation and legitimacy in the New Kingdom, where the king, identified with Atum, engenders himself through the goddess, now quite explicitly role-played by his wife and mother (Scandone-Matthiae 1985; Derchain 1970). The Story of Sinuhe and the jewellery of the 12th Dynasty royal women provide some grandeur and local colour to the rather austere vision of court pageants provided by Old Kingdom sources and the Ramesseum Dramatic Papyrus.

Although we shall return to the subject of funerals in more detail later, the close identification of the king with the Osiris myth shown in the Ramesseum Dramatic Papyrus leads us to consider other public ceremo-nies for this god.

The Mystery of Osiris at Abydos

Osiris, who in later times, with his sister-spouse Isis, was the pre-eminent god of the land, is not recorded before the later Old Kingdom, in the later 5th Dynasty (Griffiths 1980, 41, 113-14). His prominence in the Ra-messeum Dramatic Papyrus reflects his original status as a god who represented the deceased king and no one else. It has been plausibly suggested that the myth of his death, resurrection and succession by his posthumously conceived son, Horus, is an example of one that originated in royal burial rituals, such as the Rite of the Opening of the Mouth, that were performed by his heir (Griffiths 1980, 80, 105, 147). It was not until the First Intermediate Period that royal mortuary texts and practices were democratized, making identification with Osiris possible for every deceased person and beginning his development into the universally recognized god of the dead.

From this time onwards Osiris came to be associated particularly with

Abydos in Upper Egypt and with a major religious performance that took place there, which was first attested at this period. However, although Abydos was an important centre during the period of state formation and the probable burial place of most of the Dynasty 0 and Archaic Period rulers, its original city god was a jackal spirit, Khentamentiyu, 'the first of the westerners'. During the 6th Dynasty a new, large temple was constructed for the new composite god Osiris-Khentamentiyu and provided with a generous endowment and tax privileges (Kemp 1974, 30-1; Otto 1966, 32).

Like much of Middle Egypt in the lower Nile Valley, the monuments of Abydos suffered in the wars between the kings of Thebes and the northern rulers of Hierakonpolis that ended the First Intermediate Period (Redford 1986, 144-51). It was shortly after this destruction, beginning in the 11th Dynasty, that the 1st Dynasty tomb of Den was probably cleared out and fitted with an image of a resurrecting, ithyphallic Osiris on a lion-headed bed and the whole area was cleaned up and renovated (Leahy 1989, 56-7), transforming it into Upoker, the domain of Osiris, centred on his tomb and a sacred grove. According to their beliefs, which can be traced from the royal Pyramid Texts to the Coffin Texts and mortuary inscriptions of this time, it was in nearby Gehesty or on the banks of Nedyt that Osiris as murdered by his brother (Griffiths 1980, 22, 110). It was Wepwawet, a form of the old jackal god Sed, who came to his aid along with his wife, Isis, and brought him back to life in his secret resting place at Upoker, where he miraculously conceived an heir who avenged him and restored him to his rightful place, the temple of Osiris-Khentamentiyu (Otto 1966, 38-41). Not only did this story celebrate the stability of the kingship, it offered the promise of eternal life to every devotee of Osiris.

The development of these beliefs and the cultic performances they inspired can be traced in certain wishes for a happy afterlife found on many Middle Kingdom grave stelae, which are known as the 'Abydos formula'. Although found all over Egypt, the Abydos formula is most prevalent in that city, and especially in an area just outside the temple of Osiris-Khentamentiyu (Pouls-Wegner 2002, 67). The formula expresses the deceased's desire to receive offerings from this temple through the process of reversion (see Chapter 2), especially during the great festivals, as well as to be welcomed into the celestial realms with the rest of the transfigured dead. This also involved being allowed onto the ships of night and day in which the sun god circled the cosmos and being given access to the *neshmet*-barque, the ship of Osiris.

More detailed versions of the formula make clear that the deceased expected to participate in special processional festivals specifically connected with this god. The most complete lists of festivals found in Middle Kingdom texts relating to Abydos suggest that the most relevant are the Haker Feast, the First Procession, the Great Procession, the River Journey of the God and the Vigil of Upoker. Although the pious wish of these mortuary texts is to participate in these Osiris-related events spiritually after death, two other such records show they were also the preserve of those who were still very much alive.

From the reign of Senwosret III comes the stela of the treasurer Ikhernofret, who was sent to Osiris to refurbish his cult statue as well as to participate in his festivities. Ikhernofret describes them as follows:

> I conducted the Procession of Wepwawet when he goes forth to rescue his father. I repulsed the attackers of the *neshmet*-bark, I felled the foes of Osiris.
>
> I conducted the Great Procession and followed the god in his strides. I made the god's boat sail, Thoth guiding the sailing. I equipped the bark [...] with a cabin and fixed his beautiful regalia that he might proceed to the domain of Peqer.
>
> I cleared the god's path to his tomb in Peqer. I rescued Wennofer (Osiris) on that day of great combat, and felled all his foes on the shore of Nedyt.
>
> I made him go inside the Great Bark, and it bore his beauty. I rejoiced the heart of the eastern deserts. I caused jubilation in the western deserts when they saw the beauty of the *neshmet*-bark as it landed at Abydos.
>
> I brought [Osiris Khentamenthes, lord of Abydos] to his palace. I followed the god to his house. His cleansing was done; his seat was made spacious, as I loosened the knot ... (Lichtheim 1988, 99).

Although this is the most detailed early description of what later comes to be known as the 'Mysteries of Osiris', Ikhernofret's account is extremely laconic, as is fitting for a solemn religious-mythological pageant. The only other text that describes actual participation is the 11th Dynasty stela of Rudjahau, who states, 'I am ... a great rebel slayer when the *sem* priest proceeds, front ranked in the western lightland, the like of the Sole-among-them (Osiris), I am Anubis, the keeper of starched linen on the day of wrapping the poles, swift handed to hold back the foes from the ground of offerings. Of discerning heart ... on the day of the attackers ... one praised by the Foremost-in-Hesret when leading the poling, the guide on the Horus ways to the Netherworld' (Lichtheim 1989, 72-3).

The most that can be agreed upon is that the Osiris Festival, which took place sometime in the inundation and early winter seasons (between September and December), had four main episodes. They were (1) the First Procession, led by Wepwawet against the enemies of Osiris; (2) the Great Procession, in which an image of Osiris was conveyed to Upoker; (3) a vigil over the image that took place there, leading to its renewal; (4) the return voyage with the image to the god's temple (Schäfer 1964, 20-32; Lichtheim 1988, 100). It has been suggested that Osiris was attacked by his enemies and killed in the First Procession, representing his death at Nedyt

(Schäfer 1964, 30ff.). The vigil is often equated with the night of the Haker Festival, where the enemies are vanquished and Horus somehow communes with his father, perhaps in a dream, like the *sem* priest (identified with the beloved son) in the Rite of the Opening of the Mouth (Griffiths 1977). This would explain the reference to this personage in connection with the Haker feast and the repulsion of enemies (Otto 1966, 40). The Festival of the River Journey of the God and of punting the *neshmet*-barque, in the stela of Rudjahau (Lichtheim 1988, 71-2), suggests that part of the journey to Upoker took place by water (Otto 1966, 39; Geßler-Löhr 1983, 425-37).

Most of the Middle Kingdom inscriptions that have the Abydos formula were obtained from uncontrolled excavations conducted in the early nineteenth century, and were thought to originate from the northerly area, near the site of the ancient town and the temple of Osiris (Pouls-Wegner 2002, 10-23). North Abydos was not properly investigated before the 1970s, when William Kelly Simpson investigated the unprovenanced inscriptions of North Abydos. He concluded that many of them were from chapels, which allowed people who did not reside in Abydos eternal access to the processions of Osiris through the performative power of the texts. The texts themselves specified that these chapels were located on the 'Terrace of the Great God'.

Simpson was able to show that these installations contained a number of monuments of people who were related by blood or members of the same household, and in this way was able to associate stelae that had been subsequently scattered in collections all over the world (Simpson 1974). The Terrace of the Great God was finally discovered to the west of the temple, overlooking the wadi that was the main route to Upoker. This area was densely packed with mud-brick structures that ranged from buildings with courtyards and gardens to a few bricks propped against a wall and a piece of stone with a written inscription (O'Connor 1985). Down in the wadi, a large stela erected by a 13th Dynasty king threatened anyone who built a tomb, chapel or anything else in the wadi, the sacred route of the procession, with burning (Randall-McIver and Mace 1902, 64, 84-93, pl. 29; Leahy 1989, 42-6). While the effectiveness of the decree is illustrated by the fact that the route remained clear until Graeco-Roman times, the stela also illustrates the tremendous demand for a chapel or tomb that overlooked the route of the procession of Osiris to Upoker and back (Leahy 1989, 64). Is this a marker of widespread popular participation in this festival?

It is certainly true that the cult of Osiris in Middle Kingdom Abydos depended heavily on royal patronage. The Osiris bed in the tomb of Den was originally made by Sankhkare in the 11th Dynasty and refurbished by royal decree sometime in the 13th (Leahy 1977; 1989, 55-6). Senwosret I completely rebuilt the main temple (Pouls-Wegner 2002, 53), and Ikhernofret, one of the king's chief ministers, was sent by the king to participate in the Osiris Festival (Lichtheim 1973, 123-5). 13th Dynasty kings showed up in person. Many of the stelae on the terrace of the god were also monuments to high-ranking members of the elite and prominent members of the local community (Lichtheim 1988, 58-128). However, there are many more humble monuments, belonging to craftspeople and workers (Leprohon 1978; O'Connor 1985).

The extremely elaborate procession and performances, which included mock battles like those found in the Ramesseum Papyrus, and the importance placed on the participation of high-ranking members of society make it hard to believe that there were few living spectators (as suggested by Leprohon, forthcoming). If the followers of Osiris were devoted enough to erect stelae that enabled them to participate in the festival after their death, it is unlikely that they ignored it while still alive. The presence of the refurbished temple of Osiris and the many Ka chapels of kings ensured that Osiris was a strong economic presence in his great land, as well as a spiritual one. Later evidence from the New Kingdom suggests that we should expect earlier popular participation in what are essentially the same festivals.

Autos-da-fé

Evidence for another kind of public ceremony, one far less palatable to our sensibilities, is to be found in its most complete form at the Middle Kingdom fortress of Mirgissa, in Nubia, to the south of Egypt. As suggested by a number of later 12th Dynasty royal decrees and other documents, this was the site of one of a series of forts intended to facilitate the extraction of tribute as well as to control the movement of Nubians along the river valley, largely for customs and taxation purposes (Kemp 1983, 131-2). The success of this scheme was naturally dependent on military and psychological coercion of these foreigners. Anxiety about the hegemony of the Egyptian ruler and the elite was expressed in an ideological theodicy that conceptualized both internal and external enemies of the state as equivalent to the forces of chaos, out of which the universe was formed and threatened to dissolve back into (Frankfort 1948, 9). Literary and artistic expressions of this thought complex may be traced as far back as the period of state formation. It often finds expression in images of the king smashing his enemies' heads with a club, trampling them or otherwise annihilating them in either human or wild animal form (Davis 1992; Baines 1995, 109-12). The image of the king clubbing his enemy has given rise to considerable argument about whether or not it represents a real-life situation or is to be understood symbolically (Helck 1987, 6-7). As we shall see, Amenhotep II of the 18th Dynasty did indeed publicly despatch enemy captives in such a way, although whether in accordance with time-honoured practice or as a dramatic representation of a familiar visual motif cannot be ascertained. That such imagery had a performative dimension may be inferred from other types of evidence.

The so-called 'execration texts', which were produced in the Old and Middle Kingdom, apparently combine the performativity of the magico-religious rite with highly public, if threatening, gestures about social and political cohesion. The texts, which curse all known enemies of the state, were written on pottery vessels and figurines which were burned, smashed and buried in cemeteries. Only one Egyptian deposit, dating from the Old Kingdom, has a known archaeological context, being found buried in two large jars in the Giza necropolis (Junker 1947, 30-8). While such practices can be linked with other, more conventional kinds of magical spells and operations (Ritner 1993, 136-48), the Mirgissa deposit suggests how this rite could be made into a public performance.

The site is located in a depression on a rocky outcrop about six hundred metres from the wall of the fortress and roughly equidistant from the contemporary Egyptian town, a Nubian cemetery dating to roughly the same period, and the Nile River. There is little arable land and few trees, with not much apart from a sandy, rocky expanse separating these points, allowing an unobstructed if distant view of the deposit site from all sides. It consists of a central conical hole dug in the sand, containing four different sub-sites that make up the whole (Vila 1963, 136-41).

The first central deposit consists of a solid mass of deliberately smashed vessels, of which about half were inscribed with the standard execration formula aimed at Asiatics, Nubians, Egyptians and anyone evil 'who may rebel, who may plot, who may fight, who may think of fighting or who may think of rebelling on this entire earth' (Koenig 1990, 106-10). This material strongly suggests the performance of the Rite of Smashing the Red Pots, well known from the funerary ceremony, which was an operation designed to drive away evil where the pots were smashed with a special implement, in this case a round stone (Vila 1963, 147-9; Ritner 1993, 144-53). At seven separate intervals the deposition of the pots was interrupted by throwing in crudely modelled and mutilated mud figures of human body parts, animals, boats and wild animals (Vila 1963, 144, 156-9; Ritner 1993, 159-61). In this area were also found four mud containers which may be the crucibles in which all the material was symbolically burnt (Ritner 1993, 157-9).

Eleven metres north of the central deposit were four limestone figurines of bound prisoners. They were all buried upside down, one was decapitated and all the figures had been struck repeatedly on the top of the head before hair colouring was applied (Vila 1963, 147, 159, fig. 9; Ritner 1993, 161-2; 168f.). The deposit seems to resemble a fairly typical magico-religious ensemble, until we consider its two final components. Two metres west of the main deposit of sherds and figurines was found a human skull, without its lower jaw, balanced on top of a broken pottery bowl. Nearby a flint knife, the traditional Egyptian instrument of sacrifice, was driven point down into the sand. The skull had been carefully buried so that its teeth were flush with the surface of the ground, and in close proximity were found the rest of the dismembered remains of this unfortunate individual (Vila 1963, 146-7, figs 6-7). Traces of red wax close to the bowl and skull have been interpreted by Ritner as evidence for the burning of more enemy figures (1993, 163-7).

The Mirgissa deposit reveals that the performance of which the execration texts were a part was both more elaborate and more immediate than it first appears. The location of the Old Kingdom deposit in a cemetery may signify not secret magical acts in portentous locations so much as the obvious site for an operation involving the killing of a human being. Since there was no Egyptian cemetery at Mirgissa, a site was chosen that had the necessary magically purifying sand (Ritner 1993, 155-7, 172-3) as well as being visible for long distances on all sides. That cemeteries in Egypt were highly frequented public places has already been demonstrated above; they were also replete with the spiritual power necessary to neutralize dangerous adversaries.

The four separate deposits at Mirgissa enable us to distinguish a number of parts to the ceremony, although in no particular order. The cursing of enemies which was combined with the ceremony of smashing the red pots was perhaps accomplished by loud declamations of the written curses as well as the smashing of them. The burial and decapitation of the specially made and pre-abused enemy figurines, done upside down to render them powerless, may well have been choreographed for greater effect. Although there is no proof, it is not difficult to see the sacrifice of the living enemy, followed by his dismemberment and burial, as the climax of this performance. In *Discipline and Punish* Michel Foucault succinctly expressed the impact of the public execution on its audience (1977, 1ff.). The acts that took place at Mirgissa one day in the eighteenth century BCE could be seen from the walls of the fort and from the Egyptian town, and by anyone walking past the area or on the river. While the magical aspect of the ceremony would of course have had more of an impact on the spectators than we can imagine, it would doubtless have reminded them of their relationship to the performers as embodied subjects – subject to their authority, subject to their own attitude and actions towards it. At Mirgissa the desired result would have been to inspire fear among the Nubians, while in Egypt it would also serve to remind people of whatever class that serious transgressions of the political order are transgressions of world order, to be punished accordingly. And, as Foucault observes, such spectacles can also promote social cohesion and conformity, for reasons ranging from fear to self-congratulation.

Who was responsible for staging the execration ritual? Ritner has suggested that the standardized form of the texts and even the rest of the apparatus, such as the enemy statuettes, points to their being a product of the central government, and that the main actor in the Mirgissa drama was probably the king himself (1993, loc. cit.).

Magic performances

Let us briefly return to the box of secrets found in the Ramesseum in order to search for more private, small-scale performances. This container was the receptacle of not only a remarkable collection of papyri, but also an extraordinary selection of objects used in magical operations, including three wands engraved with apotropaic figures, a variety of amulets, figures of divine animals, a magical figure of a herdsman, female 'fertility' figures in faience and wood, and part of a pair of musical clappers. There was also a bronze uraeus entangled in a piece of human hair, as well as a wooden figure of a naked female grasping snakes and apparently wearing a lion's mask (Quibell 1898, 3, pls 2-3; Ritner 1993, 222-31). A similar, smaller deposit has been found in a house at Kahun, in a planned community attached to the funerary temple of Senwosret II. This house, which also contained a deposit of magico-medical papyri, had in a cache buried under the floor a pair of ivory wands, as well as a comparable, if somewhat cruder, figure of a lion-faced woman (Petrie 1890, pl. 8). While both the figure from Kahun and that in the Ramesseum have been identified with the protective domestic deity Beset (the female equivalent of the more well-known Bes) (Bosse-Griffiths 1977, 102-3) rather than masked performers, a canvas mask clearly representing this figure was found in the very next room. This object, which was almost flat and backless, was painted with pink circles on the cheeks and a lotus flower between the eyes and was provided with eye and nose holes to allow the wearer to breathe (Bosse-Griffiths 1977, 103-4; David 1991, 37-8).

While a similar Bes mask has been found in the New Kingdom settlement of Deir el-Medina (David, 1991, 38), the rarity of such masks raises serious implications for the nature of sacred and other performances within Egyptian culture. It has sometimes been asserted that the therimorphic ('animal-headed') iconography of many Egyptian gods reflects the widespread practice of masking by human impersonators, but there is little evidence of this. Only two such masks, both jackal-headed and completely solid, survive from a much later period (see below, Chapter 5). This should not surprise us, as the presence of persons who role-played Anubis at funerals is quite well documented (Ritner 1993, 249, n. 249). However, the only other masks of a comparable open-backed type are those recently discovered at late Predynastic Hierakonpolis. Since they are made of clay rather than lighter, more durable materials and are found only in graves, their practical applications have been doubted (Adams 1999, 30-1). However, on analogy with the Ramesseum deposit, it is possible that they either could have been buried with someone who used them in life or were utilized by persons acting in the funerary ceremony.

3. Performances in the Middle Kingdom

Figures in lion-style masks are also seen participating in activities shown in some Old Kingdom tomb chapels in Memphis, although the meaning of these scenes is still not well understood (Decker and Harb 1994, 628-9, pl. 249).

Whatever the nature of these activities, if they were in any way public it is unlikely that they took place in the house where the props were found. The smaller 'workers" houses at Kahun featured narrow passageways and nested groups of rooms that facilitated privacy rather than accessibility and spaciousness (Kemp 1989, 155, fig. 53). The house may well have been the residence of a magical practitioner who worked throughout the settlement (David 1991, 39). Were the mask and related implements used in private rites of healing or in more public ceremonies? While both are possible, it is noteworthy that the Kahun mask, like all the others known from Egypt, has no opening for the mouth, rendering sounds made by its wearer muffled or inaudible. My own experiments with my students have encountered the same problem (see below, Chapter 6). Given the obvious importance of the role-playing function in scripted performance, as noted in the Ramesseum Papyrus, this raises the issue of whether masked characters spoke dialogue or whether it was said for them by a reader – indeed, what their role in such performances was. Perhaps the function of masked performers was to provide an epiphany separate from the narrative and dialogue provided by the other actors. Some further light on this problem may be provided by another look at funerary ceremonies.

A good funeral

It is the Story of Sinuhe, that quintessential document of elite culture and aspirations, that provides us with our most succinct description of the obsequies of an upper-class Egyptian at this period. The passage in question occurs in a letter written by Senwosret I to Sinuhe, still living abroad, to persuade him to come home. It runs as follows:

> A night is made for you with ointments and wrappings from the hand of Tait (a funerary goddess). A funeral procession is made for you on the day of burial; the mummy case is of gold, its head of lapis lazuli. The sky is above you as you lie in the hearse, oxen drawing you, musicians going before you. The dance of the *muw*-dancers is done at the door of your tomb; the offering list is read to you; sacrifice is made before your offering stone (Lichtheim 1973, 229).

This brief passage, which shows both similarities with and differences from the Old Kingdom funerals, is to a large degree corroborated by representations in Middle Kingdom tomb chapels. The best preserved of these is found in the Theban tomb of Senet, the wife of Antefoker, a vizier of Senwosret I (Davies 1920) and roughly contemporary with the literary description.

63

Although embalming is mentioned in the Story of Sinuhe, there is no clear depiction in the Middle Kingdom representations of where it was performed, in contrast to the Old Kingdom ones, which clearly show the *ibu*, or tent of purification. However, the mummy itself can sometimes be shown, as is the case in the funeral procession in the tomb of Senet, where it appears above its rectangular wooden coffin while understood to be inside it (Davies 1920, pl. 21). The two female mourners seen in the earlier funeral scenes are now labelled as elder and younger kites, a clear reference to the Osiris myth, to which we find numerous other allusions. These women have now added headbands and waist-girdles to their costume. The bier with the coffin is dragged by men as well as oxen and is accompanied by the *sem*, lector priests, embalmers and *imy-khent* priests ('chamberlains') as before. The 'friends' of the deceased are found here again, this time carrying her coffin, right above the scene showing the transport of the bier. The stated destination, 'the cavern of the great palace', is most likely the burial chamber. The large coffin is preceded in the procession by two men, one beating sticks, the other with an incense burner. Before them walk four other men carrying statues on their heads representing a mummified figure in a lower Egyptian crown and Ihy, the son of Hathor, playing a sistrum. In front of them is another coffin flanked by both kites. The inscription says that their destination is the pavilion or tent of the *muu* dancers at the gateway of the cemetery. In front of them (Davies 1920, pl. 23) the chief officiants of the ceremony stand before the *muu*. The four male dancers are attired in short kilts and tall headdresses made out of reeds and they perform a fast-moving dance while pointing to the ground with their right index and middle fingers, saying, 'Her head is set in place for her.' This once again clearly indicates identification of the deceased with Osiris.

In the lower scene the bier with the mummy is preceded by men dragging a shrine containing the canopic jars and the Tekenu, a crudely fashioned seated figure. It is not clear how these two registers relate to each other. The most likely interpretation is that they are consecutive, showing one long procession led by the chief officiants, who encounter the *muu* dancers, followed by the statue bearers and the friends carrying either the outer coffin or the sarcophagus, in turn followed by the canopic jars and Tekenu, with the bier itself at the end. However, both the kites and the chief officiants are shown twice, and other interpretations are certainly possible.

The presence of the *muu* dancers, the Tekenu and the statue bearers suggests that we are dealing here with an elaborate routine that took place in a specially constructed space that was not fully illustrated until the New Kingdom, although separate elements can be attested from the Archaic Period onwards. The so-called Butite burial ceremony is in later representations associated with a precinct divided into a number of areas, including a hall of the *muu*, a garden with a pool and a group of shrines in

3. Performances in the Middle Kingdom

a palm grove, at the centre of which is the Tekenu (Settgast 1963, 48-51). The Tekenu has been identified with the enigmatic seated figures found in early Archaic representations of the Sed Festival and has been variously identified as a re-presentation of a human sacrifice, a royal personage or a bundle of waste material left over from the embalming process (Helck 1986). The *muu* are attested in very late Old Kingdom funeral depictions. The shrines among the palm trees, seen in some fragmentary Old Kingdom depictions, are now archaeologically attested from the Middle Kingdom at Tell ed Daba and the Dynasty 0 Period at Buto (Wilkinson 1999, 319-20).

Apparently related to this cluster are the so-called ritual voyages, such as that depicted in Senet's tomb, to Abydos and across the waterway. While the journey to and from Abydos merely shows two boats (Davies 1920, pls 17-18), the journey across the waterway is of much greater interest (Davies 1920, pl. 18). Three small papyrus skiffs are shown sailing across. The first carries the coffin on a lion-headed bed and is accompanied by the kites, the *imy-khent* and a lector priest; on the second the servant of the *rekhyt* offers a foreleg of beef to a standing mummiform figure in a crown like one of those seen in the funeral procession. In the last boat are a lector priest and an officiant called 'the great god'. The boat is rowed by a man labelled 'servant of the Meret'. The boats are greeted by a man standing on the far bank with a cloth over his shoulder and a walking stick, who raises his hand in greeting, crying, 'Come, flood!' (Settgast 1963, 67, 77). Next we see the first boat again, complete with the coffin on the lion bed and its crew, this time being dragged by six men on a sledge who are preceded by another six people, three men and three women, labelled as the people from the delta towns, who throw their hands up in the air, apparently in a gesture of mourning (Davies 1920, pl. 19; Settgast 1963, 27).

While it is possible to trace these images back in time, there is little agreement as to whether they represent ceremonies actually acted out at elite Egyptian funerals. Jurgen Settgast has suggested that the depiction of the sacred precinct in New Kingdom tombs and scattered representations of ceremonies depicted with it in the Middle Kingdom point to their actual enactment at this period. He doubts that they took place earlier, when the sacred precinct as such is not attested (1963, 72-5). However, a passage from the Middle Kingdom Coffin Texts suggests that the pavilion of the *muu* is to be identified with a hall where a vigil was held over the deceased and could therefore be the same as the earlier tent of purification (Settgast 1963, 80; Faulkner 1973, 45, 55). Settgast also suggests that the so-called ritual voyages were acted out in the sacred precinct, perhaps with model boats on one of the pools.

Although the question of how activities like the so-called ritual voyages were acted out cannot be resolved, they raise the issue of how to distinguish between performance and performative utterances or texts. Settgast is probably right to suggest that similar depictions of boats in Old Kingdom tombs, like later models, are magical rather than part of an actual performance. The suggestion that certain passages in the Coffin Texts are actually dramatic texts (Drioton 1957, 268-84) should also be considered in this light. Just because Coffin Text Spell 148, concerning the birth of Horus (Faulkner 1973, 125-7), has speeches preceded by the name of the speaker and indications of setting and action, that does not necessarily indicate that it was acted out by mortuary priests or even recited (despite the standard directions). As noted above, the performative, that is, magical force of the texts ensured their effectiveness in the next world.

4

Performances in the New Kingdom and Third Intermediate Period

Performances like the one memorialized in the Mirgissa deposit did not prevent large swathes of Egypt from falling under foreign rule as early as the late eighteenth century BCE. While the Nubians took control of southern Egypt, south of Thebes (Trigger, Kemp, O'Connor and Lloyd 1983, 173), self-described 'rulers of foreign countries', called Hyksos by the Greeks, originating in the Levant took over the north, including Memphis, and set themselves up as Egyptian-style kings. Neither propagandistic bluster nor acts of execration proved effective against this two-pronged assault and it would be over a century before native control was reasserted (Redford 1992, 98-129).

When the rulers of Thebes finally succeeded in ejecting the Nubian and Canaanite invaders they made a point of pursuing them far into their own hinterlands, laying the foundations of an imperial strategy based in 'forward defence' (Redford 1992, 148-60). While the kings of the early 18th Dynasty sought to present themselves in a traditional way, like the 'ancestors', it was Thutmose III who first displayed himself as the warrior or 'sporting' king, a persona further developed by his successors to the end of the New Kingdom in the eleventh century BCE (Decker 1992, 22-4). Obviously, this new role was a product of a more 'imperialistic' and interventionist foreign policy, involving permanent military occupation of extensive areas outside Egypt proper and a more developed programme of ideological intimidation of outlanders than had been previously tried. However, it must not be forgotten that this imperial project also involved professionalization of the army as well as expansion of the bureaucracy (Hayes, 1973, 353-63).

While wealth which began to flow into the palace and temple eventually benefited much of the population, emphasis continued to be placed on domination of the non-elite class, to which the king's new persona gave added emphasis. The rise of large urban centres and their populations led for the elite to new political challenges of persuasion and control. The well-preserved temple complexes of Thebes, with their related urban and cemetery areas, are the most well documented from this period (Kemp 1989, 211-13), but other large urban conurbations such as Memphis and Pi-Ramesse also existed.

Although the loss of the empire and, with it, foreign revenue led to

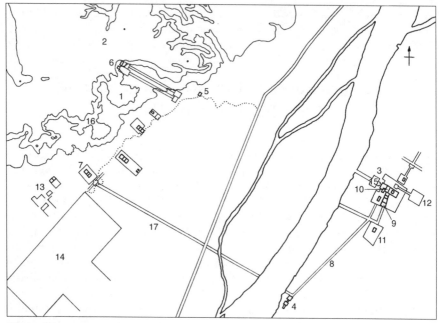

Fig. 6. Map of Thebes.

1. Nobles' tombs at Sheikh Abd el Gurna
2. Valley of the Kings
3. Temple of God Amun-Re at Karnak
4. Temple of Southern Opet at Luxor
5. Temple of deified King Amenhotep I
6. Temples at Deir el Bahari (King Mentuhotep, Queen Hatshepsut and King Thutmose III)
7. Temple of King Ramesses III at Medinet Habu
8. Processional Way between Karnak and Luxor temples
9. The 'Floor of Silver' Court of the Tenth Pylon at Karnak
10. Hypostyle Hall of Karnak temple
11. Temple of Goddess Mut at Karnak
12. Temple of King Akhenaten at Karnak with connected Palace to the West
13. Palace of King Amenhotep III at Malkata
14. Birket Habu, artificial lake of Malkata Palace
15. Quay in front of temple at Karnak
16. Village, temple and tombs at Deir el Medina
17. Processional way between Luxor temple and Djeme (at Medinet Habu temple)

undermining of the political and social cohesion of Egypt by the eleventh century, the cultural pattern established remained, with the cult of Amun and its processional cult dominating the social and political life of the country throughout the Third Intermediate Period and beyond. The thesis presented in this chapter is that, during the New Kingdom, earlier cultic and other performances were organized into an elaborate state 'theatre' whose audience was urbanized and at least partially literate. The purpose of this theatre was at once religious and political: long-established divine festivals were redesigned to showcase the ruler as the link between the gods and humanity in a fashion much more emphatically public and carefully choreographed than before. Furthermore, the presentation of the festivals was such that not only was much of what transpired visible to the whole community, but there existed mechanisms for their direct participation in some form. The opening out of these religious events can be most clearly studied by looking at the basic cultic act, the care and feeding of the god's image, and the ancillary rites attached to its creation and the reversion of offerings made to it.

Although the New Kingdom is one of the most well-documented and prosperous periods in Egyptian history, it has left us little in the way of documents directly related to performance like the Ramesseum Dramatic Papyrus. Only a handful of texts exist; two are directly related to performance of temple cult, and the other, relating to the animation of cult statues, is recorded in connection with the funerary ceremonies. We shall deal with the latter first.

The Rite of the Opening of the Mouth

The Rite of the Opening of the Mouth was a central ritual of Egyptian religion that called down spirits of gods, other supernatural beings or deceased persons into statues, magical objects or mummies. Although it is referred to in Old Kingdom tombs and temples and an abbreviated version is known in the Pyramid Texts, a full depiction and text of the ritual is not found before the New Kingdom, the most extensive being in the tomb of Rekhmire, the vizier of Thutmose III, and in the tomb of Seti I. Eberhardt Otto, who made an extensive study of the rite (1960), believed that later versions differed considerably from its original form. It makes use of the myth of Horus and his father, Osiris, to provide a narrative framework and identities for the protagonists. Otto suggested that the relationship of the *sem* priest to the statue was central and that the whole rite had a 'dramatic' character, with different characters entering and exiting the scene and moments of great emotional tension.

The Rite of the Opening of the Mouth consists of purification and preparation of a statue, the offering of certain important or magical substances to it and the imparting of sensory input and the ability to take in nourishment by touching the nose, eyes and mouth with magical instruments (one of which, the *medjedefet*, resembles a chisel). This operation is performed by the 'Beloved Son' of the statue, who re-presents Horus, the son of Osiris. The statue is offered bread, water and ointment, with which the rite concludes. In funerary contexts the statue is then presented with a traditional meal of twenty-one items which are recorded in a standard offering list (Gardiner 1915, 58-61). In a temple this action would be represented by the daily offering of food, clothing and ointment to cult statues (Meeks and Favard-Meeks 1996, 126-9, 135-6). The fullest New Kingdom depictions of the rite comprise seventy-five 'scenes' consisting of vignettes with labels and dialogue (Otto 1960, 34-171). The performance takes place in the 'House of Gold', with the statue placed on a small mound of sand to ensure its purity (Gardiner 1915, 58; Otto 1962, 36). At a much later period, the House of Gold was identified with the place of the resurrection of Osiris, but earlier it signified a sculptors' workshop or gold-working studio (Otto 1962, 36), the places where divine images were manufactured. Apart from the *sem* and the Beloved Son, the other main actors in the rite are the 'chamberlains', the 'wardrobe master', the lector priest (who possibly read out all the dialogue instead of prompting the other actors), and the 'friends', whom we have already encountered in the Sed Festival; a number of 'followers'; and one female part, the 'great mourner' – Isis, the widow of Osiris. The subsidiary actors sometimes repeat dialogue and function like a chorus.

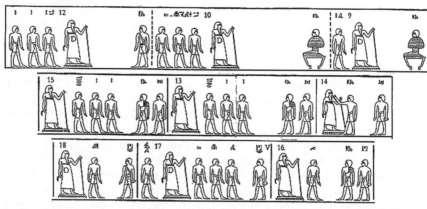

Fig. 7. Scenes 9 to 18 of the Rite of the Opening of the Mouth in the tomb of Rekhmire. Scenes are read from right to left and from top to bottom. Adapted from the original publication by Lynn Holden.

One of the most interesting and dramatic parts of the rite is found in scenes 9 to 18 and runs as follows (bold type indicates stage directions in the original text):

Scene 9
Scene takes place in the House of Gold. Sleeping by SEM in front of it [the statue]. Behind it is a CHAMBERLAIN. [*The SEM is shown wrapped in a cloak huddled on a little bed in front of the statue.*]
SEM: He has broken me! (*sleeping*) He has hit me. (*dreaming/sleeping [qed]*)

CHAMBERLAIN: My father! My father! (*Repeat four times.*)
(*Waking of the sleeper, the* SEM; *finding the* CHAMBERLAINS.)

Scene 10
SEM is opposite the chamberlains. [*The three* CHAMBERLAINS *stand opposite the kneeling* SEM, *who is before the statue.*]
SEM: I have seen my father in all his forms.
CHAMBERLAINS (*to* SEM): Your father shall not go away from you. [...] She who remembers Horus has found him. (*form of a god's companion*)
SEM: The spider has caught him. (*spider*)
CHAMBERLAINS: I have seen my father in all his forms. (*form of a praying mantis*) Protect him, lest he suffer! (*bees*) That nothing be disturbed! (*shadow*)

Scene 11
(**He grasps his staff. The qni vest** (Frankfort 1948, 133-4) **is on him.** [*Transition: The* SEM *changes costume. He has removed the cloak and appears wearing a sash.*])

Scene 12
SEM is opposite the SCULPTORS. [*The* SEM *stands opposite the statue and three* SCULPTORS.]
SEM: Stamp for me my father! (**stamping on the cheetah skin** [*costume worn by the* SEM]) Make for me my father. Gods' form. Make for me a likeness of my father. (*the* SCULPTORS) Who will make for me a likeness like him? (**making a likeness**) Very like? [...] (*statue*)

Scene 13
SEM, recitation before the BONE CARVER, **the** AXE WORKER **and the** STONE POLISHER. [*Appointment of specialized craftsmen. Enter* LECTOR PRIEST.]
SEM: Who is he who approaches my father? (*CRAFTSMEN*) Who is he who will hit my father? (*A CRAFTSMAN*) Who is it who will seize his head? (*A CRAFTSMAN*) Do not hit my father! (*CRAFTSMEN*)

Scene 14
[*The* SEM *touches the mouth of the statue with his little finger. Enter the* LECTOR PRIEST.]
LECTOR PRIEST (*speaking as statue*): Touch my mouth with your little finger.
SEM: I have come to look for you. I am Horus. I have struck your mouth for you. I am your beloved son.

Scene 15

SEM before CRAFTSMEN. [*Action of striking. The SEM and the LECTOR PRIEST face the CRAFTSMEN.*]

SEM: Don't hit my father!

CRAFTSMEN: May those who would hit your father be protected.

Scene 16

[*The SEM and the LECTOR PRIEST stand before one of the CRAFTSMEN.*]

SEM: I am Horus-Set. I will not allow you to make bright [i.e. polish] the head of my father.

Scene 17

[*Making ready the statue. Three CHAMBERLAINS and the ASSOCIATE OF HORUS stand before the statue facing the LECTOR PRIEST.*]

CHAMBERLAINS (**to the ASSOCIATE OF HORUS**): May Isis go looking for Horus (**the secret land**) in order that he come looking for his father. (*ISIS KHERSEKET*)

Scene 18

[*Handing over of the statue. The SEM and the LECTOR PRIEST face one another with the statue behind them.*]

LECTOR PRIEST (**to SEM**): Go quickly to see your father!

Helck (1987, 27-8) concluded that the main actor, the *sem* priest, contacts the spirit by falling into a shamanic trance, an occurrence that may be compared to the vision of Horus communing with his father on the night of the Haker Festival at Abydos. As noted in Chapter 3, the vigil in which this took place probably involved the *sem*. The actual manufacture of the statue, its carving, polishing and painting, is closely linked to its creation, or birth (*msi*) (Otto 1962, 3-4), which is why the priest, who speaks with both his own voice and that of the statue, tries to excuse the injury caused the spirit by its manufacture. They also remind us of the exhortations of Horus not to injure his father, Osiris, as the corn is threshed by the donkeys of Seth in the Ramesseum Dramatic Papyrus. It has also been argued that the rite's enigmatic references to the spider and the praying mantis are technical terms used by sculptors (Fischer-Elfert 1998).

While most scholars who have studied this rite believe that the statue ritual dates back to the Archaic Period, it must be noted that it is not attested before the New Kingdom. In her study of references to dreams in Egypt before 1000 BCE, Kasia Szpakowska has suggested that the word *qed*, which occurs in Scene 9, signifies 'dream' rather than 'sleep', a usage attested only in the New Kingdom (2003, 16-18, 147-51). Although the text contains a number of archaisms such as the word for sculptor (*genuty*), and its plot line and cast of characters may be linked to the Ramesseum Dramatic Papyrus and the Old Kingdom Sed Festival, it should be noted that the early 18th Dynasty produced many archaistic artistic documents (Aldred 1980, 147-63). The elaboration of this ancient rite may be connected to a much expanded version of the elite funerary ceremony (see below) as well as an interest in the theory of divine and royal images, which comes to the fore a little bit later, in the Amarna Period (Ockinga 1984, 117-22). The presentation of the ritual, known only from tomb walls and not from papyrus documents, in the form of vignettes and captions rather than tables, as in the Ramesseum Papyrus, is perhaps a function of its close connection with the tomb and funerary cult rather than indication of a different recording tradition (Drioton 1957, 256).

Funerals

Elite funerals of the kind described in Chapter 3 are well documented in Theban tomb chapels of the earlier 18th Dynasty, where they become ever more elaborate. Indeed, they are often shown on the side wall of the cult shrines of these installations, directly juxtaposed with extended depictions of the Rite of the Opening of the Mouth just described (Gardiner 1915, 28-45-6). The elaborate procession and water journeys are shown in even greater detail, and in addition we find what has been described as the 'sacred precinct'. This elaborate installation, which may have been a semipermanent feature of large cemeteries (Settgast 1963, 29), had eight components: the hall, the *muu*, the women's tent, a pool garden, 'the gods of the great door', shrines of the gods, three pools, a slaughterhouse for meat offerings, and four basins around which they were arranged. As noted above, earlier materials suggest that these rites may preserve Lower Egyptian royal ceremonies of prehistoric times (Settgast 1963, 27-8, 49-51, pl. 14). They also show similarities with the actions described in Ramesseum Papyrus E (see Chapter 3) as well as the royal obsequies uniquely shown in the Amarna Period for Tutankhamun and Akhenaten's daughter Meketaten (Freed, Markowitz and D'Auria 1999, 31; Reeves 1990, 72). Both nobles and kings could expect their mummy to be dragged to their tomb by companions, although the military and police could help with the more extensive equipment of a king (McDowell 1999, 221). Images like that of the god Menkeret and the shrine-shaped boxes for *shabtis*, best known from the tomb of Tutankhamun (Reeves 1990, 131, 138), suggest that there was a close correspondence between cultic equipment and the rituals attached to them.

The Daily Cult and the Ancestor Ritual

Two other cultic scripts are known from this period. They are the script of the Daily Cult of Amun (Berlin Hieratic Papyrus 3055) and the Royal Ancestor Ritual, known in two papyri now divided between London, Cairo and Turin.

The daily cult of the statue of the god found in the innermost room of every Egyptian temple was not, of course, a performance as we have defined it. The care and feeding of the image, which happened three times a day, was essential to maintenance of the spirit of the divinity in its statue-body, the presence of which was essential in the world to uphold the cosmic order (David 1981, 58-79). This activity, so portentous and fraught with cosmic danger, was the exclusive and secret domain of the ritually pure and expert. Only the king or his deputy, the *hem netcher* priest, was permitted to gaze upon the face of the god or to touch its image. The operations of the cult were in theory closed off from all but the lector priest and a few other officiants who assisted at the service.

Berlin Papyrus 3055 is not elaborately laid out like the Ramesseum Dramatic Papyrus. Its title, 'Book of Utterances of the Rites of the God, which are done in the temple of Amun Re, King of the Gods, in the course of every day by the great priest (*wab a'a*) on his (assigned) day', tells us that it provides a script for each action performed in the cult at the morning service (Moret 1902, 7-9). It lists the utterances under sixty-six separate chapter headings which either correspond to a specific cultic act or provide alternate scripts (Königliche Museen zu Berlin 1901). The cultic ritual presented therein, which corresponds to pictures and texts displayed on temple walls and is to some degree supplemented by them, ran as follows. The officiant began by lighting a fire and burning incense. Next he approached the shrine of the god, broke the clay seal on the doors and threw them open. He then removed the cloths in which the statue was wrapped, revealing the face of the image. He prostrated himself before it, offered incense and perfume and then removed the image from the shrine. The officiant then purified the statue with water and incense, dressed it in fresh cloths and offered it a meal (Moret 1902, 9-190). It was at this point that the officiant called the spirit of the god into his statue in order to consume the food (Nelson 1949a, 225). After the statue was purified and its vestments replaced, fresh, pure sand was placed on the floor of the sanctuary (Moret 1902, 200-2). The officiant then cleansed the shrine with a special broom and closed and sealed its doors (Nelson 1949b).

What happened next is described in the Royal Ancestor Ritual, which is preserved in very similar kinds of documents. This text, which is preserved in papyri dating from the reign of Ramesses II, originally described a rite performed for Amenhotep I, regarded by the Egyptians as the founder of the New Kingdom regime, and was later modified to include more recently deceased kings (Gardiner 1935, 101-6; Nelson 1949a, 201-2). It was intended to ensure that food offerings presented to Amun at the divine service reverted to the spirits of deceased kings, metonymically represented by Amenhotep I. The utterances which facilitated this were accompanied by the burning of incense and special candles made of fat-soaked linen. The offerings were placed on a special altar of the kings and may even have rested in a hall inscribed with their names, as found in the temples at Karnak and Abydos (Nelson 1949a, 310-46; David 1981, 83-102). After the royal ancestors had enjoyed their meal, the food reverted to other worthy dead with memorials in the temple and then to the priests and other employees of the temple and even the community at large. The reversion of offerings was always an act of fundamental religious and economic importance, but was it a performance? During the New Kingdom, vast amounts of food and live animals intended for slaughter were displayed in the 'hall of offerings' where the god appeared in its processional boat, and presented in the 'dining hall', where the priests may have partaken of them (Moret 1905, 110-11). While we have already noted the often close relationship between eating and performance in a festive context, it remains unclear whether consumption of reverted gods' food had the ceremonial or performative character that is associated with something like the Christian Eucharist. In the absence of definite evidence on this matter, let us consider further the particulars of the divine service.

In the script provided for conducting the cult, the officiant role plays various gods and the props used in the ritual are also given different identities and significance. The action as a whole is mythologized, re-presenting the story of how Horus restores his father, Osiris, to life. The similarities to both the Ramesseum Dramatic Papyrus and the Rite of the Opening of the Mouth are striking. Not only do they suggest a common origin for these routines in royal funeral rites (see above, Chapter 2), but also raise an interesting question. Do routines of a dramatic character have a ritual origin or does ritual have an inherently dramatic character?

What went on in the inner sanctum of the god may have been 'more inaccessible than what happens in the heavens' or 'more veiled than the state of the other world' (Meeks and Favard-Meeks 1997, 126), but there are many indications that, during the New Kingdom, the cult of the great temples was opened out in a way that created an audience and the possibility of interaction. Indications of this are found among the collection of documents of which the script for the daily cult is a part. P. Berlin 3055 is part of a collection known as the 'Takelot Papyri', named for the notation of a date in the reign of a king of this name on one of them (Gülden 2001, xiv), which were purchased from a dealer in Luxor in the early nineteenth century. The collection, which may well originate in the library of the Karnak temple, includes the aforementioned daily cult script for Amun, a less complete one for his wife, Mut, and a document relating to one of her festivals, as well as several collections of hymns to major deities. One of these collections, P. Berlin 3049, includes hymns similar to those found in the daily service of Amun, which are sung to awaken the god before he is taken out of his shrine (Gülden 2001). Such hymns often consist of the refrain 'Awake in peace, in peace', punctuated by a litany of Amun in his various forms. In the daily cult script they are simply written out word for word in unbroken lines (e.g. Königliche Museen zu Berlin 1901, pls 1-27; Moret 1902, 122ff.), but in P. Berlin 3049 a couple of them are laid out with the different verses in separate horizontal lines, with the opening and closing refrains in columns at either end (Gülden 2001, 22, 46, 61, pls 4, 8, 11). This 'anaphoric' or 'antiphonal' type of composition (which is also known from Middle Kingdom documents) was used in several different literary genres (Grapow 1936, 38-51; Goelet 2001), but in the present context it clearly points to a notation for a song sung in at least two parts. How could this be, when the cult was supposed to be performed by a single celebrant?

As noted above in Chapter 2, singers and musicians, mostly female, begin to be associated with divine and mortuary festivals beginning in the Old Kingdom. As the office of *hemet netcher*, or prophetess, declined in the Middle Kingdom, they became more numerous, and the *shamayt,* or chantress, made her appearance. This functionary, equipped with the sacred sistrum and *menat* necklace of Hathor, provided singing and percussion accompaniment at all manner of religious and state festivals. The office of *shemayt* was the one most commonly held by elite and middle-class women in the New Kingdom (Onstine 2000, 11-76). In the Third Intermediate Period, they occupied the highest social strata as members of the family of the high priest of Amun and were prominent in the music department of the temple of Amun, under the direction of the politically influential God's Wife of Amun (Naguib 1990; Onstine 2000, 77-9). This functionary, generally a relative of the king who took some kind of role in the actual cult (Gitton 1984, 39-42), increased in significance until by the 26th Dynasty she herself held the office of first prophet of Amun (Gitton and Leclant 1977), and with it the rights and responsibilities of performing the cult (see below, Chapter 5).

Anaphoric hymns of the type discussed above are first found addressed to Senwosret III during the Middle Kingdom (Goelet 2001, 79-81), suggesting the existence of some kind of choir. The Rite of the Opening of the Mouth, which closely resembles the cult ritual in concept and form, required that the *sem* priest be assisted by a lector and others. The Ancestor Ritual mentions servitors who move the offerings around (Gardiner 1935, 95). A badly damaged relief in the festival hall of Thutmose III at Karnak may show these women in the sanctuary during the cult (Onstine 2000, 43-8), but also raises the question of how many people can fit into such a room during the service. A study of similar issues in relation to Iron Age Israelite sanctuaries suggests that musicians would have had to stand outside the sanctuary proper (Burgh 2002). In the Egyptian New Kingdom context, this would have been in the resting place for the barque shrine in front of the sanctuary. However, the use of musical accompaniment may not just arise out of a desire to elaborate the daily cult, but may also be a reflection of a process of externalization into an expanding sphere of public worship.

How this process developed is illustrated by depictions of the cult of Aten as practised by his chief prophet, Akhenaten. Although generalized scenes of the king worshipping his god show him offering to the god with his wife and children, with their entourage shown directly behind him, a scene from the tomb of Panehesy at Amarna makes it more site specific (Davies 1905, pl. 18). In a detailed representation of the large Aten temple at Amarna, we see the king and queen standing together on top of a stepped altar in the main courtyard. At the foot of the stairs stand their daughters, playing the sacred rattles or sistra as the *shamayt* normally do. Priests and other servitors are shown bowing around the foot of the altar. Outside the wall of the temple others bow and sing songs of jubilation. As in the old Sed Festival enclosures, the outsiders are clearly conceived of as being an audience, even if they are not present at the performance. Revealingly, very few depictions of Akhenaten worshipping his god in carefully delineated settings ever show him using the main altar of the temple at its eastern end. Even though the Aten's temples were of a solar type and open to the sky, the inner sanctum was still at the farthest remove from the entrance and excluded public participation. The recurring image of the king worshipping his god in the main courtyard of the temple suggests a desire to have a real audience present, or at least close by.

The god goes out

In an inscription commemorating his building projects, Akhenaten's father, Amenhotep III, describes how, as well as rebuilding the Luxor temple ('the southern Opet'), he constructed a *maru,* or 'viewing place', in front of it. The viewing place contained offerings to the god as well as being the venue for receiving revenues and tribute from all his Egyptian and foreign subjects (Davies 1992, 3; Cabrol 2001, 600-7). Depictions of the reception of foreign tribute show a large, elaborate ceremony with the king seated beneath a baldachin, surrounded by his high officials and approached by crowds of foreign dignitaries with huge quantities of gifts. In some representations there are also musical performances and sporting events (Vandier 1964, 572-610, 691-5; Decker 1992, 77-80). We may therefore assume that the 'viewing place' must have been a large space; in the case of the Luxor temple it may be identified with the 'solar court' of Amenhotep III, directly in front of the main temple and its sanctuary. There are inscriptional indications that the *rekhyt,* or general population, were admitted into it, at least on festive occasions (Bell 1985, 275-6), principally the Opet Festival. It is likely that the god present was Amun in his processional barque, resting at one of the many stations during his great processional festival, the Opet.

As we have already seen above, Egyptian festivals typically involved a procession centred on the image of the god in its sacred barque. Such events are known from the Archaic Period onwards. The Festival of Sokar, the mortuary god of Memphis, is attested (Serrano 2002, 92-8), complete with logographic representations of his distinctive boat and his procession around the walls of the temple of King Neferirkare, as described in the 6th Dynasty Abusir Papyri (Posener-Kriéger 1976, 59-76, 549-53). We have also noted the popularity of the procession of Osiris during the Middle Kingdom. However, if New Kingdom Egypt did not invent such events, it greatly augmented them, and at this period we begin to find extensive lists of festivals on temple walls, where scarcely a day passes without a celebration of some kind (Altenmüller 1977). While they celebrated various kinds of events, from the agricultural and the astronomical to the mythological and the political, the medium of the festival, a holiday from the mundane world, was an occasion for the god to appear in procession. The divinity left the temple in the sacred barque, carried on the shoulders of the priests, and hit the road or the river to display itself to the people, sometimes visiting the temples of other gods before returning home. The gods could appear individually or in groups, in an intimate village setting or on a grand scale. Schechner describes processions as a kind of natural theatre and a bipolar model of the performances that take place in ceremonial centres. A procession is an event that moves along a prescribed path, but at appointed places the procession halts and performances are played (Schechner 1988, 158-60). In a brief examination of the growth and variety of New Kingdom festivals in the Theban area, we shall focus on their performative aspects.

The Beautiful Festival of the Valley

That processional festivals in honour of Amun of Thebes took place as early as the Middle Kingdom is confirmed by the existence of a processional kiosk for the barque of this god (the so-called White Chapel) erected by Senwosret I, which was reconstructed from fragments reused in later buildings (Cabrol 2001, 511-13). During the Middle Kingdom a procession is known to have travelled from the temple of Amun on the east bank to the funerary temple of the 11th Dynasty king Mentuhotep Nebhepetre on the west. Textual references to a procession of the god to this king's temple are found at this period, and excavation has revealed a processional way paved with bricks leading from the temple into the cultivated land of the valley. However, it is clear that this particular causeway was soon reconceptualized as a processional or 'god's way' used in the Beautiful Festival of the Valley, where Amun visited royal mortuary temples on the west bank and a shrine to Hathor, the goddess of love and regeneration, whose shrine was adjacent to the Mentuhotep temple in the western mountain (Cabrol 2001, 46-50, 78ff., 151-4).

During the New Kingdom this festival was greatly expanded. Both Hatshepsut and Thutmose III constructed temples, or shrines within them, to celebrate Hathor and receive her guest, Amun, expanding and renewing the Middle Kingdom causeways to accommodate the god's procession. During the earlier 18th Dynasty the Beautiful Festival of the

Valley functioned as yet another festival of the dead. Amun and Hathor helped revitalize the spirits of not only deceased kings, but all the noble dead of the cemetery. Elite tomb chapels of this period show family members communing with their deceased relatives by staying up all night, drinking and singing songs that celebrate the ability of Hathor to resurrect them, a theme that can be traced back to Old Kingdom funeral songs (Schott 1952, 32-45, 64-93). In the 19th Dynasty Amun visited the west bank, accompanied by his wife and son, Mut and Khonsu, and stayed in the mortuary temple of the reigning king (Cabrol 2001, 741). While courtiers and senior bureaucrats could aspire to follow the gods in procession, humbler folk like the craft workers of the necropolis had to be content with visiting Hathor's shrine and offering their prayers (Sadek 1987, 501).

The Festival of Sokar

Similar to the Beautiful Festival of the Valley was the Festival of Sokar. As noted above, this ancient celebration, originating at the beginning of Egyptian history, commemorated a falcon god of Memphis, a chthonic deity related to both death and agriculture. In essence his celebration consisted of a procession of his image, accompanied by divine standards, around the walls of Memphis on the 26th day of the fourth month of the inundation season, the time when the flood receded and the earth was to be readied for planting (Gaballa and Kitchen 1969, 13-23). The original citadel of Memphis contained the palace of the king, who also circled the walls as part of his accession to the throne or jubilee (see above, Chapter 2). Not surprisingly, the procession of Sokar was already being performed at royal funerary temples as early as the 6th Dynasty (Posener-Kriéger 1976, 549-53), and he soon became inextricably identified with Osiris, the avatar of deceased kingship. By the New Kingdom, when the procession was performed around the walls of the funerary temple of the reigning king, they were almost indistinguishable, and the festival, which lasted from the 18th to the 30th of the month, adapted many of the features of the Mystery of Osiris performed at Abydos, which were still celebrated at this time. Inscriptions in the tombs of the elite as well as texts and representations in the temple of Ramesses III at Medinet Habu show that almost all this festive time was devoted to celebration of these mysteries around figures of Osiris made of sprouting grain (Gaballa and Kitchen 1969, 36-43), which will be discussed in more detail in Chapter 5.

While these Osirian rites mostly involved the priests, the 24th to the 26th of the month were given over to Sokar, and male members of the elite vied for the honour of taking part in the procession of Sokar and the procession that preceded it. On the day before the procession they celebrated the Netcheryt Festival, when Sokar-Osiris came back to life, and they held a vigil for him, staying up all night garlanded with onions. The onions symbolized food offerings for all the dead who were included in this feast of resurrection, just as in the Beautiful Festival of the Valley (Gaballa and Kitchen 1969, 43-5). At dawn on the 26th of Akhet, the king or his deputy priest aroused Sokar in his shrine and, after offering to him and the other gods, took him out for procession in his special barque around the walls of the royal temple. It began with the priests libating and censing the way, preceded by musicians and singers. Then came the barque of the attending gods carried on the shoulders of the priests, followed by more priests carrying the divine standards and various symbolic objects related to the god. Finally came sixteen men, high officials like those who participated in the earlier Sed Festivals, pulling ropes which were held by the king (or his deputy), and finally, the barque of Sokar. To shouts of 'Victory, victory, sovereign!' the procession made its way around the outside walls of the temple before visiting the private tombs in the cemetery and returning to its shrine inside the walls (Gaballa and Kitchen 1969, 45-71; Epigraphic Survey 1940, pls 218-26). Records from the village at Deir el-Medina inform us that this was a public holiday and the non-elite were free to watch the procession and enjoy a day of feasting and merriment (Sadek 1987, 171).

The Opet Festival

A similar distribution of activity, a dichotomy between the public and the hidden that we have already noted, can also be seen in the greatest of these New Kingdom Theban festivals, the Opet, celebrated in the southern Opet temple, two kilometres south of the main temple of Amun at Karnak. This event, which took place in the second month of the year, during the inundation, consisted of a procession of Amun in his barque to the southern temple, where he rested a few days, and back again to his main temple. The route of the procession varied over time. It seemed originally to have moved along the river bank or perhaps inland, via the temple of Mut, which stood just south of the Karnak temple of Amun. The festival, which is first attested in the early 18th Dynasty, was originally eleven days long, but by the end of the New Kingdom it lasted almost a month (Murnane 1980). Of this time period, only the first and last days were public holidays, presumably when the processions between the two temples took place (Sadek 1987, 171). The time in between, when the god rested in the southern temple, was a time of intensive ritual activity centred around the person of the king. Recent work on the Luxor temple and its texts and representations, undertaken by the Oriental Institute of Chicago, suggests that it was the repository of the royal *ka*, the spirit shared by all kings of Egypt that made them fit to rule. The purpose of the festival was to imbue the king with this legitimating essence and make it manifest. The mechanism seems to have been some sort of ritual performance where the king role played the son of the god Amun, magically re-engendered by him and reborn. After the god had re-crowned the king he appeared outside the

80

temple before the general population, which explains the need for the 'viewing place' constructed by Amenhotep III (Bell 1985).

The rituals that took place inside the southern Opet are not well understood and it is difficult to decide if they depict actual performances or are just visual metaphors. However, their religious and political importance is underlined by the fact that King Horemheb made the Opet Festival the occasion for his actual coronation (Gardiner 1953). The ease with which this event was integrated into the proceedings arises from the fact that they already re-present this ceremony. Places in the temple like the House of the Officials, where Horus was acclaimed as king by the other gods, reflect a system of mythological connotation like that found in the Ramesseum Dramatic Papyrus (Bell 1985, 272-3). Likewise, priests and high officials played similar roles.

The ceremony in which the king assumed office was alluded to in temple inscriptions and pictures, as well as in biographical inscriptions of members of the elite who took part. There are no 'scripts'. After a purification ceremony when gods at the four directions (perhaps actors in masks) poured water on him, the king proceeded to the *per wer*, the ancient sanctuary first attested at Hieraconpolis in area HK29A, where, as the Horemheb text puts it,

> His noble daughter the Great of Magic, her arms in welcoming attitude
> ... embraced his beauty and established herself on his forehead (Gardiner 1953, 15).

Although the royal cobra goddess is imagined embracing him in this poetic rendition, biographies of elite officials describe how they actually placed the crowns on the king's head in the role of *imy-khent*, or 'chamberlain', familiar to us from scripts such as the Opening of the Mouth and the Ramesseum Dramatic Papyrus (Gardiner 1953, 26; Barta 1980). What follows, when Amun places another crown on the king's head and the gods assign him his royal name, which is sometimes shown being engraved on the leaves of a sacred tree by the gods, must also be taken in a metaphorical way (Gardiner, 1953; Kákosy 1980a). On a more concrete note, as Horemheb left the king's house (part of the temple corresponding to the Sed festival 'palace' where he changed costume), 'the entire people were in joy and they cried aloud to heaven' (Gardiner 1953, 15), strongly suggesting that their acclamation was not incidental to the proceedings.

The Divine Oracle

The importance of this public legitimation of the king by the god is emphasized by its repeated use for these purposes by rulers with rather thin claims to rulership. Horemheb, who came from a non-elite background, had rescued Egypt from the godless chaos of Akhenaten and his successors, but he still needed the public endorsement of the gods, especially Amun, whose establishment and clergy had been the object of particular hostility. A century earlier, the female king Hatshepsut stated that Amun called her to rule in the hall of the southern Opet temple. Her successor, Thutmose III, for whom she was originally regent, had a similar experience at Karnak. The mention of the approach (*pech*) of a god singles out the experience of Hatshepsut as one of the earliest records of this form of oracular event (Cabrol 2001, 748). While the selection of a ruler by the god is highly unusual, mentions of oracles become increasingly common during the New Kingdom and Third Intermediate Period.

The god responded to yes-and-no answers or distinguished between written petitions through sudden movements of his processional barque (Kruchten 1986, 337-54). The oracle of Amun, king of the gods, settled administrative problems, appointed members of his clergy, blessed infants and even intervened in political disputes. While lesser village gods arbitrated on everyday problems, the Wisdom of Ani suggests that anyone could approach a god with an oracle, although decorous behaviour was urged (20.12-14):

> Offer to your god
> Beware of offending him
> Do not question his images,
> Do not accost him when he appears
> Do not jostle him in order to carry him,
> Do not disturb the oracles.
> (Lichtheim 1976, 141; Quack 1994, 109, 175-6)

All of this suggests that enthusiasm for the oracular performance could on occasion overwhelm its operation. The responses of the god were of inclination (*hon*) towards a petition or rejection (*nay en ha*) or 'stepping back'). On occasion the god could also be angry at petitioners or salute them, although how is not specified. Petitions could be submitted to the god orally or in writing (Černý 1962, 36-47). While these oracles do not have an elaborate script, there is clearly a set procedure or routine, and of course there are witnesses – as many as possible. That is the whole point. The validity of oracles is demonstrated by their careful recording in papyrus documents and inscriptions, sometimes illustrated. Such an event has an obvious theatrical character apart from its religious and other significance. Indeed, the prominence of the oracle validates the public nature of the Opet procession as well as drawing strength from it.

The procession itself is shown in the most detail in reliefs in the Luxor temple dating from the reign of Tutankhamun (Epigraphic Survey 1994) and alluded to in many other New Kingdom sources (Murnane 1980). These reliefs show how, following the Amarna Period, the god's journey to Luxor was transferred to water and his great ceremonial ship, the Userhat, was towed along the shore by the military and highly placed members of the elite who vied for this honour, to the accompaniment of drums, trumpets, singing and dancing. When the procession arrived at the southern temple, the shrine of the god was removed from the boat and carried to the temple on the shoulders of the priests, where it was met by welcoming crowds, and the whole land was said to be in jubilation (Epigraphic Survey 1994, pls 17-40). Given the nature of the festival, the king was more often present than at other such celebrations. As it travelled on land the procession formed up with the god in front followed by the divine standards and the king, who is often shown carrying them as a token of his participation (Cabrol 2001, 744-6). Behind him followed the other priestly and official participants.

Processional ways

Nothing demonstrates the importance of the Opet procession and the oracular and other events that were a part of it better than the processional ways that dominate the architectural landscape of ancient Thebes. Hatshepsut was the first to construct a sphinx-lined processional way from Karnak to Luxor and Amenhotep III completely rebuilt the Luxor temple. Thutmose III began work on the northern end of this route, south from the existing entrance of the Amun temple of Karnak to the temple of Mut, which over the centuries evolved into a spectacular series of pylon gateways and courts enclosed with three-metre-high walls (Cabrol 2001, 21, 35).

The more common sphinx-lined ways, which by the end of the New Kingdom connected all the major temples of the area, have recently been studied by Agnes Cabrol (2001). Cabrol notes the political and religious symbolism of these installations: not only did the face of the king on each sphinx emphasize his permanent presence at the festival, but its leonine form recalled the twin gods of the horizon so that the passing of the god's boat was like the transit of the sun on the cosmic plane. The sacredness of the way was protected by low walls about a metre high and plantings of flowers and trees. The reason for this was that in ancient cities unused land was always liable to be built on, unencumbered as they were by modern planning regulations (Cabrol 2001, 171-482, 731-48). The sphinxes also ensured that there was space for people to watch the procession, not to be excluded. Some of the processional sphinxes were even the object of informal popular devotion, like the large ka statues of the king or large reliefs of gods on the outer walls or gates of temples (Cabrol 2001, 477-80, 714-21). All along these routes where constructed open kiosks of brick or stone, of design similar to earlier Middle Kingdom examples, where the image of the god (and its bearers) could rest, often outside the temples of other gods. It was here that petitioners could approach the god or address their prayers directly and make informal offerings.

During the Third Intermediate Period, when the oracle of Amun played an increasingly prominent role in the political and social life of Thebes and Upper Egypt, it came to be sited permanently at the tenth pylon on the north-south processional way between the main Amun temple and that of Mut (Kruchten 1986, 333; Cabrol 2001, 743). This area had long been a focus of public devotion; statues of Amenhotep III's famous minister Amenhotep, son of Hapu, placed there to intercede with the god were rubbed smooth by beseeching hands (Sadek 1987, 45-6) or laden with offerings. Here, at the 'Floor of Silver' (i.e. a pure place), all kinds of dramatic scenarios unfolded as Amun decided inheritances, disputes over the assignment of priestly office and even succession to the throne (Cabrol 2001, 483-7)

The oracular Floor of Silver located in the centre of the tenth pylon court (Kruchten, 1986, 325-36) clearly functioned in the public space, as did the more humble oracle of King Amenhotep I, across the river in the village at Deir el-Medina (Černý 1962, 41-3). It may be that one or all of the great courtyards that connect the seventh to tenth pylons were also designed to accommodate large crowds. The forecourt of Ramesses II at Luxor contains inscriptions referring to the *rekhyt*; it seems to have replaced that of Amenhotep III as a point of public access (Bell 1985, 259ff., 270-2, 274-6; Sadek, 1987, 47). The implications of all this for the sacred architecture of ancient Thebes should be clear. The gods' ways, the broad halls, the vast courtyards and gigantic gateways were built to accommodate large crowds and provide a dramatic setting for festive events such as the processions of the gods and king and the eruption of the oracle. The repetitious character of the architecture, with its endless rows of sphinxes, gateways and decorative motifs, was geared to the stationary spectator, as were the words and acts of the appearance of the god, echoed in later compositions such as the Triumph of Horus that were most likely devised with a processional venue in mind (see below). However, a procession allows for spectators to follow along as well as to remain stationary. In a procession an event moves along a prescribed path, but at appointed places the procession halts and performances are played, albeit not highly scripted or elaborate ones.

The Sed Festival

Although it has been argued that routines like those enacted at the Opet Festival to some degree replaced old performances like the Sed (Cabrol 2001, 748), this festival was still regularly celebrated throughout the New Kingdom and beyond (Martin 1984). However, since its main venue was at Memphis rather than Thebes, many instances remain poorly documented. Amenhotep III celebrated three spectacular Sed Festivals from the thirtieth year of his reign (years 30, 34 and 37) (Kozloff, Bryan and Berman 1992, 38-41). The accumulated wealth from Egypt's foreign conquests was brought to bear on these celebrations, which are well documented in both the textual and the archaeological records.

One of the most interesting aspects revealed is the important role that the high officials of the realm played in this festival. While earlier records clearly indicate that they played parts in the dramatic performances and were rewarded for their participation, the inscriptions of King Amenhotep's time not only indicate exactly who these people were, but document their material contributions to the festival (Kozloff, Bryan and Berman 1992, 38-41). At the site of the king's palace on the western edge of the city of Thebes, where the festivals were actually celebrated, were many inscribed jar fragments and sealings left over from the feasting that accompanied them. Among the remains of these containers for perishable foodstuffs such as alcoholic beverages and meat products, we find the names of royal and temple estates, those not only of high officials, but sometimes even of the hospitality professionals who provided the supplies. Other records credit a ship's captain with bringing valuable incense from overseas (Hayes 1951, 83-104, 156-62), and Amenmose, a scribe working at the turquoise quarries of Sinai, tells of how he supplied precious stone to his superior, the overseer of the Treasury, for the third Sed (Davies 1994, 47). While most of the provisions and the venue for the celebration were obviously provided by the king, there seems to be considerable emphasis on the communal nature of the effort. While it is possible that this state of affairs is peculiar to the reign of Amenhotep III, the patterns of communal contribution to and participation in festivals can be seen elsewhere in New Kingdom society, and they have considerable importance at later periods (see below).

Led by the aforementioned minister Amenhotep, son of Hapu, the king's officials were not only most competent administrators, but highly cultured, creative thinkers with antiquarian interests. Of particular interest is Kheruef. This man played an important role in the third Sed Festival in Year 37 (Kozloff, Bryan and Berman 1992, 44-56). His beautifully carved tomb chapel, situated not far from the king's palace, which records his contribution, is also carved with esoteric cryptographic inscriptions on the subject of royal theology, on which he was clearly an expert (Epigraphic Survey 1980, pls 15-15, 35-40). Representations of the Sed Festivals of Amenhotep III which are found in his temples, as well as in the tombs of his officials, included the usual scenes: the king enthroned in the double booth, being carried by his officials, in the procession of the standards, entering the palace, visiting the shrine of the gods and rewarding them at the final levee (Gohary 1992, 11-18). However, in the tomb of Kheruef we see a detailed depiction of the king raising the Djed pillar with the help of his officials, who tug on long ropes (Epigraphic Survey 1980, pls 47, 55-7; Davies 1994, 33-5). This event takes place in the midst of a great gathering of musicians, dancers, wrestlers, stick fighters and boxers. When the pillar has been set up, the king makes offerings to it and cattle and asses are driven around it. In this scene the pillar is identified with Sokar-Osiris, whose festival was celebrated in Amenhotep III's own funerary temple, as it was later in that of Ramesses III.

The event depicted bears an extraordinary resemblance to scenes 13 to 15 and 18 and 19 in the Ramesseum Dramatic Papyrus. Both sources show the pillar being moved by ropes and mock battles, as well as the driving of asses and cattle, which are later sacrificed. Indeed, the close resemblance is what suggested the Sed as the subject of the papyrus, as raising the pillar is not associated with it in earlier periods. Quite apart from the issue of whether this activity was actually added to the Sed under Amenhotep III, we may ask if Kheruef, a man as learned as the owner of the Ramesseum Papyrus, had a similar document at his disposal. Despite the similarities of the scenes, there are also many differences. The wall relief in his tomb is a detailed pictorial record of an event, while the Ramesseum Papyrus provides only a rough sketch of the basic activity. All the tomb figures are labelled and some are even provided with dialogue. However, the explanations of mythological significance and the place of this act in an overall narrative that are found the Ramesseum Papyrus are lacking. We are faced with either an alternative method of recording such ritual performances, as has been suggested for the Rite of the Opening of the Mouth, or, more likely, a memorialization of a particular performance. In the papyrus the king is not represented as acting, and the presence of the queen behind him is not found in earlier versions of the festival.

Another previously unknown event at Amenhotep III's festival is also recorded by Kheruef, 'the sailing of the sacred barque of the king on the lake of his majesty' (Epigraphic Survey, 1980, pls 43-6; Davies 1994, 37), towed by his officials. One of the purposes of the festival seems to have been to display the king as a fully divine being while still alive, crossing the waters in his boat like the immortal sun in the sky. A huge basin or harbour excavated in front of the king's palace earlier in his reign admirably suited this purpose. However, excavations on the site of the king's palace, his 'house of rejoicing', do not provide much more information on how the festival was celebrated. Its structures were mostly of mud-brick and poorly preserved. While a large temple to Amun along with a pillared hall and large court were constructed, debris is scattered all over the site. It is likely that new buildings were constructed for each festival (Hayes 1950, 177-80, 236-42; Kemp 1989, 213-17).

While Amenhotep III celebrated his Sed in the seclusion of his own palace, his heterodox son Amenhotep IV/Akhenaten, within a few years of coming to throne, mounted the same festival right in the middle of the city of Thebes. Almost immediately on becoming king, the new king began constructing a huge temple to his solar god, which he called Gem-pa-aten, or 'the Aten is found', immediately east of the existing Amun temple. It was in this gigantic rectangular space, far larger than the existing Amun temple, that he celebrated a bizarre version of this ancient festival (Redford 1999, 53-6). Although this structure was later completely destroyed, enough of its ground plan and relief carved blocks used in its construction survive to show its appearance and uses. Since this structure was intended for sun worship, it was unroofed. Its walls were constructed to form a series of bays which were decorated with reliefs commemorating events connected with it and separated by piers with large statues of the king. At the eastern end of the temple, in the sanctuary, was the main altar, and much of the rest of the space was filled with hundreds of smaller ones (Redford 1984, 102-17). The general idea of the Sed Festival seems to have been that after a generation on the throne, a king would offer thanks to the gods of the land and they would renew his power. Amenhotep IV did neither. Although the traditional deities of Egypt were not yet proscribed by the king, he managed to greatly downplay their role at this event. All the divine offerings were to the Aten, not to other gods (Redford 1999, 56-7), whose presence was relegated to the traditional standards that led the royal progress and to minor players like Meret, all shown on a very small scale (e.g. Gohary 1992, pl. 20). However, most of the usual events such as the enthronement, levee and offerings took place. Throughout the festival the king was carried in procession every day between the temple and the ceremonial palace, where he changed his costume and stayed for the duration. This building, shown in considerable detail in the temple reliefs, may have been on an axis with the entrance of the Gem-pa-aten temple, with which it was connected by a processional way (Redford 1999, 57), and probably lay west of it, just north of the entrance to the Amun temple. It served as the 'green room' for the king, who was, at least in theory, the main actor for all the temple performances. It also lay right in the middle of the city of Thebes, so that its inhabitants could see the king periodically emerging from the festival enclosure, as in earlier times (Redford 1984, 128-30; see also Chapter 2). The suppression of the individual identities of the officials who acted in the festival stands in contrast to the practice of Amenhotep III and suggests that the new king wanted to appeal more directly to the non-elite classes. Later, when he changed his name to Akhenaten and moved his residence to the new city of Akhetaten in middle Egypt, the king travelled every day in his chariot from his residence in the north of the city to the ceremonial palace in the centre of town (Kemp 1976, 98-9; 1989, 276-9). Some have argued that this daily event substituted for festival processions of the gods (Lacovara 1999, 67), but in hindsight it may underline their growing importance and that of more 'public' religious performances.

The only other Sed Festival known in any detail was celebrated by king Osorkon II of the 22nd Dynasty around 850 BCE in the delta city of Bubastis. Enacted in a specially built courtyard, it was depicted in reliefs on the inner gateway (Naville 1892; Kitchen 1973, §277, 80). Attention has been drawn to the close similarity between these texts and representations and those made for Amenhotep III (Naville 1892, 4; Kitchen

1973, §280, n. 432). Apparently iconographically unique is a representation of an area completely filled with gods' shrines and offerings, labelled as the 'dining hall' already mentioned in connection with the divine service (Naville 1892, pls 7-8). The only possible parallels are depictions of temples from the reign of Akhenaten which would have been completely inaccessible at this period (Gohary 1992, pls 82-3). In this context we recall the words of Kheruef, director of Amenhotep III's Sed Festival, when he said:

> It is His Majesty who does these things, as one who conforms to the writings of old, and the generations of people since the time of the ancestors (when) they did not perform the Sed festival (Davies 1994, 37).

In other words, although every attempt was made to follow the traditions connected with this ancient festival, research revealed to the Egyptians, as it does to us, that it was done a little bit differently every time. The directors of the festival took what they wanted from earlier celebrations as well as adding something of their own. Even within a few years the Sed as celebrated by Amenhotep III and his son showed considerable differences. Over a longer period of time this ancient festival continued to be creatively reconfigured.

Other performances

Rites not known from earlier periods which centred on the king also took place in temples at this period. For example, the Rite of the Foundation of the Temple, first depicted showing Thutmose III in the Amun temple at Karnak, depicts the king going through the motions of laying out the plan of the building. He first determines the site and the orientation of four corners by surveying with a cord, then breaks the ground and builds the damp courses, which he fills with sand. Next he protects the building by placing inscribed plaques at each corner, puts a block of stone in place, and finally purifies the whole site with incense. The king is assisted in this performance, which represents the actual surveying and foundation of a building, by Sefkhet Abwy, the 'seven-horned one', the ancient goddess of literacy, who helps him stretch the cord, then survey the building (Moret 1964). New Kingdom and later more elaborate depictions of the ceremony give the king dialogue. Foundation deposits from every period of Egyptian history that contain metal plaques engraved with kings' names may provide proof that such ceremonies actually took place (Letellier 1977). Are we to imagine the king being present to inaugurate every major temple construction, along with an actor playing the part of the goddess? While such representations cannot be dismissed as purely symbolic, the problem of how to interpret them remains.

Another such performance, also first known from the reign of Thutmose III at Deir el-Bahri, is 'Striking the Ball' (Decker and Harb 1994, pl. 62,

132-3). The king is shown hitting red clay balls with a stick that are caught and brought back to him by priests. Other depictions, from the Ptolemaic Period, explain that the ball represents the eye of Apophis, the great serpent that threatens the sun god and the cosmos, although it also seems likely that this activity mirrored a game originally played for fun. Indeed, both the foundation ceremony and the Rite of Striking the Ball illustrate how more everyday activities have been ritualized and made into a spectacle of some kind (Decker 1992, 114-15).

Other, less formal performances such as games, sports, music, singing and dance also found a home in religious festivals. We have already noted the importance of the chantress, or *shemayt*, who was found at all the processional festivals, public offerings, the Sed Festival and probably even the daily cult of the gods. Male and female singers were also found at such events and so were musicians such as harpists, drummers and flute players (Manniche 1991; Teeter 1993, 84-6). The Beautiful Festival of the Valley featured overnight celebrations in the tomb chapels of the ancestors, with dancers, musicians and especially songs by old male harpers which celebrated the glories of the hereafter and the brevity of life (Schott 1952, 64-84; Lichtheim 1945). Acrobatic female dancers, like those attested in the Old Kingdom, where an important part of religious processions and especially the ancient Sed Festival (Decker 1992, 136-45), but they were also a highlight of private parties such as those given in the Canaanite district of the capital, Memphis (Caminos 1974, 334-5). Although chantresses were plentiful among women of the elite or middle class, dancers, musicians and singers are poorly represented in the written record, suggesting they were mostly illiterate and lower class, despite their popularity. Perhaps, as in other traditional cultures, they were regarded with suspicion (Manniche 1991, 58-60, 108-17, 124-5), although this cannot be proven.

From the Old Kingdom onwards, men and some women are depicted in strenuous, non-utilitarian physical activity. Some of this is clearly for military training, which is recognized as the origin of most combat sports and tests of skills with weapons. Wrestling, stick-fighting and boxing, which were presented at many of the festivals (Decker 1992, 5, 170-89), clearly had training and entertainment value quite apart from the symbolic significance accorded them at events like the raising of the Djed pillar. However, they provided an ideal vehicle for the dramatization of conflict and resolution essential to the myth of Horus and Seth, which was central to the monarchy and the general world view of Egypt. Men are seen wrestling before the barque shrine of the deified king Thutmose III inside a temple and stick-fighters are even shown on top of a cabin of the boat ferrying the image of Montu, the god of war (Decker and Harb 1994, pls 310, 316-17, 567-8). While it may seem that religious festivals provided a venue for sports in Egypt as they did in Greece, there are indications of less formal venues. As a prince, King Amenhotep II is said to have performed great feats of archery in 'the great hall (*weskhet*) of the king at This' north of Thebes, a columned hall of the type favoured by the Egyptians for large gatherings (Decker and Harb 1994, pl. 69, 146-7; Spencer 1984, 5-6).

The athletic prowess of the king became a subject of ideology and tool of theocracy at this period and he is sometimes shown in temple reliefs being trained by gods rather than mortals. Exhibitions of royal excellence were by their nature not competitive, but could be witnessed by large numbers of people, whether it was the crew of the boat rowed single-handed by the king or the admiring members of his mess on the parade ground or the royal estate, suggesting a potential audience for different kinds of sporting activities (Decker 1992, 34-59).

However, it has been plausibly suggested that most public events in which the king or his officials participated made use of the public space provided by the temples with their processional ways and public spaces. Trials may have been held at the doorways of temples or large spaces like the hypostyle hall at Karnak, with public executions somewhere off to the side (Cabrol 2001, 749-54). Amenhotep II vividly describes how he despatched his foreign captives in a way reminiscent of both traditional depictions of the smiting of enemies and the Mirgissa deposit:

> It was to the delight of his father Amun that he returned after he himself had slain with his club seven chieftains who were in the district of Tekhay (in Nubia) and who were placed upside down at the brow of the falcon ship of his majesty .... Thereupon six men from among the foe were hung in front of the rampart of Thebes and the hands likewise. The other enemy was then transported south to Nubia and hung on the rampart of Napata in order that men should see the victories of his majesty for ever and ever ... (Cumming 1982, 27).

In much the same way, Prince Osorkon, the son of Takelot II, struck down the instigators of a Theban rebellion against his father and had 'every one burned with fire in the place of his crime', i.e. in the Karnak temple (Caminos 1958, 50-1, 55). Such public appearances of the king or high officials, who are shown in artistic representations under a low, stepped baldachin, have been identified by Cabrol with square bases of stone and brick found adjacent to the processional ways and main entrances of the Theban temples. The king also showed himself at his palaces, at the 'window of appearance', actual examples of which have been found at the ceremonial palaces of Akhenaten at Amarna and Ramesses III at Medinet Habu (Kemp 1989, 211-12, 278).

We have noted how the roles in ritual performances at the great New Kingdom festival not taken by the king or the priests were filled by high officials. They dragged the boat of Amun at the Opet Festival as well as the barque of Sokar, they followed closely the images of the gods, they participated in the Sed Festival and even took a role in organizing such performances. Although the more important positions in the priesthoods began to become hereditary at this period, many of these officeholders filled other important government posts (Hayes 1962, §3). In other words, the priests and the high officials who assisted them at the great festivals were all members of the elite, as where the chantresses who accompanied their performances (Onstine 2000, 88-9). However, at some celebrations members of other classes also had close access to the gods.

The festivals of Mut, the wife of the Amun of Karnak, although subject to royal and elite patronage, appear to have been somewhat less restricted. In the tomb of the Khabehenet, a 'workman' at Deir el-Medina, we see this man and his relatives in the sacred boat of the goddess as it sails on the lake, depicted twice, from each side. Only one of the names of these men survive, that of Nebre, the scribe of the Place of Truth, as the village was called (Černý 1949, 25-7). On the stela of another villager, Hesy-su-nebef, the head workman, Neferhotep, shown on the barque of Mut, has pride of place on top of the monument (Quibell 1898, pl. 10.3). (It must be remembered that the cultured and affluent craftsmen of Deir el-Medina, while not members of the elite, were hardly poor and unconnected.)

Apart from participating in the festivals of east Thebes, the workers of the necropolis also had their own celebrations and local shrines. There was the large temple of their patron, Amenhotep I, as well as devotions to Hathor and other deities such as Ptah, god of crafts. Detailed records of life in this community enable us to distinguish public holidays from celebrations restricted to the temples (Sadek, 1987, 85-142, 169-82) and reveal that the most important festival was that of Amenhotep I, when the villagers spent four whole days celebrating (Černý 1927, 183-4). The image of Amenhotep I also gave oracles and was, in fact, the court of final appeal in village legal cases (McDowell 1999, 172). The divine cults of the village were run by its inhabitants, with men fulfilling the priestly roles and women occupying the role of chantresses (Sadek 1987, 79-82). It was during festivals that communal judgement of a different kind was passed on unfortunate individuals like the 'hot' or demonic man who was beaten with sticks (Borghouts 1980). Although they were government employees, the villagers supported the cults and their festivals from their own contributions, in a way that reminds us of the contributions of high officials to the Sed Festival of Amenhotep III (Sadek 1997, 177-9). Evidence from the village suggests that its religious festivals reflected the large state ones on a small scale, although they do not provide evidence for which came first.

Even at Deir el-Medina there is very limited evidence for performances outside the sphere of religious festivals. However, an outstanding exception is the series of demonstrations staged by the workers in the reigns of Ramesses III and IV when their rations failed to appear. In Year 29 of Ramesses III the workers marched to the riverbank, provocatively crossing the boundaries of the cemetery, inside which they were supposed to remain, in order to confront the 'children of the vizier' about their plight.

They even staged torchlit processions (Edgerton 1951; Frandsen 1990). While these demonstrations, which were apparently effective, where staged out of the desperation attendant on hunger, another notable eruption was intended to protect the honour of the village.

In Year 16 of Ramesses IX, the discovery of robberies from the tombs of the necropolis led to suspicion falling on the workers. When one of their number was questioned and exonerated, 'the great magistrates caused the administrators, the captains, and the workmen of the Necropolis, and the chief policemen, policemen and all the supply staff of the necropolis to go around West Thebes in great celebration as far as Thebes'. They all crossed over to the temple of Ptah, where they confronted the mayor of Thebes, Paser, by whom they believed they had been framed. 'This mayor of Thebes spoke to the people of the Necropolis in the presence of the butler of Pharaoh, saying, "As for this celebration you make today – it is not a celebration, it is your song of triumph that you are making." He then swore by the king that he would write to him and have them all arrested for tomb robbing, a capital offence' (Peet 1930, 28-45; McDowell 1999, 196). The tomb robbery trials recorded in P. Abbott eventually led to the conviction and execution of a number of the villagers, but the demonstrations described, where the workers are swept up in a power struggle between the mayors of east and west Thebes, may be described as a form of political activity of a type more familiar from our own time. Marches and other large gatherings by non-elite people were probably of more importance in Egyptian life than our meagre records would suggest.

5

Text and Context: Performances in Late Period and Graeco-Roman Egypt

The Third Intermediate Period came to an end about 710 BCE, when the Kushite ruler Shabaka took control of the whole of Egypt and appeared as King of Upper and Lower Egypt in the temple of Ptah in Memphis (Morkot 2000, 208). Some years before this, an elder relative and former king of Kush, Piye, had invaded Egypt, defeating the numerous rulers of Middle and Lower Egypt in battle, but had afterwards withdrawn (Lichtheim 1980, 60-84; Kitchen 1973, §§324-8). Shabaka's reign and that of his Kushite successors marks a brief period of political unification when, for the first time in many years, country-wide resources could be concentrated on large building projects on sacred sites and literary and artistic capital could be expended on these sites (Leclant 1965) as well as on elite tombs (Smith 1981, 409-11). The Kushite kings drew attention to their care for the gods and their rites and festivals (Myśliwiec 2000, 85-105), and the continued presence of a female family member in the office of God's Wife of Amun only strengthened that relationship (Morkot 2000, 237-9).

In 664 BCE the Kushite rule of Egypt ended with the Assyrian invasion, the occasion of much bloodshed and destruction of sacred sites, including the great temple of Amun at Karnak. This mercifully brief period ended when Assyrian power collapsed, and by 656 BCE Egypt had come to be controlled by the house of Niku, from Sais in the western Delta, the erstwhile governors for the Assyrians (Morkot 2000, 259-80, 293-304). These rulers, although politically hostile to their Kushite predecessors, continued their preoccupation with embellishment and refurbishing of sacred sites, and it was during this period, the 26th Dynasty, that interest in literary and artistic achievements based on the emulation of old styles reached new heights (Manuelian 1994, 357-410). However, this prosperous period ended with the Persian conquest in 525 BCE. While the Persian rulers initially took great pains to respect the customs and gods of the Egyptians, even appearing as pharaohs, relations quickly declined, and Egypt was in revolt for over forty years, from 404 to 343 BCE, a period corresponding to Dynasties 28 to 30 (Myśliwiec 2000, 135-59). After a brief reconquest by the Persians the country surrendered to Alexander in 332 BCE and political independence ended.

Foreign rule did not mean the end of native culture. The first Persian kings, as well as the native rulers of Dynasties 28 to 30 and the Greeks and Romans who came after them, all to a greater or lesser degree continued upkeep of the temples and their cults, taking on the role of king of Upper and Lower Egypt. Although this policy was sometimes more honoured in the breach than the observance, it really only came to an end in 312 CE, when the Emperor Constantine converted to Christianity. Furthermore, the later periods of Egyptian history, especially the Ptolemaic and the Roman, are better documented than any other. This is partly because, as the latest in a temporal series, traces are more numerous.

Deliberate policies favouring immigration of Greek and other peoples and the aggressive expansion of agriculture led to a rise in population. The expansion of trade and industry also made possible a higher level of affluence and with it, material culture (Bowman 1986, 17-20, 122-6, 166-7). Remains of a vast bureaucratic archive and of private documents, of extraordinarily well-preserved settlement sites and vast cemeteries, along with almost perfectly preserved temples and other sacred sites and an unrivalled collection of liturgical and ritual books would seem to suggest that the later period of Egyptian history could provide us with all the evidence we need to fill in the gaps in our ideas about the nature and role of performance in this culture. However, for several reasons, this is not actually the case.

As noted above, the later period, at least at its beginning, was riven with political ruptures and discontinuities, which often translated into the destruction of the physical settings of life as well as its material and social fabric. Secondly, the assumption that the Egyptian cultural materials of the Ptolemaic and Roman Periods either imitate or simply extrapolate the intellectual formations of earlier periods cannot be assumed. Thirdly, the better preservation of the archaeological record points up the importance of regional variation, which is not so obvious in earlier, less well-documented periods. Fourthly, the importation of large, culturally foreign communities, most notably the Greek and Jewish, cannot have failed to influence indigenous culture.

All these parameters need to be taken into consideration and to be played off against a striking continuity of practice and belief that apparently characterizes this long period: namely the cult of Osiris, which can now be seen to influence all other such formations, and whose pull is felt outside Egypt as well as in it (Witt 1971).

This chapter is arranged thematically around groups of sacred texts that are generally agreed to have a performance component. Although they are loosely arranged in chronological order, they are connected by topic rather than exact period. Other materials such as temple reliefs and architecture, documentary sources and material culture are also arranged under these headings where appropriate, or else placed at the end of the chapter.

5. Late Period and Graeco-Roman Egypt

The Shabaka Stone: Horus and the 'political' doctrine of Memphis

The Shabaka Stone, a large basalt stela of rectangular shape now displayed prominently in the British Museum, has no archaeological provenance (Sethe 1928, 1). Its content, however, closely ties it to the cult of Ptah and his temple in Memphis, which was at the heart of the political and spiritual hegemony of Late Period Egypt. Its striking layout consists of two horizontal lines at the top made up of a heading and an introduction, with sixty-two vertical lines of text below (Breasted 1901, pl. 1-2). The text, which is read from left to right, is written in retrograde, as is common in funerary and other sacred texts. The left and right halves of the stone vary markedly in content, although it begins and ends with an account of the doings of Ptah, the city god of Memphis and creator of the universe as we know it. The right-hand or concluding portion of the text explains how he accomplished this through vocalization of his thoughts and that his city of Memphis is the 'great seat' or throne of the kingship, because there Osiris' drowned body was pulled from the water and his son Horus was acclaimed king of Upper and Lower Egypt. The left-hand portion, which shows a greater degree of formal complexity, consists of a narrative describing how Geb came to give his inheritance to his grandson Horus instead of Seth.

Embedded within this section is another, created by the horizontal division of the vertical columns, in which utterances by various gods are shown facing the names of others. This arrangement, which we have already encountered in the Ramesseum Dramatic Papyrus, suggests that we are dealing with a dramatic text of a similar sort. The characters in the play are those mentioned in the story, namely Geb, Horus, Seth, Isis, Nepthys and the council of gods (Sethe 1928, 8-16, 18-19). Unfortunately we do not know how this drama developed or segued into the creation story, as the stela was at one time reused as a millstone, obliterating most of the middle portion of the inscription. The beginning of the main text, which would have gone a long way to answering some of these questions, is likewise incomplete (Sethe 1928, 5-6).

Adolf Erman, the prominent nineteenth-century Egyptologist and philologist, was the first to suggest that the text had a dramatic character, drawing attention to the groups of hieroglyphic signs that faced each other as an indication of dialogue. Erman also divided the text into sections, distinguishing between the narrative and dramatic portions of the left-hand portion (1911). His work was continued by his pupil Sethe, who was thereby able to recognize the nature of the Ramesseum Dramatic Papyrus (1928, 13-16; see above).

Although the Shabaka Stone has a number of similarities to the earlier document, there are some important differences. For one thing, the narrative, which is confined to short explanatory passages in the Ramesseum Papyrus, is much more extensive and detailed, and the speeches given by the gods (nearly all by Geb in the surviving portion) are even briefer. There are also fewer scenic indicators and no mention of props. When Geb tells Seth to go to the place where he was born and Horus to go where his father drowned, this may be an embedded stage direction. This is also suggested by the fact that underneath each speech the column is divided into boxes with logographic writings of their names and the names of Upper and Lower Egypt. The next speech of Geb, addressed to both of them – 'I have separated you' – has the logograms of both Upper and Lower Egypt.

After a narrative interlude, in a box formed by the lower part of the vertical lines below this, where Geb decides to give all of Egypt to Horus, another dramatic section is laid out in a singular fashion. Geb addresses the divine assembly six times, in each speech bequeathing Horus a part of his inheritance. The name of the god is written logographically and placed in a separate box, below which is an epithet belonging to him as the heir. The first three speeches give an idea of this dialogue:

> Geb to the Nine Gods: 'I have appointed Horus the first born.'
> Geb to the Nine Gods: 'Him, alone, Horus, the inheritance.'
> Geb to the Nine Gods: 'To the son of my son, Horus, the jackal of Upper Egypt.'
>
> (Lichtheim 1973, 52-3)

There seems to be no obvious reason for the text to be laid out in this way. The speeches are all given by one character, although it may be possible that others present shouted or repeated the name of Horus, as it occurs in all of them. Sethe thought that the text recorded a performance in which tableaux with dialogue and narrative explanation were enacted, much in the style of a medieval mystery play (1928, 16-19). However, this explanation does not adequately accommodate the cosmological text recorded on the other side of the stela, one notably lacking in dramatic possibilities. Although recitations of such texts may have taken place in Egypt (see below), they are not characteristic. A text of the second century CE from the temple at Esna, which describes the creation of the world by the goddess Neith, is thought to have been recited like the Babylonian Creation Epic, but this is pure speculation (Sauneron 1962, 251).

Sethe also noted that the layout of the text resembled that of the offering lists found in tombs and temples from a very early period. These documents are performative rather than performance texts, in that they are intended to facilitate recitation of the list, by any visitor to the tomb or on their own, to produce the desired results. The offering lists, like other such effective texts, also make use of both aural and visual puns, which while lost in the translation are obvious in a tabular inscription like the one under discussion (1928, 10-11). Somewhat similar devices are found in the cosmology section, where different forms of Ptah are enumerated under a horizontal line of text inserted over lines 48 to 52, reading, 'the gods who came into being with Ptah'. Indeed, the lack of indicators of human actors, props and *mise-en-scène* like those found in the Ramesseum Papyrus, as well as the predominantly literary character of the text, suggests that it might not be a dramatic text at all. After all, it is engraved on a stone, not on a papyrus, suggesting a performative or effective function rather than an *aide-mémoire*. The statement of King Shabaka in the introduction, that he had the text copied from a worm-eaten old book he found in the temple of Ptah (Sethe 1928, 1-2; Lichtheim 1973, 52), also points in this direction, although it should not be taken as literally as has been done in the past. While this text has been dated anywhere from the Archaic Period to the 19th Dynasty (Schlögl 1980, 110-21; Allen 1988, 42-3), it is more helpful to see it as a product of the 25th Dynasty (Junge 1973), although no doubt influenced by a long line of sacred texts, as is to be expected in any traditional society.

Season	Egyptian	Coptic
Inundation		
Month 1	Djehuty 'Thoth'	Thout
Month 2	Pa-en-Ipet 'The One of Opet'	Paope
Month 3	Hut-Heru 'Hathor'	Hathwr
Month 4	K3-her-K3 'Ka upon Ka'	Koiahk
Growing		
Month 1	Ta-'3bet 'The Offering'	Twbe
Month 2	Pa-en-Pa-Mekherw 'The One of the Censer'	Meshir
Month 3	Pa-en-ImenHotep 'The One of AmenHotep I'	Paremhotep
Month 4	Pa-en-Renenutet 'The One of Renenutet'	Paremoute
Harvest		
Month 1	Pa-en-Khonsu 'The One of Khonsu'	Pashones
Month 2	Pa-en-Inet 'The One of the Valley (Inet)'	Paone
Month 3	Ip-Ip 'The Most Hidden One'	Epeep
Month 4	Mesut-Re 'Birth of Re'	Mesore
(3 = aleph)		

Fig. 8. List of month names. During the later period many of the months were named after festivals originating, for the most part, in the Theban area.

Legitimation through visiting the most holy shrines of Egypt and especially coronation in the temple of Ptah at Memphis were extremely important to the Kushite kings, as can be seen in Piye's account of his visits to these sites (Lichtheim 1980, 71, 76-7) and his celebration of the cult, as well as Taharqa's statement that his mother came all the way from Kush to see him crowned at Memphis (Eide, Hägg, Pierce and Török 1994, 154). This inscription of Shabaka, no doubt publicly displayed at somewhere like a colonnade in the principal forecourt of the temple, artfully uses a number of literary genres and the layout of an old sacred book (complete with lacunae!) to suggest to the reader that he, Shabaka, is the heir of Geb and Osiris, just like Horus – for many reasons, not least of which is his ability to adumbrate the storied heritage of this the most politically significant temple in Egypt. While it is possible that the dialogue presented in what looks like 'dramatic' format was enacted at Shabaka's actual coronation or one of its re-presentations, it may also be used here as a kind of graphic and literary *tour de force* intended to dramatize the document for the reader as well as make it performative or 'effective' for all time. A demotic papyrus of the late Ptolemaic Period which contains a closely related account of the creation by Ptah is not a dramatic text either (Erichsen and Schott 1954). Junker's doubts (1941, 10-20) about the 'dramatic' character of this work may be allowed to stand. It does, however, draw our attention to the ever-increasing importance of the Osiris myth in both the ideology of kingship and the wider religious life of the community in this later period.

Secret rituals

Anxieties about the legitimacy of rulership may also be detected in the intertext of two documents that may be dated to the fourth century BCE. The first document is Brooklyn Papyrus 47.218.50, a liturgical handbook with no actors specified other than the king and a 'master of ceremonies'. Actions are interspersed with indications of hymns to be sung or books to be read at the appropriate time (Goyon 1972a, 8-13, 17).

The actions consisted of a long and complex ritual that was intended to protect the king during the dangerous unlucky days between the end of the old year and the beginning of the new. Because the Egyptian calendar had only 360 days, five 'intercalary' days were added after the end of the last month, which were the days of the 'plague' of Sekhmet, the eye of the sun, and the goddess of fire and destruction (Vandier 1936, 80-4). They were of danger to not only the individual but the kingdom, and even the cosmic order of which the king was a guarantor. The ceremonies were so crucial and dangerous that after the beginning ceremony a priest took the place of the king. They began the last day of the old year and lasted fourteen days (Goyon 1972a, 19-20, 41-2).

During this time many activities were performed, among which the following stand out. The substitute king was covered with amulets and surrounded by protective sand. He then slept with seals signifying the royal inheritance, afterwards performing elaborate execration rites (Goyon 1972a, 23-32). Four live birds – a falcon, a goose, a hawk and a vulture – were anointed with oil and made to spread their wings around the king, the actualization of an image common in literature and art. Then a tear was taken from the eye of the falcon and used to anoint the 'king', again a concrete version of the powerfully protective eye of Horus amulet. The birds were then sent off in the four directions to announce the renewal of royal power (Goyon 1972a, 30, 77-81). Not only was this rite associated at this period with the coronation and the Sed Festival, later it was also part of a ceremony in which a living falcon was enthroned in the Ptolemaic temple of Edfu (Goyon 1972a, 30-1, 36-7, 78-9; Watterson 1998, 97-103).

Although it is clear that the confirmation of royal power was not a public performance, it clearly entailed the participation of more actors than the master of ceremonies and the king/substitute. Extrapolating from other royal ceremonies, we might imagine that the king's palanquin was carried by his 'friends'. Singers performed the hymns and proffered unguents, perhaps accompanied by musicians, and servitors must have been present to move around the offerings. The lack of earlier documentation for this ritual suggests either that it was very secretive affair or, more likely, that it developed as a response to the political instabilities of the Third Intermediate and Late Periods, when reigns were short and more than one ruler often claimed the inheritance of Horus at any one time (Myśliwiec 2000, 159-60), even foreigners.

The Demotic Chronicle, a crypto-political and prophetic text dating from the early Ptolemaic Period, examines the Egyptian kings of the fourth century, when the Brooklyn Papyrus was written, and finds them wanting. Most of them failed to uphold Maat, did not carry out acts for the gods properly or consistently and consequently failed to pass on their inheritance to their sons (Felber 2002). The institution of these New Year rites could have been intended to boost royal prestige, not only in priestly circles but also among a wider public consisting of the elite and maybe even the general population.

Also likely dating from this same period is Papyrus Salt 825 (British Museum 10051), a work that describes rites that, like the Confirmation of Royal Power in the New Year, also took place in the pavilion of the House of Life and were apparently also designed to propitiate the 'plagues of Sekhmet' marking the turn of the year (Derchain 1965, 25-7). Papyrus Salt 825 is profusely illustrated with diagrams of objects to be used and vignettes showing how to make a small image of Osiris, around which the rites are centred. A number of cryptographic writings, using hieroglyphs instead of hieratic script, are used to transmit esoteric and potentially dangerous knowledge. Although this text provides very detailed directions, it also supplements them with a mythological *aperçu* and numerous glosses or asides referring to other versions of the text and its links to other ritual performances.

The ritual, which took place sometime in the first month of the year, was intended to avert the periodic risk of universal dissolution attendant on this dangerous time. The aim of the rite was in fact the merging of Re with Osiris, of the principle of creativity with that of eternity to produce 'Life', the name given to the figure of Osiris made during the ritual (Derchain 1965, 35-7, 153-6). These absolutely secret acts were undertaken by the people of Re: 'they are the scribes of the House of Life' (Derchain 1965, 139; Gardiner 1938, 170-1). Their work is safeguarded by extremely elaborate prophylactic and execration rites.

The Osiris figure was composed of special sand and clay mixed with various aromatic substances in precisely specified quantities and moulded into the shape of Osiris. It was then placed in a closely fitting mummiform container of pine, then inside a cedar shrine ten and a half palms (78.75 cm) high. The placing of the figure inside the shrine was accomplished after first removing the figure from the previous year. Because the shrine was momentarily empty, this was a very dangerous operation, necessitating that the actor, the *fekety* or 'shaven' priest, recite powerful spells and wear a protective amulet, as shown in the vignette, which depicts gods rather than the priests who played their parts.

The rites described in the Salt Papyrus aim to protect not just the king or the body of Osiris but life itself, not so much re-presented as concentrated in the image made of clay and sand. The enormously elaborate magical apparatus and performative utterances are an indicator of a globalized anxiety evinced in not only ritual but also prophetic texts (Derchain 1965, 19-20).

The Mystery of Osiris in the month of Khoiak

This festival, which in its most developed form took place over nineteen days in the fourth month of the inundation season, may be traced back to its origins in the secret celebrations of Osiris enacted in Abydos in the Middle Kingdom (see above, Chapter 3). While its basic purpose was to commemorate and re-present the death and resurrection of Osiris, over time it became complicated by the identification of this god with Sokar, the funerary deity of Memphis, and incorporation of his own triumphal procession (Gaballa and Kitchen 1969). We have already witnessed the earlier stages of this development in the Sokar Festival celebrated in western Thebes during the New Kingdom (see above, Chapter 4). While the visits of other gods to cemeteries were always an occasion for the living to remember their departed relatives and friends, Osiris was a special case, in that every deceased person became assimilated with him and hoped to share his revival. This explains not only the great popularity of the festival but the name of the month. Khoiak, which is the later Coptic Egyptian version of *Ka her ka*, 'soul upon soul', roughly translatable as 'All Hallows' month' (Allen 2000, 108).

References to this festival are found throughout the textual record of the later period and occasionally even in the archaeological one. Although the Egyptian calendar shifted because it did not have a leap year, the festival was often celebrated during the winter, sometime around the solstice (Griffith 1970, 178-80, 448; Cauville 1997a, 76ff.), making it analogous to such celebrations as Saturnalia, Christmas, Hanukkah and Diwali. The official name of the festival, *Hebes Ta*, or 'Breaking the Earth' (Meeks and Favard-Meeks 1997, 168), and its timing at the end of the inundation season signalled the beginning of planting, as well as the return of the light. The Khoiak Festival, which featured the burning of lights and the making of figures of Osiris in which seeds were germinated, held the promise of collective as well as individual rebirth.

Such manufactured figures of Osiris, the secret work around which the festival was celebrated, are already attested in connection with the New Kingdom Sokar Festival, where the figures were already identified with both gods (Davies and Gardiner 1915, 115; Kitchen and Gaballa 1969, 37). Other applications of this idea may be seen in the seeded Osiris figures that began to be placed in tombs at this time, as well as the Ptah-Sokar-Osiris figures used in Third Intermediate Period tombs, in which funerary texts were placed (Raven 1978-9; 1982). The other important event, the procession of the resurrected Sokar, which took place on the 26th of the month, is known from the Archaic Period (Gaballa and Kitchen 1969, 13-19). However, the absorbing and moving calendar of events that we know as the Khoiak Festival is not attested before the fourth century BCE, from which the earliest documents survive.

The most revealing of these is Louvre Papyrus N 3176 (S). The document divides neatly into two parts, probably written by different hands (Barguet 1962, pl. 1, viii). The first four columns, written by the divine father and *hap* priest Pa-sheri-khonsu, contain two processional hymns to Sokar-Osiris. In the first one the reciter role-plays Horus, and in the second, Anubis. It also contains a litany of offerings and the gods' names as well as a personal prayer signed by the holy man (Barguet 1962, 3-13). There is little indication that these texts relate to the Khoiak Festival (ibid., 14), but the rest of the document is a very valuable source for it. The texts consist of directions for the conduct and route of processions during the festival and observances made during stops. The document also gives indications of what hymns or other sacred works are to be performed or read and when, although the works are not quoted in full (ibid., 44-56). The activities of the festival all took place at various sites within the precinct of the Karnak temple, although identifying them is not always easy.

From the 18th to the 23rd of Khoiak, the text 'Protection of the Bed' was recited in the temple of Isis (ibid., 17). This no doubt referred to the bed on which the mummy of Sokar-Osiris was placed while the seeds germinated or while it was being embalmed. On the 24th day it was taken in procession to a hall in the Akh-menu, the old festival temple of Thutmose III in the east of the temple precinct (ibid., 6, 10, 18); this building had always had a connection to the cults of Osiris and Sokar (Gaballa and Kitchen 1969, 27-8). A number of texts were recited, including the 'Protection of the Bed' and the 'Return of Osiris', and the Rite of the Opening of the Mouth was performed in the House of Gold. The procession then returned to the temple of Isis. This all seems to suggest that the mummification of the figure was complete and the stage set for its transformation and resurrection at the hands of Isis and Nephthys. On the nights of the 24th and 25th was performed a 'sailing' of Osiris on the south side of the sacred lake, and a text called 'Opening of the Neshmet Barque' was read (Barguet 1962, 18). These activities recall the Middle Kingdom ceremonies at Abydos (see above, Chapter 3) when a procession may have travelled at least part of the way by water from the temple to the Archaic cemetery and the tomb of Osiris.

After leaving the sacred lake the procession went to the *djajda* or 'kiosk' of Amun, where members of the community spent the night in vigil as in the New Kingdom festival (see above, Chapter 4). There they could contemplate the god and listen to the recitation of sacred texts before he was taken to the house of Sokar (Barguet 1962, 19). During the day of the 25th the god was again taken out in procession to the kiosk of Amun, to the collective refrain of the old anthem 'Victory, Victory, Sovereign!', and the Going Forth of the Procession of Sokar was enacted. Protective rites against the enemies of the god were performed before he was returned to the temple of Sokar. On the night of the 25th and 26th the god was taken in procession towards the kiosk of Amun, ending up at the temple of Isis in the 'northern domain'. At dawn on the 26th, the actual day of the Festival of Sokar, the god was taken in procession first to the house of Sokar and then to the tomb of Osiris, which it briefly entered before going back to the kiosk of Amun. Sometime after the 26th there was a procession to the Opet temple in the southern part of the precinct of Amun (ibid., 22-4, 48-9).

The reference to the northern domain allows us to place the shrines of Osiris, Sokar and Isis mentioned in this text in the north-eastern part of the Karnak precinct, where a number of chapels to Osiris were constructed from the Third Intermediate Period onwards (Barguet 1962, 31ff.; Leclant 1965, 262-86; Coulon, Leclère and Marchand 1995, 220). This 'mound' or domain of Osiris was further defined by the great brick enclosure wall built around the Amun precinct by Nectanebo I, who also provided a special entrance for it with his eastern gate (Barguet 1962a, 31-2). The kiosk of Amun is almost certainly the structure of that name inaugurated at his temple by Ramesses II for public prayers, at the eastern end of the temple of Amun, to which Nectanebo's gate also gave access (Cabrol 2001, 580-1).

It was just north of this temple, up against the back wall of the main structure, that French archaeologists have discovered the actual 'cavern' or tomb of Osiris. This was a brick structure with three vaulted crypts lined with small niches which contained objects of indeterminate material moulded in the shape of Osiris. Fragments of wall paintings on plaster depicted the traditional tomb of Osiris, a mound with plants, as well as a twenty-four-hour vigil by divine and human beings that took place as he was embalmed, and seventy-seven divine guardians who were believed to watch over him. Other paintings showed King Ptolemy IV running with the Apis bull, an event often associated with the resurrection of Osiris (Coulon, Leclère and Marchand 1995). The existence of this structure answers the question of how such images of Osiris were disposed of in the 'sacred necropolis' after they had been used, as, for example, in the Salt Papyrus. Before Ptolemy IV built this structure the figures were buried in the same general area, in pots or small holes (ibid., 221).

Apart from the fact that sites mentioned in the text can be identified on the ground, Papyrus N 3176 also gives valuable indications about how its actions were to be performed. At one point the astronomer priest, who fixed the times for the different parts of the ceremony, is indicated to say 'in a loud voice, "There is no god", to which there is a response "all at once" or "in chorus" in the first person plural: "Don't take him away from us" ' (Barguet 1962, 23-4; cf. Alliot 1954, 519, n. 7). Given that this happened in procession to a kiosk in front of one of the temples, it seems reasonable to assume that the response was given by members of the public who were watching the procession, indicating once again the interactive possibilities of the processional form. The papyrus also indicates when the members of the procession were to walk slower or faster, as when they were approaching the god's tomb (Barguet 1962, 24). The main actors are the Scribe of the God's Book, a priest who could be responsible for conducting the proceedings as well as reading out the sacred texts indicated by their titles in this document, and the astronomer priest who fixed the times of the different activities (Gardiner 1947, *61-2; Barguet 1962, 24). Reference to the two sisters, Isis and Nepthys, who played a key role in mummification and resurrection of Osiris, is found in an allusion to the 'Glorifications of the Two Sisters'.

Be this as it may, another fourth-century document puts the participation of the goddesses in a whole new light. As already noted, all the papyrus documents so far discussed list hymns, invocations and protective magical texts to be read out during the proceeding described. Titles of such works are also listed on the walls of Ptolemaic temples, sometimes in connection with particular ceremonies. The so-called Bremner-Rhind Papyrus (P. British Museum 10188), unlike the other texts from this period, is precisely dated to Year 12 of Alexander, son of Alexander, fourth month of the inundation season – in other words, to the month of Khoiak of 311-12 BCE (Faulkner 1936, 121). This book contains the texts of four works that were recited at the festival, no doubt copied into one book for this exact purpose. They are the Songs of Isis and Nepthys, the Bringing In of Sokar, the Overthrowing of Apep (a great serpent who threatened to devour the sun) and an execration of all his names (Faulkner 1936; 1938; 1938a; 1939). Nesmin, a priest of the temple of Amun who owned but did not copy the text, emphasizes the secret nature of its contents, suggesting that these books were not read at the public part of the Khoiak celebrations (Faulkner 1938, 10-11).

The first text, the Songs of Isis and Nepthys, gives the most specific instructions for performance. It is to be celebrated in the temple of Osiris, Lord of Abydos, from the 22nd to the 26th of Khoiak:

> The entire temple shall be sanctified, and there shall be brought in [two] women pure of body, their wombs not having been opened [i.e. not having borne children, or prepubescent], with the hair of their bodies removed and their heads adorned with wigs. [...] small drums in their hands, and their names on their arms, to wit Isis and Nepthys, and they shall sing from the stanzas of this book in the presence of this god (after Faulkner 1936, 122).

These women are pure, nulliparous or prepubescent, probably to avoid menstrual contamination. Like priests in service in the temple they are washed clean and all hair is removed from their bodies. Writing on their arms the names of the goddesses they role-play serves to magically strengthen their identification with them and, being temporary, was likely done with pen and ink rather than tattooed. The text indicates more than a simple recitation. Sometimes they alternated, other times they sang in unison, accompanied by the beat of hand drums interspersed with the pronouncements of the lector priests (Faulkner 1936, 122-32). While it may appear strange that they are not mentioned in the Louvre Papyrus, not only may it be of an earlier date, but it is by no means an exhaustive description of the ceremonies. It also appears that these texts could have uses other than for the Khoiak Festival. For example, 'The Felling of Apep' was recited every day in the main temple of Amun (Faulkner 1938a, 167).

Although the many details given about the Khoiak Festival in these texts are supplemented by numerous other papyri and temple inscriptions from this period, the most exhaustive treatment is to be found in the Osiris chapels on the roof of the temple of Dendara, which date from the first century BCE. These chapels, which were constructed by Cleopatra VII between 51 and 42 BCE (Aubourg and Cauville 1998, 767), were perhaps intended as a memorial to her father, no doubt intended to make her appear as his heir rather than her two brothers, with whom she was locked in a struggle for control of the land (Huß 2001, 705ff.). The chapels were likely inaugurated on the 28th of December, 47 BCE, the 26th of Khoiak, when the full moon, the celestial manifestation of Osiris, rose and passed at the zenith right over the middle of the roof of the temple, a very rare occurrence (Aubourg and Cauville 1998, 770-2).

These six chapels not only concentrate in one place the site of the celebration of the secret (in Greek, *mysterion*) of Osiris' resurrection, but they also record every step of the process in a long hieroglyphic text found in the first chapel as well as in the texts and representations on their walls. These records suggest that most of the events of the Khoiak Festival were celebrated here in secret, even the procession of Sokar, which paraded through the chapels following the circuit of the moon in a counter-clockwise direction (Cauville 1988). They also inform us of details about the making of the Osiris figures which are not supplied in the Theban material and are reminiscent of the methods used to make the Osiris figure in the Salt Papyrus.

According to the main text, although the Mystery of Osiris is celebrated in the sixteen towns of Egypt where parts of his body, dismembered by Seth, were found, it is done differently in each one (Chassinat 1966, 77-98; Cauville 1997c, 14ff.). This is something we should bear in mind as we try to build a general picture of these rites using materials from different places and dates. The records provided by the Dendara chapels have the festival begin on the 12th day of the month, when work begins on the first of two model figures. Made of barley and sand, it is created by placing these materials in the two halves of an Osiris-shaped mould and watering it for twelve days, from the 12th to the 21st of the month. After this the two halves of the mould are joined with gum and reeds to make a figure called Khentamentiyu (Cauville 1997c, 14). On the 14th, preparations begin for making a similar figure of Sokar. This consisted of crushing minerals and precious stone and mixing them with various aromatic ingredients, binding the mixture together with earth, water and crushed dates, and forming it into an egg. The egg was kept moist for two days before being pressed into the mould of Sokar, which closely resembled that of Khentamentiyu. Three days later, on the 19th, the shapes were turned out of the moulds, dried out and stuck together with a previously prepared 'salve' made of bitumen. Between the 21st and the 23rd both the figures were properly dried out, painted and embalmed. On the 24th they were placed in the 'Upper Tomb' (Cauville 1990, 80), identified at Dendara with two niches in the second western chapel, replacing figures from the previous year, which were rewrapped and placed in miniature coffins.

As at Thebes there was a sailing of Osiris on the sacred lake on the night of the 25th. The procession of Sokar took place at dawn on the 26th when the god, accompanied by all the priests of the temples of Upper and Lower Egypt (at least in theory), came out of the western chapels and, perhaps after public procession to a local temple of Horus, returned to the open court in front of them. There Sokar-Osiris was touched by the sun and his bird spirit flew up to heaven. On the 28th was celebrated his great going forth. On the morning of the 30th and last day of the month, the Djed pillar, the emblem of Osiris discussed above (Cauville 1997c, 24), was raised. Finally, in the ninth hour of the night the remains of the figures from the previous year were taken to the sacred necropolis, where they were secretly buried to protect them from the depredations of Seth (ibid., 26).

Although the records of the Mystery of Osiris at Dendara are much fuller than those elsewhere, we should be aware that they show a process of continuing development and elaboration. They also appear to be firmly in the tradition of magical ritual texts such as the Salt Papyrus. The main text in the first chapel is also illustrated, with figures showing the moulds, and is replete with learned glosses and explanations, although the mythological explanation found in the Salt Papyrus is lacking. The directions for making the figure of Sokar closely resemble those found for the Osiris figure in the earlier document, with the added complication that the materials are to be measured out in containers shaped like the body parts of Osiris. This illustrates one of the striking characteristics of these performances that we have already noted, that they make concrete and act out literary and visual imagery.

Related to this is the deployment of actors in the mystery. The figures are made by Shenty(t), a figure representing Isis as widow, in her house. According to the mystery text she is placed upright and naked on a bed (Cauville 1997c, 34). The reliefs in the second chapel show the clothed figures of Isis and Nepthys kneeling on a lion-headed bed measuring out the ingredients with scales, assisted by the creator gods Ptah and Khnum (Cauville 1997b, pls 39-42). These scenes are supplemented with speeches by them as well as by the king and other gods who are present. The imagery of the bed relates to the idea of sexual self-regeneration alluded to in Chapter 2, as well as the myth about how Isis conceived Horus after reviving Osiris. Although it is possible to act out this scene, it may be that small statues were used to represent all or some of the characters. The embalming of the figures and the Rite of the Opening of the Mouth required the participation of the *sem* priests, lector priests and others normally associated with it (Cauville 1997d, 229-31). Likewise it is the *fekety* priest (also appearing in the Salt Papyrus) who presses the egg mixture into the moulds of Sokar. Clad in a panther skin and wearing a lock of hair made from lapis lazuli, he sits on a stool before an actor or an image of Nut, the mother of Osiris, with the vase containing the egg in his hands, saying to her, 'I am Horus who comes to you, O powerful one. I bring to you these (things) of my father.' He places the vase on her knees before taking it back and pressing the contents into the moulds (Cauville 1997c, 26).

Another event during the festival that apparently involved a number of actors was the 'Hour Watch', a twenty-four-hour vigil that took place while the figures were being mummified on the 23rd to 24th of the month. The most detailed depictions of this are found in the temples of Isis at Philae and of Horus at Edfu and in the second eastern chapel at Dendara (Junker 1911). At each hour Osiris is attended by different gods and protective spirits as well as *hem netcher, sem* and *wer maaw* (solar) priests who offer incense and salves and make libations. In addition, the lector priest recites texts. While it cannot be ascertained whether the gods and spirits are represented by actors or images, at Dendara the two great kites, or mourners, are specified to be played by eight different women:

> The kites enter and mourn in the temple, two women at a time, eight women in all, performing the purification which is incumbent on them. They stand inside the door of the courtyard of the divine assembly (Cauville 1997c, 69).

In some scenes the women speak, and they no doubt sang dirges like those preserved on the Bremner-Rhind Papyrus and similar documents. They are also shown playing hand drums (Cauville 1997b, pl. 49). Since the vigil took place in the chapel at Dendara where the reliefs of it are found on the walls, the images of the protective gods carved in a frieze around the wall would probably have sufficed to summon their participation. The priests and women (in four shifts) would have actually been present (Junker 1911, 6-7).

Among the many other activities associated with this festival was the sailing of thirty-four miniature boats with images of gods at the eighth hour of the day; they carried 365 lamps, one for each day of the year (Cauville 1997c, 22). This activity, which doubtless took place on the sacred lake of the temple, may have been open to wider participation. It suggests a relationship to the winter solstice, around which time it was celebrated. The Opening of the House Festival was also celebrated between the 16th and the 24th (ibid.). Comparison with the rite of the same name in the Salt Papyrus suggests that it should refer to removing the old figures from the temple and replacing them with new ones, but it seems to have been a public procession by a statue of Osiris that went around the temple, cemetery and countryside, providing a public spectacle and celebration at the same time the mystery was being enacted. It is also possible that the procession of Sokar and the raising of the Djed pillar had a public aspect, as in earlier times, for they represented the emotional and ritual climaxes of the month. However, according to Cauville the Djed pillar was raised in the forecourt of the roof (Cauville 1997d, 224).

Also of interest is the extreme site specificity of the Dendara Mysteries. The six chapels were each designed for different activities, as indicated by their wall decoration. After the first chapel, an open court that contained the main text along with representations of the procession of Sokar and propitiatory rites connected with it, was the second chapel, where the moulds where made. One wall was completely taken up with a representation of the 'garden', or water table, where the barley-and-sand statue was left to germinate surrounded by gods and protective spirits, including the seventy-seven shown in the tomb of Osiris at Karnak. On the ceiling are two representations of the sky, one at night, when the figures were made, and one during the day. The night sky, the domain of the lunar Osiris, is shown as a Graeco-Babylonian-style zodiac. The positions of the stars and planets enable us to date these chapels. On the left is a traditional image of Nut giving birth to the sun that represents the day. As in the Salt Papyrus, the aim of the ritual is an assimilation of Re and Osiris.

The third eastern chapel is filled with protective images. Most striking is the roof. Between two similar celestial designs is a skylight with an image of Osiris lying on his bed on each of the four sides. This is where the mould sown with seeds was placed in order to germinate (Cauville 1997a, 70-4). The third western chapel, opposite it, has scenes of embalming on its wall and was where the figures were wrapped. In the second western chapel were two niches where the figures were placed until the next year after they were wrapped. These last three chapels were also decorated with pictures of protective spirits and the resurrection of Osiris on his bed, both a vegetal and a sexual event. The last chapel on the western side was the open court where the statue of Sokar was exposed to the rays of the sun and brought back to life before being taken on procession (Cauville 1988, 31-2).

Most other surviving Egyptian temples made use of sites for various purposes, as at the temple of Amun at Karnak. It is most unusual to see such a dedicated installation, suggesting it may have had a performative function as well as a spatial one.

The Obsequies of the Apis Bull

The next work to be considered, P. Vindobonensis (Vienna) 3873, gives very detailed, if incomplete, instructions for how to embalm the divine Apis bull of Memphis, and is now thought to date from the early second century BCE (Vos 1993, 1-16, 42). Surely this is a practical rather than a dramatic operation? The answer to this question involves a wider look at the cult of this god, one that goes back to the earliest period of Egyptian history but achieved its greatest flowering in the later period.

As noted in Chapter 2, the Apis bull is attested right from the beginning of the 1st Dynasty, in a ceremony where it ran around the walls of the city of Memphis, apparently driven by the king himself. While it can be argued that this event was tied to both the coronation and the Sed Festival, in the first instance it was obviously closely connected with kingship. There is, however, no evidence for the cult or burial of these animals before the reign of Amenhotep III, when their remains began to be buried in the farthest reaches of the cemetery of Memphis, north-west of the Step Pyramid (Dodson 1995). From the reign of Ramesses II onwards Apis was placed in his own fully equipped tomb (Vercoutter 1972, 341). Throughout the New Kingdom we can also witness the growth of private people's devotion to this god, who came to be seen as an incarnation of the souls of Ptah, Re, Horus and Osiris.

5. Late Period and Graeco-Roman Egypt

The cult of the living bull was clearly of great social significance; P. Louvre 3176 describes his run as 'dazzling' (Barguet 1962, 5). Perhaps the spectacle engendered the kind of the religious experiences expressed in New Kingdom devotional texts. Greek travellers like Diodorus Siculus, who visited Egypt in the middle of the first century BCE, describe his oracular activities, which, however, did not take place in procession but in his own precinct within the temple of Ptah at Memphis. Diodorus also describes in detail how a new incarnation of the god was chosen according to his particular markings (Oldfather 1933, 290-5). The murder of Apis, along with other divine animals, by foreign conquerors was a common motif in later Egyptian literature and Greek accounts.

Nevertheless, the life of Apis has left fewer traces than his death. Khaemwase, a pious son of Ramesses II (Gomaà 1973, 39-47), constructed the 'lesser vaults', which consisted of underground tunnels off which were cut the individual burial chambers. It was apparently customary after a chamber was sealed for devotees, especially participants in the funeral of the bull, to place on the wall of his tomb inscribed stelae asking for the intercession of the god in the next life. This practice was continued in the 'greater vaults', a greatly enlarged and magnificent continuation of the tomb which, with its huge granite sarcophagi (Vercoutter 1972, 344-5), is as major a tourist attraction today as it was in antiquity, although of course for different reasons. This great tomb, called *kem* in Egyptian, which was used between the reign of Psamtik II of Dynasty 26 and the Roman conquest, was named in Greek – after the god ('Osiris-Apis' or 'Serapis') – the Serapaion, or, in Latin, the Serapeum (Vercoutter 1972, 341-2; Ray 1972, 699-700). Although the Serapeum is a spectacular site in its own right, by far the most valuable items that were found there from our point of view are the dedicatory stelae, which date all the way from the 22nd Dynasty to the end of the Ptolemaic Period. They reveal an elaborate processional ceremony and its antecedents which involved participation of not only the elite class but society as a whole, and even foreigners (Vercoutter 1972, 341-6).

The stelae, dating between the 22nd and 27th Dynasties, reveal public practices that not only involve public display of emotion but also record the earliest ascetic practices known in the Mediterranean world. These practices were closely tied to the actual embalming process. During the first three days that the body was in the embalming house, the worshippers of Apis went on a complete fast. On the fourth day they broke the fast in order to subsist on bread and vegetables for the next sixty-seven days, on the last of which they joined the great funeral procession to the tomb. These privations were not endured at home but outside, in a vigil that lasted day and night (Vercoutter 1962, xiii-xiv, 29-31; Vos 1993, 31 n. 34). This event suggests a real-life equivalent to the 'Hour Watch' performed at the Khoiak Festival, but one in which the watchers were involved for over two months rather than a twenty-four-hour day. They spent their time squatting on the ground bewailing the fate of the god, no doubt beating and tearing at themselves in traditional gestures of mourning. They did not bathe or tend to themselves in the usual way (Vercoutter 1962, 28-30, 50). Even if the mourners, who included the future king Psamtik III, had to endure winter cold (Vercoutter 1962, 37-9), they seem to have been clad only in special scanty costumes (Vercoutter 1962, 29). And mourning for Apis was not just an elite affair. In a stela from the reign of Amasis, the King's Friend Neferibre states, 'I dressed myself as a poor man among persons of little account. ... [When the god] descended into his barque I was before it, lamenting with the paupers' (Vercoutter 1962, 50-1, 52, 54-5). Although only highly placed priests and officials could leave these devotional records, it is clear that there was general mourning for Apis. The day of the funeral procession was probably a national holiday.

Let us return to the embalming process. The Vienna Papyrus informs us that apart from certain logistical modifications mainly due to his size, Apis was treated after death like an Egyptian human, albeit an elite one (Vos 1993, 34-6, 123-4). Herodotus, the Greek traveller who visited Egypt in the mid-fifth century BCE, informs us that in the most expensive mummification process, the body was eviscerated and the cavities were cleaned out with palm wine and spices and then dried out with natron – a naturally occurring substance composed of sodium carbonates, sulphates and chlorides with strongly desiccating properties – before being wrapped in gummed linen bandages (Sélincourt 1972, 115; Ikram and Dodson 1997, 104). It is remarkable that apart from Herodotus' description and those of other Greek writers, there is no clear description of the process other than this papyrus (Spencer 1972, 611). The reason for this may be that the process was a craft transmitted only within the embalming profession, but it is also likely, in the light of what the Vienna Papyrus tells us, that it was conceived as one of the most powerful of secret ritual performances – indeed, the one that brought the deceased back to life through identification with Osiris. Not surprisingly, the priest in charge of the process is the *hery seshta*, the one who is 'over the secrets', like the owner of the magic box that contained the Ramesseum Papyrus (Vos 1993, 37 n. 33; Ritner 1993, 231-2).

Unfortunately, the Vienna Papyrus does not give a coherent description of the process, but consists only of notes from different sources and in no particular order. Right in the middle we find instructions for removing the dead Apis from his stall in the temple by the west door, to be taken to a tent on the roof near the ceremonial palace of the king. This tent is clearly the *ibu*, or tent of purification, where the body was washed before being taken to the *wabet*, or embalming house (Vos 1993, 31-2, 150; see also above, Chapter 2). In our document there is no clear description of the process of evisceration but there are descriptions and measurements for a very large number of pottery and copper vessels, as well as copper instruments that had to be constantly cleaned. R.L. Vos, who made a study of the Vienna Papyrus, has noted their similarity to those found near the well-preserved burial place of Buchis, the sacred bull of Montu, near Thebes, and has suggested that they were used in this part of the process (Vos 1993, 35-6, 53-6, 92, 123-4, 169).

It should be remembered that violence to the deceased – the Osiris – while necessary, was regarded as an unlucky and unclean act and, like his death, was seldom mentioned. Diodorus of Sicily provides us with a fascinating glimpse of this drama of mummification:

> Then the one who is called the slitter cuts the flesh, as the law commands, with an Ethiopian stone and at once takes to flight on the run, while those present set out after him, pelting him with stones, heaping curses on him, and trying, as it were, to turn the profanation on his head; for in their eyes everyone is an object of general hatred who applies violence to the body of a man of the same tribe or wounds him or, in general, does him any harm (Oldfather 1933, 310-11).

It has been suggested that this performance re-presents the murder of Osiris by Seth, thereby further strengthening the identification of the deceased with this god. It also appears that a completely different group of priests was in charge of this process than of the better-documented later part (Vos 1993, 185-6, 198).

After the god was eviscerated and dried out, he was removed from the so-called 'butchering room' to the 'wrapping room' (Vos 1993, 32-6). As the *hery seshta* and the four lector priests assisting him enter the wrapping room, the mourners of Apis let out a great cry of lamentation (Vos 1993, 37, 43, 73). The actual embalming house of Apis has been identified at the south-western corner of the site of the temple of Ptah at Memphis. This building, of which the lower parts of the walls and foundations survive, seems to have been used from the 22nd Dynasty up to the Roman Period. Graffiti, including some in Greek, on the outside walls testify to the presence of the vigil-holders, and the great limestone embalming tables with their lion heads remain in place (Jones and Milward Jones 1982; 1983, 31-3; 1988).

The Apis was bandaged and salved by the *hery seshta* and his assistants (called 'friends', as in the archaic royal ceremonies and Opening of the Mouth) (Vos 1993, 35-6, 47) and he was affixed to a board with sixteen clamps, using an elaborate bandaging method to fix him in an upright kneeling position, with his front legs stretched out like those of a sphinx (Vos 1993, 49-50, 133-4). These details would have remained obscure to modern-day readers but for the discovery of the Buchis bull mummies at Thebes (Mond and Myers 1934a, 58-61; 1934c, pls 34-5, 162-5). No dialogue is preserved in this text, and although the *hery seshta* performs the most important operations, such as mummifying the head and eye sockets (Vos 1993, 45-8, 63-5, 66-7, 92, 105), there is little to indicate that this is little more than a technical operation. This lack is remedied by a later document, 'The Embalming Ritual', a text known from two copies from the first century CE (Sauneron 1950, vii-xiv). This document supplies the prayers and invocations that accompany the embalming of each part of the body. Much of it resembles the Opening of the Mouth in that the deceased is offered the ointments and amulets as he might be offered the eye of Horus. When the wrapping was complete Apis was lowered into a coffin and a priest went outside and tore a cloth, at which signal the assembled devotees burst into great cries of grief (Vos 1993, 30-1, 144).

On the 69th day a number of elaborate ceremonies took place, centred on a 'sailing' like that of Osiris in the month of Khoiak. The coffin was taken on a processional barque, accompanied by Isis and Nepthys, to the 'lake of the king', where the god was set up on a mound of pure sand on the bank. Then two priests got into a boat on the lake and read nine books re-presenting the struggle and victory of Osiris, including the Overthrowing of Apep, preserved in the Bremner-Rhind Papyrus. After this the god was taken to a tent of purification set up on the shore of the lake. He went in by the western entrance and, after the Rite of the Opening of the Mouth was performed, he left by the eastern entrance, thereby undoing his death. After this the priests returned the god to the embalming house and threw a brick over the threshold to show that he had been reborn (Egyptian women traditionally gave birth squatting on bricks). After this Apis was ready for his funeral on the 70th day, and the papyrus ends (Vos 1993, 40-1, 50-3, 157-68).

Two young women who actually played the parts of the goddesses (the kites) at the funeral of an Apis that died in 164 BCE are documented in a collection of Greek papyri from near the site of the Serapeum; they came on the market in the early nineteenth century. The archive in question belonged to Ptolemaios, son of Glaukios, a man who lived in the cemetery area of Memphis because he had been 'taken' by the god (Thompson 1988, 88-91, 213-14). He apparently met the girls through an Egyptian friend with whom he shared a room. Ptolemaios helped represent them in the Greek legal system, writing letters on their behalf, when a dispute with their mother threatened to deprive them of their inheritance and the allowance paid to them in their position as the kites (Thompson 1988, 233-45, 253-65). Clearly members of the property-owning classes, the youthful Taous and Thaues were also twins, likely identical ones. That they are almost always referred to as such in Ptolemaios' archive points out that they owed their celebrity, and no doubt their role in the obsequies of Apis, to their being freaks of nature. The particular mystique of twins is well documented in Egyptian culture, as elsewhere (Baines 1985). The documents tells us that their presence was required downtown at the embalming of Apis, at ceremonies (not mentioned in the Vienna Papyrus) that can probably be identified with the sailing on the 69th day, as well as the funeral procession itself. After the funeral the twins were retained to make offerings to Apis for the benefit of the royal house, and paid in kind with full rations (Thompson 1988, 235-9).

The funeral procession of Apis is most well documented in the dedicatory stelae of the Third Intermediate and Late Periods. These sources tell us that the extremely heavy bier of the god was dragged by the highest officials of the realm, just as in a royal funeral (Vercoutter 1962, xii-xiv; Vos 1993, 164-5). Military divisions were also involved in this activity, as they had been in transporting the body of the king in the New Kingdom (Vercoutter 1962, 60-1; 1972, 340; and see above, Chapter 4). Although such a duty goes back to the earliest times, these texts introduce the notion of personal devotion to a god (as opposed to a king) and the expectation that he would intercede to provide them with eternal life in the future. Devotion to Apis went beyond even the boundaries of Egypt. Darius I of Persia stated that he loved him more than any other king (Chassinat 1901, 77-8). An Egyptian official under the Persians describes how a levy from all over the empire was required to finance the elaborate obsequies (Vercoutter 1962, 60-1). The embalming and burial of Apis, along with readying the sepulchre, which consumed enormous amounts of rare materials and many thousands of person-hours, was the most costly of many public performances based on conspicuous consumption. According to Diodorus, the official in charge of the burial of Apis under Ptolemy I could not meet the cost, which was covered by the king to the sum of over fifty talents (Oldfather 1933, 290-1) – the equivalent of millions of US dollars.

More details about the procession of the Apis come from archaeological evidence dating to the fourth and third centuries BCE. Nectanebo I, who undertook to renew all the sanctuaries of the land, was responsible for constructing the sacred way of the god. This stretched over two kilometres from the valley to the tomb of Apis and was paved with stone and lined with four hundred sphinxes in the royal image (Smith 1974, 14). At the other end of the god's way (in Greek, *dromos*) the king built a small temple for the celebration of the funerary rites (Smith 1986, 4-8-19). Many small buildings of stone or brick which lay along this road were uncovered by Auguste Mariette in the nineteenth century, but few were recorded except for a small stone chapel containing a statue of the bull. This was found on a broad stone esplanade in front of the time at the end of the processional way proper (Lauer and Picard 1955, 1-27).

Some idea of what took place at the service is provided by an inscription on the sarcophagus of Djeho, an individual who 'danced at the everlasting festival' at the tomb of both Apis and Mnevis, the sacred bull of Heliopolis, across the river. As the text and pictures on his magnificent sarcophagus make plain, Djeho was a dwarf. From the Old Kingdom, dwarves were said to perform in the 'dances of the gods' and it is thought that their resemblance to newborns helped facilitate resurrection. Like the twins, Djeho was a freak of nature, and was handsomely rewarded in both life and death through the offices of his aristocratic patron Tjaiharpta, who was no

113

doubt responsible for his getting a role in the festival as well as a place in his own tomb (Baines 1992).

The Triumph of Horus

While the Apis Papyrus of Vienna may be associated with a cult that is well documented over a long period, our next source appears isolated – and quite problematic.

The text and representations known to modern scholarship as the Triumph or Victory of Horus, which are engraved on the outer western enclosing wall of the temple of Horus at Edfu, are part of a large ensemble describing the Festival of the Victory of Horus, a celebration which took place from the 21st to the 25th of the second month of winter. It celebrated the struggle of Horus against his enemies, led by Seth (Fairman 1973, 14-17, 27).

The temple of Horus at Edfu replaced an earlier New Kingdom temple and was reoriented to face south, towards the temple of Isis at Philae, instead of the more usual direction of the river. The new construction was begun in 237 BCE by Ptolemy III, but most of it was not completed until after suppression of widespread revolts in Upper Egypt in the early second century BCE (Watterson 1998, 25-8). The temple seems to have been intended as a shrine to the kingship of the Ptolemaic house, and much of its decoration foregrounds performances of royal elevation and renewal like the coronation and the Sed Festival, as well as other re-presentations such as the Enthronement of the Sacred Falcon (Cauville 1987).

The reliefs of the Festival of Victory were carved during a period of civil war between Ptolemy X and Ptolemy XI, both sons of Cleopatra III, for control of the country. Although one or the other may have intended such performances to bolster his claims, their identity in the texts is kept purposefully vague (Fairman 1973, 16-17). The texts and representations of the festival are in two parts. One, a myth about Horus' form as a winged sun disk, is written in the form of a royal historical narrative illustrated with vignettes (Fairman 1935). The other, the Triumph of Horus, takes a similar form, except that the pictures are much more closely related to the action of the story.

The Triumph of Horus consists of eleven tableaux, each with a horizontal label, captions on the figures and a block of text. Eight of these pictures show Horus in a boat armed with a harpoon and accompanied by other gods. In most of these he is shown spearing a very small hippo with the harpoon (Fairman 1973, 79ff.). The story told by this ensemble is of how Horus defeated Seth with a harpoon when he took the form of a hippopotamus. The text includes the ancient 'ritual of the ten harpoons', a protective rite that had its origin in a hippo hunt conducted by the king in Archaic and prehistoric times (see above, Chapter 2). Such protective acts had long been incorporated in funerary rites and were also part of the protective rituals we have seen enacted in the Salt Papyrus and Khoiak Mysteries.

The text describes how Horus, aided by his mother, Isis, goes after Seth in hippo form. Aided by other gods and protective spirits, he places a harpoon in every part of Set's anatomy before bringing him captive to shore, where he is serenaded by the princesses of Upper and Lower Egypt. The king and Horus are also shown in an execration rite in which they stab small figures of a hippo and a bound captive (Fairman 1973, 27-9). Until the capture of the hippo, the king is shown watching or participating in the proceedings. Afterwards he disappears, indicating his complete assimilation with the triumphant Horus (Fairman 1973, 29-30, 105). The last scene depicts a butcher, like that mentioned in the Salt Papyrus, cutting up a cake of *shat* bread in the form of a hippo while the chief lector priest reads out a book of execrations. After this a goose is brought and grain is poured into its mouth (ibid., 113-15). The goose presents in concrete form the name of Geb, the 'heir' of the gods, the father of Osiris and the one who bestows the inheritance (Helck 1950). Isis divides the hippo between the different gods and commands that the remainder be burnt (Fairman 1973, 110). The text ends with a litany of the gods and holy places whose enemies have been overthrown, and a fourfold repetition of the royal titulary concludes the text (ibid., 119-20).

The text and representations of this composition certainly have more of a narrative character than many such works found on temple walls. While it is quite normal for captions on figures to give the words spoken by them, the longer texts that accompany these tableaux are more unusual, being a mixture of narrative, dialogue, hymns, invocations, and directions. Sometimes the speeches are attributed with the usual phrase 'words spoken by', but often the speaker must be deduced from the speech itself or from the surrounding narrative. A.M. Blackman and H.W. Fairman (1942) saw in this portion of the work the key to its dramatic character, although this was denied by both Étienne Drioton and Maurice Alliot, who had closely studied the whole temple. They saw the ensemble rather as a collection of materials consisting of hymns and recitations with some performed elements, but not as a unified whole (Alliot 1954, 677-86, 807-22; Fairman 1973, 19-27).

Although all the elements that occur in the long sections of the Edfu text can be found elsewhere, it must be admitted that their use all in one text, and in combination with pictures describing the same story with additional dialogue, is very suggestive. In the first scene we also see Thoth holding an unrolled papyrus in front of him as if reading from it. Behind him are the figures of Horus and Isis and before him is the scene with the boat (Chassinat 1934, pls 495-6). This implies an action narrated by a reader, perhaps as suggested with regard to the Shabaka Stone and the Ramesseum Dramatic Papyrus. The cutting up of snakes, the stabbing of the figurines and the cutting up of the hippopotamus cake (Fairman 1973,

95, 111-14) are all actions that were actually performed during various rituals and ceremonies. Likewise, the scene where Horus is serenaded by the queen and the princesses, while perhaps inspired by New Kingdom representations, also suggests an actual event. Lingering scepticism has dogged Fairman's publication of this text in the form of a play and the performances that it has inspired. However, the recent discovery of a demotic text that clearly records speeches and actions of actors in another, very similar version of this story has vindicated his theory (Gaudard 1999).

The Triumph of Horus still has problematic features that call for explanation. Fairman argued that the horizontal labels on top of each scene were the utterance of a 'chorus', largely on the basis of their declarative character and the fact that some were written in the first person plural (Blackman and Fairman 1942, 35; Fairman 1973, 37ff.). However, the expression 'all at once' found in Louvre Papyrus N 3176 does not occur here, although it might have been present in the papyrus from which the Edfu text was adapted. Fairman also attributed marked repetitions to the chorus and added an appropriate execration of Apep from the Bremner-Rhind Papyrus where the text indicated it (Fairman 1973, 43-4). The pictures also seem to indicate that the principal characters stood on individual podia of the kind used in medieval mystery plays, suggesting that an actual performance had the appearance of a static tableau not unlike the pictures themselves (ibid., 133-42). The appearance of Thoth with the book-roll and the lector role-playing the wise man Imhotep imply that the latter provided the narration of the play and may even have spoken the actors' lines for them (Blackman and Fairman 1942, 36; and see further below).

One of the chief problems connected with this work is the place of performance. The constant repetition of lines, the succession of very similar scenes and actions, two different incarnations of Horus for Upper and Lower Egypt, and the presence of the king who also harpoons the hippo (Fairman 1973, 42-4) could be used to argue for a processional setting, if it were not for the presence of the podia and the obvious inference from the text that the setting is the sacred lake ('Pool of Horus', Blackman and Fairman 1944, 16) where the boat could sail. Fairman argued that enacting the play on the lake would present too many logistical problems and would be too difficult for a large audience to see, and suggested the front of the temple as a possible location (Fairman 1973, 47-50). While this would suit a processional presentation, it must be admitted that the precedent provided by the sailings of Osiris discussed above and the text itself favour the lake as the site of performance. Furthermore, there is no certain indication of a large audience, the only general direction for participation referring to 'the prophets (*hem netcher* priests), fathers of the god and the priests' (Fairman 1973, 115).

5. Late Period and Graeco-Roman Egypt

Some feasts at Esna

At Esna, the site of the ancient Egyptian town of Iunyt, only the forehall of the temple survives, but it contains some of the latest and most interesting Egyptian religious texts. Foremost among these are the column texts, consisting of direct transcriptions of ritual and liturgical books used during the major festivals celebrated at this temple in the first and second centuries CE (Baines and Malek 1980). These cannot be precisely dated, but other inscriptional indications give a time span between the reigns of Domitian and Antoninus Pius (81-161 CE) (Sauneron, 1962, 1-6). The texts themselves are heavily encrypted, more so than any others in existence, making them very difficult to read even for scholars well versed in Ptolemaic temple inscriptions. The matters described in these books were not intended for profane readers; they were for setting up ritual performances as secret as they were vital to the stability of the cosmos (Derchain 1965, 4-7). Since the Esna texts were apparently copied straight from liturgical handbooks, they lack illustrations, although internal evidence and other sources can often make up for this lack.

The main god worshipped in this temple was Khnum, a creator god who made the world through craft on his potter's wheel (Meeks and Favard-Meeks 1993, 54). His animal spirit was the ram, a creature known for its virile behaviour. Although most of the festivals celebrated at the temple involved the type of cultic performances and processions with which we are already familiar, three festivals celebrated in the third months of winter and summer (Pharmenoth and Epiphi) give some very interesting evidence for performance activities.

The Festival of the Raising of the Sky and the Setting up of the Potter's Wheel took up the whole of the first day of Pharmenoth, the third month of winter and the seventh of the year. The organizing concept was the creation of the universe by Khnum, who was identified with other creator gods like Amun-Re of nearby Thebes and Ptah of Memphis. Given the amount of space the texts devote to the festival, it must have been the most important celebrated in the town (Sauneron 1962, 71).

After the morning service, in the first and second hours of the day, and the celebration of Khnum as the creator, a special portable image of the god was taken out of the temple and placed in its front porch, where the 'Touch of the Sun' revived and re-ensouled the image (Sauneron 1962, 119-24; Meeks and Favard-Meeks 1997, 195-8). Offerings were presented and hymns were sung and the Opening of the Mouth was performed, the face of the god was uncovered and he remained in the porch until the beginning of the Mystery of the Divine Royal Birth (Sauneron 1962, 125-7). For this event the divine image, accompanied by attendant gods, was taken from the porch of the temple to a small kiosk or shrine with an enclosed sanctuary and an open space within which non-priestly observers could gather, although it still lay within the temple precincts. The title of the book that describes this event says that it consists of the acts of Khnum and his divine college, and glorifies what appears on his potter's wheel – all of the gods, but especially a child who is Horus – for the purpose of glorifying the king. The text records the words spoken by Khnum as he makes the child on his wheel, those of the gods who bestow gifts on him like fairy godmothers, and the words of the child himself. Along with the speeches there are hymns of praise to the gods, especially to Khnum (ibid., 185-9).

The story itself is easily recognizable as that of the divine birth, first seen in the Middle Kingdom Papyrus Westcar, which tells how the first three kings of the 5th Dynasty were born to a woman inseminated by Re. Later we find this story used by 18th Dynasty rulers such as Hatshepsut, Thutmose III and Amenhotep III, most notably in the southern Opet temple at Luxor (Brunner, 1964). Since the focus of this version of the story is the royal *ka*, it seems likely that it played some role in the secret rites enacted at the Opet Festival (Bell 1985, 25ff.). The story resurfaces at the end of the Late Period, when the identification of the child with an actual king is played down in favour of the god-child of a divine couple. The myth was celebrated in special shrines, or 'birth houses', in the grounds of the temples. These shrines resembled a shelter made of clumps of reeds or papyrus and were probably intended to recall the temporary structures where Egyptian women actually gave birth. The most elaborate examples had a closed sanctuary area, with a hall or courtyard surrounded by columns in front of it (Daumas 1977).

Although there are a number of representations of the divine birth story in these structures, none are supplied with substantial texts. Together with the New Kingdom material the plot can be developed along these lines: the expected birth of the young god is announced; the union of the parents takes place; the god is conceived; Khnum forms him on his wheel; the birth is announced; the divine mother is taken to give birth; the child is recognized by his father; he is nursed by goddesses; he is enthroned before the gods and given the attributes of royalty. Not all stages of the story are present here. This text presents only the forming of the child by Khnum and his presentation to the gods, who bestow their gifts. As his mother, Neith, the creator goddess from the north of Egypt, hails the child, suggesting that he is not an earthly king but the divine prototype of a king (Sauneron 1962, 190-2). In contrast to the short speeches found in documents like the Ramesseum Dramatic Papyrus and the Shabaka Stone, the words attributed to speakers here take the form of longer poetic compositions, and the independent narrative so central to the Triumph of Horus is lacking. Of course it is possible that it may have existed in another document that was not selected for transfer to the temple walls, but this raises the issues of both regional and diachronic variation.

Allowing for regional variation, we may use this text to visualize a kind of mystery play that took place in the Birth Houses of this period. Since

Hathor was the goddess of love and childbirth, her prominence in these places ensured the presence of her female devotees, as was the case in her own temples (Daumas 1977, 464). The beautiful, joyous hymns that no doubt interspersed the speeches would have been performed by the women shown in the temples playing the sistrum rattles and small hand drums. Under the influence of Hathor's sacred intoxicants they apparently performed whirling trance dances like those of the Islamic zikr. It is uncertain how much of this festival would have been public (Daumas 1968, 13-15). The mysterious forming of the god-child no doubt took place in the depths of the temple. It is uncertain whether Khnum and the other gods were played by actors in masks or represented by statues. Horus may have been played by a child or adolescent. It is likely, however, that he was shown to the people waiting outside the shrine, and the presentation of kingly attributes may also have happened in the open (Sauneron 1962, 186-94).

The Mystery of the Divine Royal Birth was over by the third hour after noon, when the god left the kiosk and made a circuit of the city before returning to the main temple amid general rejoicing of the community. The processional statue was returned to the crypt and the time came for the final rite of the day, 'Transmission of the Wheel to Female Beings' (ibid., 233-4). This remarkable text, almost entirely lacking in indications of where or how the rite was performed, addresses the obvious contradiction between a creation myth that attributes all activity to a male god and the fact that only females can give birth. The text exhorts prostration before not only Khnum, who created all people and gods on his wheel, but also Menhyt, another name for the uraeus snake on the brow of the other creator, Re, as well as that of the king. In this other creation story the snake, the eye of both the god and his daughter – identified with Sekhmet and Hathor (see above, Chapter 4) – was the source of the tears that grew into the human race. In other words, it is the creator of people. The text commands the worship of Sekhmet and Hathor through the setting up of the Potter's Wheel (ibid., 235).

The Potter's Wheel of Khnum, which has already figured in the Mystery of the Divine Royal Birth, was a sacred object kept in its own shrine somewhere in the temple. At this point in the proceedings it may have been lifted up or offered libations and incense. The pronouncement that follows is entitled 'Utterance for the establishment of the Wheel in the bodies of all female beings'. The text then asks the god to transfer the creative power of his wheel into the bodies of female beings and to protect the creatures so formed. The prayer concludes,

O gods and goddesses of this town, All-Powerful Ones, rulers of this district, who seek to multiply births, as a gift to make rejoice our hearts, place the egg in the bodies of women, to provide the country with younger generations, for the favour of the King of Upper and Lower Egypt, Pharaoh living forever, beloved of Khnum (after Sauneron 1962, 236).

It was followed by the rite that bestowed this creative power on women, which consisted of tying a ribbon or garland on three young girls like those mentioned previously. They represented a pregnant woman, the child conceived by her, and one other, one who is either born or about to give birth. The garland placed on the head may be the same as the bonnet sometimes worn by the woman in the logogram for 'birth' (ibid., 237-8).

Quite different to the women-centred rites of the first of Pharmenoth were two festivals celebrated at Esna in the second and third months of summer, on the ninth of Payni and the 19th and 20th of Epiphi. Both of these celebrations were based on the myth of the destruction of humanity, in which an attempted revolt by people against the creator god led to his sending his daughter and eye, the lioness Sekhmet, against them before having a change of heart and tricking her into sparing those who were left. In this version of the story the creator hides in terror from the rebels and abdicates power in favour of his son Shu, who overcomes them. Here the rebels represent the generalized forces of chaos as much as rebellious humanity (Sauneron 1962, 321-5).

The myth was re-enacted at a sacred precinct just outside the town; it consisted of two temples with a lake in between them called the Red Lake. The northern temple, which was called the House of the God, represented the tomb of the old creator gods and Osiris. Like similar sanctuaries elsewhere, its purity was not supposed to be contaminated by the footfalls of animals or the presence of women. The other temple, to the south of the lake, was the House of Khnum where the god went on vacation from his main temple as the spirit of the countryside (ibid., 315-22).

On the festival of the ninth of Payni, Khnum, who functioned here as the creator Re, came to hide in the House of the God and found his son Shu. The rebels, discovering his whereabouts, marched to the temple. Meanwhile, inside the temple the face of the god was turned away from the door of his shrine and all the officiating priests and the male singers made a great noise around the statue, as did the 'men surrounding this temple'. This was kept up until the penultimate hour of the day, when the god's statue was taken south to the House of Khnum (ibid., 323-30). The feast of the 19th and 20th of Epiphi, which is much better documented, involved the god going in procession to the temples by the lake and spending the night there (ibid., 332-7). Lights were permitted only inside temple and were not to be made with wood from the sacred grove:

> Making a great offering of every good thing. Singing by the male singers of the temple, before the god, right up to the fourth hour of the night. But no singing to the accompaniment of the harp, beating of the drum or blowing of trumpets inside his temple (after Sauneron 1962, 351).

This interesting passage recalls an observation by Plutarch in his treatise on Isis and Osiris that the blowing of trumpets was forbidden at the ceremonies of Osiris because it recalled the braying of an ass, an animal associated with Seth (Griffiths 1970, 410-11).

Even more remarkable were the extraordinary prohibitions that hedged around this celebration. Not only was the road to the temples at the lake completely closed to normal use, but any men who entered the temple precinct had not to have touched a woman in twenty-four hours or eaten forbidden food in four days. They also had to be purified, washed and appropriately dressed (in linen). No man who was widowed, possessed or bewitched could enter. The proper place for the townspeople was on top of the large enclosing wall – they were forbidden to go past the kiosk. No one was allowed to sleep on either side of the sacred way, and naturally admission to the temple was forbidden to anyone in a sheepskin. Those taking part in the procession were expected to have refrained from touching a woman for four days. Those who actually worked inside the temple were not to have touched a woman for nine days and to have abstained from forbidden food for five. They were to shave themselves all over and cut their nails, and to enter the temple only from the side entrance. All access to Asiatics (i.e. foreigners) was forbidden. Women were forbidden access at all points and within a zone around the temple that covered almost three hundred square metres (Sauneron 1962, 340-9).

It seems obvious, from the mention of the enclosing wall, that these prohibitions refer to the main temple as well as the shrines at the lake. Although Serge Sauneron, the editor of these texts, thought these prohibitions referred only to the Festival of Taking Up the Club that we are describing here (Sauneron 1962, 349), it is not unlikely that they were of a more general nature. Prohibitions against foreigners are common in temples of the Ptolemaic Period, for example. Such practices certainly have implications for religious performance, and we shall return to them below.

This festival concluded on the 20th with a 'battle' on the lake between the god and the forces of chaos. While it is likely the divine image was positioned to watch in a kiosk like those beside the sacred lake at the temple of Amun at Karnak, the nature of this battle remains unclear. The name Red Lake recalls the story of how the human race was saved from Sekhmet by the ruse of a lake of red beer masquerading as blood, although here the blood may be thought of as real. The re-presentation of the struggle could have taken a number of forms, from the manipulation of magical figurines or larger images to an actual fight between men in boats (ibid., 373-8), like those seen in much earlier tombs and reliefs (Decker and Harb 1994, 573-600, pls 324-37). There might also have been the kinds of choreographed duels that were enacted at the raising of the Djed pillar for Amenhotep III. Herodotus reports a rite that took place at Papremis, an unidentified town in the Delta, where

there is a special ceremony in addition to the ordinary rites and sacrifices practised elsewhere. As the sun draws towards setting, only a few of the priests continue to employ themselves about the image of the god, while the majority, armed with wooden clubs, take their stand at the entrance of the temple; opposite these is another crowd of men, more than a thousand strong, also armed with clubs and consisting of men who have vows to perform. The image of the god, in a little gold-plated shrine, is conveyed to another sacred building on the day before the ceremony. The few priests who are left to attend to it, put it, together with the shrine which contains it, in a four-wheeled cart which they drag along towards the temple. The others, waiting at the temple gate, try to prevent it from coming in, while the votaries take the god's side and set upon them with their clubs. The assault is resisted, and a vigorous tussle ensues in which heads are broken and not a few actually die of the wounds they received. This, at least, is what I believe, although the Egyptians told me that nobody is ever killed (Sélincourt 1972, 108-9).

While the particular myth that Herodotus associates with this activity cannot be identified any more than the town where the rite took place, it bears a remarkable resemblance to the ceremony of the Victory of Khnum, when men surrounded the House of Khnum, in which the image of the god was hidden. Another such festival might have provided the material for the Roman poet Juvenal's Egyptian satire (Ramsay 1928, 290-5) where he portrays a clash between the Osiris worshippers of Dendara with the devotees of Seth from Ombos, which results in an act of cannibalism. As to whether such mock battles were more controlled than these foreign observers thought cannot be ascertained. To this day, large faith-based gatherings can be volatile occasions and often lack adequate crowd control. Perhaps this is why public participation in Egyptian religious events became more restricted over time.

Other evidence for performance in the later period

As noted above an enormous amount of textual material documents religious festivals and related activities from this period. In particular, a great deal is found on the walls of temples of the Ptolemaic and Roman Periods. Apart from direct transcriptions of ritual books, there are also innumerable scenes of the daily cult as well as many other ceremonies known from earlier periods, and some that are not. For example, the Festival of the Beautiful Union, which involved the sailing of Hathor of Dendara to Edfu (Watterson 1998, 105-11) to marry Horus at his temple, is known from the First Intermediate Period (Fischer 1968, 211), *c.* 2100 BCE, although the ritual in the House of Life which forms a part of it (see above) is not known any earlier than the Salt Papyrus. The Foundation of the Temple (Montet 1964) and the Striking of the Ball (Decker and Harb 1994, 123-37, pl. 63-60) are attested in the New Kingdom, but are depicted more frequently and in greater detail at this time. The Sed Festival is alluded to in texts and representations, but no full depiction of it exists. Were conditions too unsettled to permit its celebration? The temple calenders show continuity with those from the New Kingdom, although they record more local celebrations, implying not a greater number of festivals but better documentation.

Architectural evidence for processional and other public performance is also found at this period. The Kushite kings of the 25th Dynasty paid special allegiance to Amun and his main sanctuary in Thebes. Piye celebrated the Opet Festival (Lichtheim 1980, 71). Taharqa built four huge porticos consisting of four rows of columns at the four entrances of the main Karnak temple. These structures, which are found in front of almost all the temples erected by these kings and were later widely imitated, are referred to as 'porches' in Egyptian (Leclant 1965, 200-7). Contemporary texts do not specify their use, but it was likely for the Rite of Touching the Sun, which we discussed in relation to the temple at Esna, where the image of the god was placed in the porch of the temple to receive the sun. Other rites that mention a porch or gate may also refer to these kinds of structures, which provided an opportunity for public communion with the god, like the kiosks placed at other venues outside the temple.

A particularly popular festival at this period was the Festival of the Decades, which marked every Egyptian week which was ten days long. It involved the visit of Amun-Re to a temple on the west bank at a place called Djeme, which sheltered the tombs of the primeval gods. It involved propitiatory rites undertaken by the king and the God's Wife that consisted of throwing clay balls and shooting arrows in the four directions. When the god returned to Karnak his image was taken into the crypt of a subterranean structure near the sacred lake. Contact with the primeval waters led to a cosmic rebirth in which Re and Osiris were one. Above ground the king also become spiritually recharged. While the beginning and end of this processional rite were secret, the middle part allowed the god and the king to interact with the community (Parker, Leclant and Goyon 1979). The exalted status of the God's Wife was also advertised in her festive sailings on the river, shown in reliefs of both the 25th and 26th Dynasties (Morkot 2000, 300ff.).

Apart from the institution of the God's Wife, the northern Egyptian kings of the 26th Dynasty continued other cultic institutions in the domain of Amun, such as his oracles. A document commemorating a divine decision at the Floor of Silver early in the reign of Psamtik I is illustrated with a beautiful vignette. It shows the shrine of the god without the barque carried by the priests, faced by the lector and the four prophets of Amun, resplendent in their leopard skins. Behind these men, who just happen to be four of the most powerful figures in Upper Egypt, is seen the priest Harsiese, who is asking the oracle about changing his position in the hierarchy (Parker 1962, 1-34). At this period the site of the oracle seems to have moved from the court of the tenth pylon to a site within the main temple – either the entrance to the hypostyle hall or the Portal of the Kings of the 22nd Dynasty to the south of it, in front of the temple (Cabrol 2001, 488-9). This last site would certainly have been a public space where the operations of the god could have been generally observed. Although it is known only from a description of Herodotus, the columned courtyard where the Apis Bull appeared at the temple of Ptah in Memphis, which was constructed by Psamtik I (Sélincourt 1972, 143), resembles the 'viewing place' of Amenhotep III at Luxor temple. It was in this pubic space that the bull performed oracular acts (Pietschmann 1894, 2808). Although not as well documented in Egyptian sources, divine oracles remained popular throughout the later period and were even adapted to Christian use (Černý 1962, 47-8; Frankfurter 1997, 193-5).

A processional way for the Festival of the Decades of Djeme in western Thebes was constructed sometime in the Third Intermediate Period and was still in use in Roman times (Cabrol 58-9, 65-6). During the fourth century BCE the kings of the 28th to 30th Dynasties constructed a large number of processional kiosks and processional ways before the Karnak temple (Cabrol 2001, 309-10). Nectanebo I constructed a sacred way lined with sphinxes and paved with stone that connected the temple of Mut with the riverbank. It intersected with a longer one that ran south to the temple of Luxor, following the route of an earlier way built by Hatshepsut. The beautifully carved limestone sphinxes, which were backed by a low wall and a bank of trees, still retain traces of the bright colours they were painted with. Their inscriptions boast of how the king rebuilt all the temples of Egypt (a not entirely baseless claim) and aim to draw the attention of both gods and spectators in the celebration of the Opet Festival (Cabrol 2001, 143-8, 283-96, 445, pls. 27, 29).

Nectanebo and his successors were also responsible for the construction of the enormous and unfinished first pylon in front of the temple of Amun (Cabrol 2001, 209) and the massive three-metre-high mud-brick wall that surrounds the Amun temple and its associated buildings. The appearance at this time of these massive walls, with distinctive undulating brick patterns that re-present the waves of the primeval chaotic waters (Barguet 1962a, 31-2), raises the same questions about accessibility as are posed by the Esna texts. Although Egyptian temples had always had boundary walls, they do not seem to have been quite so formidable. They ensured that access to the entire area of the temple could be strictly controlled and also made them into defensible enclaves that could be very useful in times of war. This was certainly the case during the rebellion of the early second century BCE when troops loyal to the Alexandrian government besieged native rebels within these walls (Huß 2001, 506-13). The continuing presence of these ramparts in late temples as well as the presence of apotropaic texts on the main entrances suggest that the temples were not quite so public as they once had been. In some cases rites that might once have been public or semi-public, like the touching of the divine images by the sun, were carried out on the temple roof instead of the porch (Meeks and Favard-Meeks 1997, 193-8). Nectanebo's wall at Karnak enclosed the whole Osiris precinct, where the ceremonial mummies were buried and the rites of Khoiak were acted out. At Dendara everything happened in secret, up on the roof. According to the rules for access given at Esna, the townspeople were supposed to watch the ceremonies sitting on top of the wall inside the precinct, and indeed the wall surrounding the temple at El-Kab has a ramp that may have been intended to give access for such a purpose (Sauneron 1962, 342-3).

The apparent exclusion of women from temples in the Ptolemaic and Roman periods is disturbing and puzzling. At earlier periods they seem to have been present even at the cult service, if not actually in the sanctuary. The office of God's Wife had existed at Thebes up until the Persian conquest (Gitton and Leclant 1977, 801-2), and a few women with religious duties, including *hemet netcher* priests, are known from Ptolemaic times (Johnson 1998). Several of the ritual dramas we have examined have female parts.

Some of these exclusions may be the result of regional diversity or the differing requirements of each festival, as suggested above. Still, there does seem to be a common theme of restricting access by women and foreigners. The requirement for pre-pubertal girls to play the roles of Isis and Nepthys in the Osirian rites might have been a way around this. Sauneron suggested that the pregnant woman and child *in utero* blessed in the Setting Up of the Wheel at Esna would also have been played by children (1962, 237). Of course women took part in the Mystery of the Divine Birth, although they were probably outside in the courtyard. Indeed, the court of the Birth House at Philae, where similar rites were celebrated, had a bilingual royal decree of Ptolemy V on the outside wall of the pronaos (Daumas 1977). These documents were specifically intended for public places such as the *weskhet mesha*, or 'public hall', of the temple (Cabrol 2001, 705-6). The exclusion of women from many cultic spaces is perhaps ironically the result of the very foreign influences that the priests tried to curtail in their proscriptions and ever more numerous execration rites.

No doubt increasing political instability and repeated foreign invasion created an elaborate cultic theatre, the product of a priestly culture that became increasingly preoccupied with apocalyptic scenarios (Derchain 1965, 3-6), as well as the ever more improbable prospect of salvation at the hands of the gods and a 'true' king who would drive out all the interlopers (Blasius and Schipper 2002, 277-302). It is doubly ironic that the generous subvention of foreign rulers made possible an ambitious programme of textual representation in Egyptian temples. It has been suggested that the extremely elaborate representations of the rites and ceremonies found in Ptolemaic and Roman temples were intended not just to record them in a more permanent form but to create truly 'performative' documents that would work forever all by themselves (Derchain 1989). And what sense of impending doom drove the priests of Esna to copy the contents of their most important rituals directly onto the columns of the outer hall of their temple? Of course, paranoia eventually has its own reward: after the social and economic crisis of the third century, Christianity became the official religion of the Empire. Any state support for other religion dried up and soon the Egyptian gods were back to being celebrated in people's homes and in village processions, as in the prehistoric period (Frankfurter 1998, 131-44, 224-37).

The rise of animal cults in the Late Period seems to be part of the same general climate. Although the Apis and Mnevis bulls went back to the third millennium (Vercoutter 1972, 338; Kákosy 1980b, 165), the other animal cults do not seem to be much earlier than the 30th Dynasty. It was Nectanebo I and Nectanebo II, the builders of the temple and sacred way for Osiris-Apis, as well as the tombs of the sacred ibises, cats, baboons and hawks in the Memphite necropolis (Smith 1986, 418-20), who founded the cult and burial place of Buchis, the sacred bull of Montu at Thebes (Mond and Myers 1934a, 10-11). Other such installations, like that of the sacred ram at Mendes in the Delta or of the Hesat cows of Isis at Atfih, are either Late Period or Ptolemaic (Grieshammer 1972, 519; Kessler 1986, 579-81). As the desire to number years by Apis instead of by a human king suggests, these incarnations of divinity seemed more worthy of veneration as god's representative on earth than an unworthy or foreign king (Brugsch 1884).

The observances due to these animals varied. Some, like Apis and Buchis, appeared as a single incarnation and were treated like a divine ruler, who was venerated in both life and death. For example, Cleopatra VII participated in the installation of the Buchis bull, which entailed her rowing him across the river, just as the king rowed the barque of Amun in the Opet Festival (Mond and Myers 1934b, 11-13). In other cases, whole species such as cats or baboons were thought to take part in divinity (Meeks and Favard-Meeks 1997, 60-3). Although they received no particular cult, they were treated with respect and after death embalmed and buried together in a sacred vault (Smith 1974, 34-9). Oddly enough, it appears that the demand for dedication of such mummies led to the animals being despatched before their time (Ikram and Dodson 1998, 135-6).

The copious documentation of the Graeco-Roman Period shows plenty of evidence for continued private devotions and participation in festivals. Although priestly offices were hereditary by the Late Period, and under Roman rule one had to pay to join up, there seems to be no shortage of priests in Graeco-Roman Egypt until the mid-third century CE (Frankfurter 1997, 198-203). They ranged from the likes of Pesherenptah, high priest of Memphis, who conducted the royal coronation for Ptolemy XII and dined with his family (Reymond 1981, 145-51), to lower-level functionaries like the shrine carriers (in Greek, *pastaphoroi*) who carried out menial tasks in the temples and liaised with the public. But while some of these people were little better than porters (Sauneron 2000, 54-5, 70-2), others who interpreted oracles and had prophetic dreams were often in a place to influence royalty, like Hor of Sebennytos, who told his prophetic dreams about the liberation of Egypt from Antiochus IV to Ptolemy IV and Queen Cleopatra II at the temple of Serapis in Alexandria (Ray 1976, 117-44). Was this a royal audience or a public spectacle?

Priests also formed self-regulated groups, as in the case of the *choachytai*, or water pourers, the mortuary priests of this period (Sauneron 2000, 109). They set up their own observances and festivals, kept accounts and sometimes made use of the temples or processional ways we have discussed (Cabrol 2001, 71). We also hear of private individuals having time off work to participate in their own personal or community festivals, like the individual who was allowed to go to the Festival of Seth (Frankfurter 1997, 52-60; Te Velde 1967, 140 n. 1).

So far all the evidence we have examined for this period is for religious performance and festivals. Did any other kinds of performances take place in the Egyptian cultural sphere? Drioton long ago suggested that a number of the tales preserved on papyrus from different periods, especially those with a lot of dialogue, could have been performed (Drioton 1957, 261). Demotic literature of the Graeco-Roman Period is particularly rich in these kinds of narratives, which may have influenced the development of the Greek and Latin novel (Quaegebeur 1987). Works like 'The Lion in Search of Mankind', a story similar to that of the lion and the mouse in Aesop's fables, and the Setne Khamwas cycle, about the adventures of Ramesses II's son, the high priest of Memphis (Lichtheim 1980, 125-51, 156-9), could well have been vividly performed by storytellers. An American scholar, Steven Vinson, has recently gone even farther in suggesting that these tales were presented by actors in stylized costumes in a form that resembled the Roman (non-silent) kind of mime or Greek comedy (Vinson 2000). As his research has not yet been published, we are not able to evaluate it. However, the mention of the Greek theatrical tradition brings us to the issue of how it survived in Egypt and how it may have influenced Egyptian performances.

Anxieties of influence

Greek dramatic performances originated in Athens in the sixth century BCE, where they were part of the spring festival of Dionysos, a god connected with fertility, intoxication and artistic inspiration. At first they consisted only of a group of men and boys who sang a poetic narrative to the accompaniment of a flute. Later one actor appeared, and still later two. Finally three were permitted. The *skene*, a tent or booth at the back of the stage where the actors changed their costumes, was also used to set the scene. The plays always took place in daylight on the side of a hill overlooking the Acropolis with its temples. This site was called the *thea-*

tron, or 'viewing place'. Plays about gods and heroes were called *tragedoi,* or goat songs, thereby connecting them to Dionysos through his familiar, an animal closely associated with fertility, as in Egypt. Originally they were part of a full day's activity consisting of three tragic plays around a single theme and a satyr play, or parody, of it. The satyrs, also associated with Dionysos, were part man and part animal and given to anarchic revelry. This spirit was more evident in the comedies, which were presented at a different festival of the god, the Lenaia.

Before the plays began, an animal was sacrificed in the *orkhestra,* the circular space that divided the seats from the *skene,* where the chorus danced as it sang its songs. The seat in the middle of the front row was reserved for the chief priest of Dionysos, who, aided by a group of citizen men, would award a prize to one of three poets who each authored a day of plays. The *agon,* or competition, was a central feature of Greek religious festivals and was considered a sacred mode of behaviour. The competitors aimed to please the god, not themselves (Bieber 1961, 1-79; Pickard-Cambridge 1968, 40ff.). Attendance at these events was considered a sacred duty for all citizens, who in Athens were adult males born in the city-state of citizen parents who owned property or who were rowers in the fleet. There is some controversy as to whether anyone other than the male citizens was allowed to watch the plays (Pickard-Cambridge 1968, 261-70).

The Athenian plays are distinguished by the prominence of the actors who role-played the gods and heroes; like the chorus they were exclusively male. Although they were costumed in a highly stylized way and wore masks, their long, poetic speeches increasingly emphasized their interaction with each other and their inner feelings (Bieber 1961, 80-6; Pickard-Cambridge 1968, 156-209). This kind of dramatic expression was no doubt influenced by the Homeric poems, which were publicly recited at the festival of the city god Athena every four years (Nagy 1996, 64-112), as well as the popularity of lyric poetry, which portrayed emotional states in the first person. Although the actors were probably not capable of violent movement, they were able to disappear from view and change costume to appear as new characters (Pickard-Cambridge 1961, 137ff.). Later dramatic presentations featured increasingly elaborate costumes and scenery as well as special effects (Bieber 1961, 108-28).

Athenian drama spread across the Mediterranean and Near East, at first by way of the Greek colonies in Italy and Sicily, but most notably through the Macedonian elite who took control of Alexander's empire after his death (Rice 1983, 52-3). The earlier kings of Macedon, which was to the north of Greece, enthusiastically adopted its culture, and one of them lured the tragic poet Euripides to his court, where he composed *Bacchae,* a play about the secret things in the cult of Dionysos. The house of Ptolemy connected itself closely with this god, tracing descent from him through Alexander (Rice 1983, 83-5; Hazzard 2000, 70).

All the kingdoms founded by Alexander's generals staged elaborate dramatic festivals, but nowhere were they favoured more than in Ptolemaic Egypt. From the early third century BCE the kingdom had its own Guild of the Artists of Dionysos, which included persons who financed, wrote, acted in and provided music for the plays. These men where servants of the god and they were not be harmed for any reason. They even had a chapter at Ptolemais Hormou, the Greek-style city set up in Middle Egypt by Ptolemy I. In 276 BCE Ptolemy II celebrated a great festival in Alexandria to present his father as a god and honour Dionysos as the god of the royal house. Its main event was an enormous procession that lasted a whole day, with tableaux made up of statues and precious materials as well as people and animals to illustrate the myth of Dionysos. It also featured the actors who celebrated the drama associated with the god (Rice 1983, 52-8). Although drama may have been promoted initially because of its connection with the ruling house, it was undoubtedly popular. There are many references to theatrical performances in documentary sources; after the Homeric poems, the most plentiful literary manuscripts to survive are excerpts from the tragedies of Euripides and the comedies of Menander (Bowman 1986, 162).

Despite the survival of all this textual material and many references to theatres, the only well-constructed stone structure of a recognizable theatrical type is a small late Roman building at Kom el-Dik in Alexandria (Bowman 1986, 206, 215-16). This is probably not a theatre of the classic type but a *bouleuterion,* or lecture hall (Alston 2002, 174, 272). Ancient descriptions of Alexandria describe hundreds of theatres, but they are all gone, along with those in the hinterland, with the exception of one at Antinoopolis, the remains of which survived until the nineteenth century (Alston 2002, 242-3). For example, the theatre at Oxyrhynchus, just south of the Faiyum, housed council meetings, mass gatherings to honour public figures, athletic displays, mimes, dramatic performances, recitations of Homeric poems and chariot races (Bowman 1986, 144-5; Bagnall 1993, 230ff.). These activities no doubt took place in lighter constructions of mud brick (wood, used elsewhere in theatre construction, was in short supply) and have apparently all vanished. It is possible that performances also took place at the bottom of hillsides or mounds in a way that imitated the original theatre.

Even more problematic than the location of the actual theatres is their effect on indigenous culture. By the second century BC it is extremely difficult to pinpoint the 'ethnic' identity of persons mentioned in our documentary sources. Ptolemy I made Alexandria the capital and created a Greek citizen body and supporting institutions such as the *gymnasion.* Ptolemy II established the city of Ptolemais as another such foundation in the hinterland and settled large numbers of veterans in the Faiyum. Although the ethnic Greeks were initially a military and social elite, they soon intermingled with Egyptian bureaucrats, who were essential to the functioning of the government, and they intermarried with local women.

The ruling class was forced to deal with the Egyptian elite in the form of the priesthood, and the whole community adopted the Egyptian gods (Bowman 1986, 209-10, 124-5, 62-3, 61, 18, 122, 186ff.). Since Greeks were reluctant to learn other languages, it is likely that the Egyptian priests translated bilingual decrees into Greek from demotic and not the other way around, using notes forwarded from the royal chancellery. There are more than a few passages, even in Ptolemaic temple texts, that suggest a familiarity with Greek philosophical ideas. It is possible that the use of a 'chorus' in the Triumph of Horus or the long poetic speeches in the Mystery of the Divine Royal Birth at Esna may reflect the influence of Greek drama. Furthermore, although access to dramatic performances was wider in the Hellenistic Period than in classical Athens, we cannot assume that Egyptians would have been admitted to them, especially in the early Ptolemaic Period.

In the Roman Period documentary sources show the popularity of mimes, a less formal theatrical form very popular in Italy and exported throughout the Empire. Mimes were not silent and featured very broad comedy as well as highly realistic, if not actual, violence. They were more widely presented than the older Greek plays (Bieber 1961, 165-6). As noted above, they were possibly linked to a native storytelling tradition to create an indigenous form of theatre. Another performance introduced by the Greeks was the athletic competition. One is recorded in 267 BCE at an unidentified Greek city in Egypt, where colonists from northern Greece and Macedon competed in foot races in celebration of Ptolemy II's birthday (Walker and Higgs 2001, 115-16). However, as late as the second century CE, hieroglyphic inscriptions describing funeral games for Hadrian's lover Antinous suggests they elicited scant interest or understanding from the native population (Decker 1992, 107), unlike the chariot races of the Byzantine Period (Bagnall 1993, 92).

Other cultural influences were also at play in Egypt in the late first millennium. The use of mercenary soldiers from Judea by the kings of the 26th Dynasty and the Persians allowed for cultural interaction as well as conflict (Porten 1996, 18-19, 74-88). Aramaic texts written in the demotic script, as well as stories known from Biblical sources, show a high degree of multiculturalism. An interesting effect that relates to our topic is the introduction of the horned altar into Egypt from the Levant. The altars, which were originally used for burnt offerings and incense, were set up outside the doors of Egyptian temples, where they were often used in protective and execration rites. The door of the temple or the nearby processional way seems to have been the place where capital sentences were also carried out, as suggested by a trench filled with human remains found near the sacred way between Karnak and Luxor (Cabrol 2001, 664-8). These horned altars were also used by persons unable or disinclined to go inside the temple. Cult worship as practised by the Greeks did not revolve around a statue as in the Near East but a burnt offering on an outdoor altar, often in front of the temple, whose statue was seen merely as a token of esteem (Burkert 1985, 60-3). Accommodation to Greek practice became increasingly common in the Roman Period, when altars could often be seen erected outside the doorways of temples (Varille 1942). Feasts of Hellenic character, like the Amesysia, or birthday of Isis, were known from the time of Augustus onwards, and were celebrated in shrines like the so-called Serapaion on the sacred way running between Karnak and Luxor. The members of the cult held sacred banquets to which they sold tickets, a purely Greek custom (Bagnall 1993, 267; Cabrol 2001, 716-17).

Some general observations

The extraordinary amount of material about performance in the later period that is available for discussion makes it difficult to draw conclusions. While many of the religious festivals and performances known from earlier periods continued, it is clear that they were celebrated in ever more elaborate ways. There seems to have been a shift in emphasis from public, interactive spectacles to crucial but secret operations whose successful conclusions were later announced publicly.

The preceding statement actually conceals more than it reveals. Many of the earlier performances were also obviously secret, and likewise processional festivals like the Opet or the funeral of Apis were still clearly central to the life of the community in the Late Period and beyond. The Festival of the Victory of Khnum at Esna apparently entailed a large crowd of men surrounding a small temple in the countryside and making a great din. Still, most of the documents we have examined emphasize secrecy, and site-specific rituals like the Mystery of Osiris at Dendara were largely self-contained on the roof of the temple. Huge enclosure walls, seemingly a 30th Dynasty innovation, controlled access to the sacred precincts. The temple of Isis at Philae, founded by the prolific Nectanebo I, did not require a wall because it was located on an island. Still, even here many pilgrims visited the site and crowds of local people witnessed the divine festivals as they clustered under the colonnades, erected under Augustus, that flanked the sacred way that ran between the door of the temple and its quay. While these structures have been linked to the colonnades found lining the streets of Roman Period cities (Arnold 1999, 236-7, fig. 195), they also resemble the earlier Kushite porticos discussed above.

What these performances looked like becomes an ever more pressing question with the existence of so many scripts. Activities that had a strong constructive component, like the manufacture of the figurines of Osiris for the ritual in the House of Life or the mystery in the month of Khoiak, involved the actions of priests clothed in pure linen and white sandals or with the addition of a leopard skin or a lapis lazuli sidelock as in the case

Fig. 9. Colonnade of Augustus at Philae.

of the *fekety* priest. The girls who play Isis and Nepthys in Papyrus Bremner-Rhind are completely shaved, wear wigs and have the names of the gods they play written on their arms, but no indication of their clothing is given. Presumably it is linen and resembles the archaic costume worn by goddesses in the customary representations. However, it must be remembered that the priests also role-play the gods. The *fekety* priest is not depicted as such in the Salt Papyrus, but as the theriomorphic god Shu. Sauneron was uncertain whether Khnum is re-presented in the Mystery of the Divine Birth by a statue or an actor. Did masked actors play the part of theriomorphic gods? Did they do so all the time, sometimes or not at all? There is considerable disagreement among scholars on this point (Wolinsky 1986; Ritner 1995, 223). While the metaphorical character of Egyptian texts and representations must be strongly emphasised, it must be noted that these later-period performances in particular show a tendency to present them in a very concrete fashion. The king is anointed with a tear from the eye of the living falcon that re-presents the eye of Horus in the Ceremony for the Renewal of Royal Power; a goose is given grain at the end of the Triumph of Horus, representing the transmission of patrimony through Geb, who transmits the inheritance to Horus and Osiris, in that the name of this god is written with a goose. Male virility and the power of craft are given concrete expression in the potter's wheel

132

of Khnum, and so on. Given such a penchant for concrete visualization, the use of masked actors to play theriomorphic gods cannot be ruled out.

Apart from the two masks mentioned in Chapter 3, only two Egyptian masks survive – from this period. They both represent the jackal, the animal spirit of Anubis. As the embalmer god and *sem* priest, Anubis was a popular figure, both at the funerary ceremony and in the myth of Osiris. His jackal-headed form survived his transference to the Graeco-Roman cult of Isis and Serapis (Witt 1971, 198-209). As noted above, references are found as early as in the Coffin Texts to 'Anubis' men at funerals, and he is often shown playing the role of the chief embalmer or assisting in the Opening of the Mouth ceremony at the funeral from the New Kingdom onwards (Ritner 1993, 249 n. 1142). However, the two surviving Anubis masks are quite different from the earlier type discussed above. Both are of heavy ceramic material and cover the entire head, with no holes for eyes or mouth. A unique depiction of a priest wearing this kind of mask, shown in cross-section, is found in the reliefs of the Procession of Sokar in the first western chapel on the roof at Dendara (Cauville 1997b, pl. 13; Schäfer 1986, 121-2). The man is being steered along by another priest behind him because he obviously cannot see where he is going. Such a mask would make it impossible for an actor to speak his lines or move around the stage, a observation that for some puts paid to the idea that masked actors could ever have functioned in any kind of performance unless they stayed absolutely still and someone such as the lector priest read their lines for them. In this regard it must be noted that the vignette in the standard embalming ritual, in which the Overseer of Secrets appears to play the role of Anubis, shows him as a man in standard priestly attire (Sauneron 1952, 10). The question of whether masks were used in Egyptian cultic performances is not one than can easily be decided, but this does not make it any less crucial.

We have mentioned that Egyptian cults suffered an irrevocable decline with the social and economic crises of the third century, followed by the rise of Christianity (Bagnall 1993, 261-8). However, they did not disappear overnight. Worship of the gods, along with their attendant festivals and performances, can be documented into the sixth century (Frankfurter 1997, 20-33, 76). Late antique and Christian sources indicate the existence of small-scale celebrations in private homes and the celebration of important festivals like that commemorating the arrival of the Nile flood (ibid., 42-6). A fourth-century Christian source describes in rather loaded terms such an event that took place near Hermopolis:

> There was a huge temple in one of the villages which housed a very famous idol, though in reality this image was nothing but a wooden statue. The priests together with the people, working themselves up into a bacchic frenzy, used to carry it in procession through the villages, no doubt performing the ceremony to ensure the flooding of the Nile (Frankfurter 1997, 44).

While performances that openly celebrated the forces of nature as epitomized by the old gods fell into desuetude, they did not entirely disappear. Up until the nineteenth century the Nile flood was celebrated in a festival near Cairo, where a major canal left the river for the site of Heliopolis (Corteggiani 1979, 138-9, pl. 25). Even today, a festival honouring the Luxor saint Abul Haggag takes a model boat four times around the mosque (Naguib 1990a; Hoffman, 1995, 109-110), which is located in the old southern Opet temple. Actions, it seems, speak louder than words.

6

Learning about Past Performances
in the Present

Ever since Erman first suggested that the left-hand side of the Shabaka
Stone represented some record of dramatic activity (1911), scholars have
not been idle in suggesting ways that this might or might not have come
about. Doubts about the existence of Egyptian 'drama' seem well justified.
The putative scripts that we have examined give their actors no lines that
reveal state of mind, intention or feelings about other characters. There is
almost nothing in the way of interactive dialogue and very few stage
directions, unless we count indications embedded in the speeches themselves, and there is no attempt to suggest or even describe a setting in a
recognizable, everyday world. The actors are unlikely to move or speak in
a convincing or lifelike way, chanting or shouting their lines, and they are
perhaps costumed in outlandish old clothes and possibly even masks.
Since those wearing masks are unable to see or make themselves heard,
their lines are spoken by a reader and they must be moved around the
stage by another person. Even if there is an audience, which in many
instances is not the case, if we exclude the actors themselves, they cannot
actually follow the words of the actors because they are in an ancient,
unintelligible dialect. While the audience may know the story, they cannot
experience the emotional crescendo and release that we expect from
theatre, because they can't follow what is being said.

While these observations are valid to a point, they can be met with two
major objections. First, what we recognize as theatre is a very particular
phenomenon known in only a few cultures (Schechner 1988, 103ff.), and
the version familiar to those in western culture is even more specific still.
As noted in the Introduction, theatre is a subset of drama and of performance in general, an activity most closely related to ritual, but connected
with others that form a spectrum from total self-focus to community-wide
participation. The second problem with this argument is that there is and
has been more than one kind of theatre current in even our own culture.
It seems highly likely that ancient Greek theatre may have resembled the
Egyptian performances described more closely than our own, particularly
in its minimal stage directions and indications of setting as well as its
highly stylized acting and costuming. Like the Egyptian events it also
appeared in the context of a religious festival. And if the audience was
supposed to be engaged by the actors' speeches, that was not always the

case (Schechner 1988, 193-6). The polite, undivided attention of a modern theatre audience was as unknown to Shakespeare as to Euripides. Even in the seventeenth century playwrights repeated themselves to allow for periodically absent or inattentive listeners. The mystery plays of medieval Europe closely resemble Egyptian performance in many ways, but no one would deny their dramatic character. In more recent theatrical history, playwrights and directors such as Bertolt Brecht (1964, 33-41, 69-77) actively sought to distance their audience from the play in order to make them become more critical of it and aware of their own relationship with it. As noted above, performance and performance art have looked to other kinds of performance such as ritual, play, sport and so on in order engage and create an active audience. Of course, other non-western cultures have their own kinds of dramatic and other performances that bear little resemblance to the three-act play with a 'realistic' setting enacted under the proscenium arch.

Two other, minor observations may be made. The use of masks is a difficult problem and the very small number of surviving specimens offer little help, especially since they are of two radically different types. The earlier, lighter ones with eye and nostril openings, which cover only the face, have been found in both settlement and mortuary contexts. The two later ones, heavy ceramic objects with no openings that cover the whole head, have no known provenance. The conceptual character of Egyptian art makes is very difficult to identify masked figures. The unique cross-sectional view of the priest in the Anubis mask at Dendara may suggest how the later type of mask was used, but it could also have a specific significance in the procession of Sokar, in which special sacred objects were carried (see above, Chapter 4). An unplaced relief fragment from an Old Kingdom tomb depicting the so-called 'foreigner game' seems to show a figure in a lion mask that resembles the earlier type, but it has not been successfully interpreted (Decker and Harb 1994, 628-9, pl. 249). While it is true that the Ramesseum Dramatic Papyrus and the Embalming Ritual (see above, Chapter 5) do not show masks on any of the actors in the activities, the question of the role of masks in these performances must ramain open.

The notion that performances of the later period, such as the Triumph of Horus, were recited in ancient, incomprehensible language was clearly enunciated by Fairman in his 1973 publication of this text (Fairman 1973, 56-7). Since the texts on temple walls were in a form of Middle Egyptian, a literary dialect that fell out of use in the early second millennium BCE, they could be understood only by learned men and would be as incomprehensible to a vulgar audience as Latin or Old English today. Unfortunately Fairman's analogy rests on the assumption that the Egyptian writing system functioned like ours. It did not. Egyptian scripts, which were all versions of the same writing system, operated on a mixed non-alphabetic system with a strong logographic component which may be more closely compared with Chinese than with western alphabetic scripts (Goldwasser

1995, 41 n. 30). Such a writing system offers its users the advantage of being easily able to read across dialects or time periods, since it is not totally dependent on a phonetic component. The existence of several of these performance texts in hieroglyphic, hieratic and demotic versions suggests that they were actually vocalized in the contemporary dialect and quite comprehensible to any listener.

One last point – while we have defined a performance as something that has witnesses, it is not impossible for those enacting it to also bear witness, as is frequently the case in religious ritual. Furthermore, as we have seen, the wider audience for many an Egyptian performance is often off site, but that does not make them any less important.

Modern imaginings: the mediated imagination

The most basic problem in imagining, reconstructing and re-presenting ancient performances in the present time is the environment that we ourselves live in. Our attempts in this direction are always already over-determined by mass-mediated structures of perception. When confronted with the Ramesseum Dramatic Papyrus, even Kurt Sethe, a consummate scholar, could imagine it only as like being at the movies (1928, 17). Not only have we to try to imagine alien culture and belief systems that existed in the distant past, but we must somehow extricate ourselves from the 'lonely crowd' (Riesman 1969) in which we find ourselves. While we still live within community structures, generally we respond to cultural prod-ucts and moments – with the exception of sport – singly rather than as a group. The audience at the cinema is a group of strangers in the dark; reading a printed book is a private activity. The consumption of television, recorded music and its hypostasis on the World Wide Web are on an ascending scale of atomized action. Few of these activities are truly interactive and most require some kind of commercial transaction. The mass-mediated network is normally the vector of entertainment, of per-sonal gratification, not of information or empowerment as sometimes suggested (Jameson 1983). And the effect is not an enhanced sense of personal integrity, but rather disassociation with the self. We watch ourselves watching whatever we watch, and when we create something it often feels like we are reflecting our own reflection of what we have seen (Deleuze and Guattari 1983, 1ff.). In other words, although we share with the people of pre-modern societies common mental abilities and the basic parameters of existence, our perceptions of the world and of ourselves are mediated in a way that is quite alien to their experience.

Fairman's text: the moment of re-inauguration

The Edfu texts that Fairman had originally published with Blackman were edited by him for performances which took place at two English

137

educational institutions in 1968 and 1973. *The Triumph of Horus* was presented on a proscenium stage in an auditorium before an audience. The 1973 production was influenced by the study of medieval drama (1973, 59ff.), although it is not known if the audience joined in the exclamation 'Hold fast, Horus, hold fast', as Fairman thought their Egyptian predecessors did. Although photographs exist of this production, a film made of it has been lost. Generally speaking the play was well received, although anecdotal evidence suggests that the repetitious uncut text made the audience a little restless. Fairman was proud of being able to facilitate these productions. However, the necessarily speculative nature of the enterprise did not recommend it to the scholarly community. Yet more anecdotal evidence suggests that, while scholars from time to time performed Fairman's text or other similar documents from the later period with their students, it was not a topic for discussion.

Pedagogical strategies: Horus in the suburbs

My initial decision to mount a performance of *The Triumph of Horus* in 1998 was based on pedagogical considerations. It was the inaugural year of a course taught with Paul Swarney, a papyrologist, in the Programme in Classical Studies at York University in Toronto. York University is a very large institution with over 50,000 students and a sprawling, not very picturesque campus surrounded by industrial parks and high-rise apartment buildings. It offers a mix of general arts courses and vocational programmes ranging from law to computer graphics. The course we offered was part of a programme of general education requirements in the humanities which focus on the teaching of critical skills in writing, thinking and communication. This course, Egypt in the Greek and Roman Mediterranean, looked at Graeco-Roman Egypt as a multicultural society, using literary and documentary sources in translation.

At the outset we experienced the frustration felt by many academics at the lack of preparedness of students and their manifest lack of interest in the material. Instructors who are strongly committed to their material often find themselves facing students who take their course on account of general programme requirements or because it fits their schedule. Those who are apparently interested in the material are generally acquainted with it through mass cultural outlets such as movies or cable TV networks such as the History Channel or Arts & Entertainment. Though such vectors claim to educate, their real intention is to entertain (cf. Postman 1985, 142-54). Furthermore, Egypt and the classical world are most familiar as floating signifiers that are scattered in random fashion throughout the advertising-based mass-cultural zone. Although primary and secondary teachers have made a commendable effort to engage students on these and related topics, both teachers and students are ineluctably implicated in this wider matrix. University instructors are certainly not outside it either, but they have their own set of cultural predispositions that both help and hinder their interactions with students.

The academic life as it now exists, although it has undergone radical transformation in the past thirty years, is still based on the unspoken assumption that it is an elite cultural activity undertaken by the leisure class. The enormous investments of time and money attendant on a graduate education were originally predicated not on scholarships and student loans, but on class position. The opening up of higher education to those outside the elite has led to pressures on the culture of both groups. On one hand we have a 'greening' or proletarianization of both the culture and content of university education (Jasen 1989; Fiske 1989, 1-21), and on the other, the transformation – or as some would have it, the destruction – of working-class culture embodying earlier folkways (Docker 1994, 51-63). These pressures are still much more obvious in undergraduate life than in graduate school and among the faculty, where those attaining positions tend to take on the culture of their new environment rather than holding on to what they leave behind. In addition, issues concerning the representation of women and minority communities come into play among both faculty and students (Bannerji 1991). Apart from the cultural gulf that separates instructors from students, there also exists the problem of changing approaches and expectations in high schools with respect to basic literacy and critical skills. So while many students have excellent self-presentation skills and are highly technologically and media-literate, they lack both the cultural capital and academic skills to perform in conventional academic routines.

So my colleague and I faced the task of enculturating our students, imparting to them a knowledge of our academic content and providing them with the tools to express and use that knowledge. The teaching of critical skills, a practice that has migrated from schools to universities in the past twenty years to meet such needs, features practices such as free writing, brainstorming and small group discussions, combined with inter-active lecture or classroom time. I had encountered role playing and acting out as techniques learned by students in high school and had utilized them with small groups. We made the decision to use acting out and role playing in a large setting when we contemplated the pitfalls of major written assignments in lower-level university courses, which include lack of atten-tion to detail and widespread plagiarism. As we searched for an assignment that would force them to put in the time, I came upon a copy of *The Triumph of Horus* on the shelves on another university library. Our announcement of this 'surprise' assignment at the beginning of the second semester was initially greeted with disbelief and hostility. However, in the end, both the class and the instructors came to regard the public perform-ance of this work to be the most rewarding and interesting school assignment they had ever participated in. In undertaking this strategy my colleague and I became part of a growing number of university instructors

139

who use the performance-based assignment, which has in the past been confined to primary and secondary education (Cohen 2004; Angelo and Cross 1993).

Over the years the major performance-based assignment in this course has evolved to include three preliminary reports and a final report by each student. While the task is based on small groups in separate tutorials and a final, class-wide activity, the mark gained by each student depends not only on their participation in them but also in submitting a final report in which they demonstrate an ability to clearly describe and understand what they have been doing. One of the greatest pedagogical benefits of this programme is the marked improvement in many students' writing skills. These are tracked from the first semester, when more conventional assignments involving reading and commenting on texts are given. The success of this strategy illustrates the truism that it is much easier to understand and write about something that you did rather than something you just read about. Work on such projects also enhances organizational and communication skills (Gillam 2002a).

Over the years that this course has run, the following projects have been undertaken: a public performance of the Triumph of Horus; in-class theatrical performances of skits based on Apuleius' *The Golden Ass*; an enactment of the Mystery of Osiris in the month of Khoiak according to the Dendara text; an imaginative reconstruction of an Isiac mystery using a variety of Egyptian and classical materials; an enactment of the mummification and burial of an Apis bull; and performance of the mystery of Osiris according the Dendara texts and the Bremner-Rhind Papyrus. The Triumph of Horus, the mystery of Osiris and the obsequies of the Apis bull, which are most relevant to the present discussion, will be described in a little more detail.

All the performances used scripts written by the students that were based on the original materials. The rewriting of the materials is an essential part of the process of understanding and re-presentation that facilitates the learning process. It generally happens that in this process the texts are greatly abbreviated, reflecting the different allocation of time and attention span between twenty-first-century university students and ancient Egyptians. It also happens that acts or characters are cut for convenience or clarity. The aim is to present a version of the essentials of the event, all the while keeping in mind that no ancient performance would have been the same as another. Costumes and props are also used and made at the discretion of those involved in the activity, but subject to consultation with the instructors. What is actually used generally depends on what is available. Skill- and resource-sharing among the students help solve many of these problems, and sometimes friends and family step in to help. Since there is no institutional financial support for these projects, students are encouraged to fundraise in order to cover costs. This exercise brings them extremely close to the ancient practitioners, for whom such

140

support was vital to continuance of their large-scale activities. All the performances took place at the end of the school year, in late March or early April, when it is generally warm enough to be outside but not always with certainty. Although this timing may theoretically not coincide with the original calendar date, the Egyptian year did wander, and in any case, the seasonal and agricultural year is quite different in Canada.

The Triumph of Horus, a twenty-five-minute presentation based on Fairman's text, was mounted in the Vari Hall rotunda, a well-lit indoor public space with a high volume of pedestrian traffic. Not only does it connect two of the major building complexes on campus, it is also surrounded by two storeys of classrooms opening off balconies. The costuming included masks as well as a two-dimensional representation of the ship of Horus, behind which the actors stood. The audience consisted of members of the class not directly involved in the performance as well as anyone strolling through the rotunda. Over two hundred programmes that included participatory lines for the audience were distributed. Music and sound effects were provided by a student and a friend of his who were adept at the synthesizer. A hippopotamus was created for the production by papier-mâché artist and puppeteer Leslie Ashton. This controversial animal, who was larger and more explicit than the figure in the Edfu reliefs, also stood in for the cake and was later disembowelled of pieces of fruit wrapped in red tissue paper.

The performance began with the *sem* priest getting the attention of the

Fig. 10. Performance of the Triumph of Horus, 7 April 1998, showing the ritual of the 10 harpoons watched by the king in the foreground (lower left, seated).

141

crowd by circumambulating the rotunda while burning incense as the props were being put in place. Then a way was cleared for the procession of priests and chorus, followed by the king and queen in purely Greek costume. The king clapped his hands and the performance began. Midway, after the ritual of the ten harpoons and the disembowelling of the hippo, the king took the spear of Horus and was crowned with the double crown. He was the last to leave the performance space, carrying the spear (Gillam 2000). The audience, which consisted of passers-by, non-acting members of the class, friends and children from the York daycare centre, displayed varying levels of interest and engagement. A few stayed for the whole thing, but most casual viewers spent a few minutes before moving on. While perhaps not displaying the commitment of an ancient audience, the behaviour of the spectators more closely approximated their reactions than one in a conventional theatre would (Schechner 1988, 193-206). *The Triumph of Horus* was the most 'theatrical' and most tightly structured of our performances. It was also one in which the instructors played a highly interventionist role. Later activities have moved away from this model and have tended to emphasize process over product.

Our students re-presented the mystery of Osiris on two occasions, in 2000 and 2004. Here the emphasis was not on one public performance but an activity that unfolded over a three-week period. The first presentation used only the Dendara texts and representations and focussed on the central activities of making the mummies, the procession of Sokar and the raising of the Djed pillar. Most of these activities unfolded in private, either in class or at specially scheduled times. The sailing of the 22nd of Khoiak took place on the campus lake. Only a few class members were available for the procession of Sokar, which took place around the complex where classes were held. It was early spring and there were no spectators. The raising of the Djed pillar took place at sunrise one week before the end of term and was a compulsory activity for the entire class. Since no detail is given about it at Dendara, a script was developed using the scene in the tomb of Kheruef, including dancing and stick-fighting. This event took place on the common in the middle of campus and the end of the ceremony was witnessed by early risers arriving by bus. After dark on the same day, the mummies were secretly buried in the campus woodlot (Gillam, 2002a).

In 2004, with a larger number of students and tutorials, an attempt was made to open out the celebration and include material from the Bremner-Rhind Papyrus as well as the ancillary activities mentioned in the Osirian chapels and the Dendara calendar. Although the making of the figures proceeded well, it proved difficult to coordinate the activities of different groups, and colder weather for the most part put paid to processions or other outdoor activities. However, the rerouting of the procession of Sokar through the shopping mall and the raising of the Djed pillar in the rotunda generated more of a public reaction. The large amount of additional material provided by the Bremner-Rhind Papyrus was a challenge for

Fig. 11. Funeral procession of the Apis Bull, 5 April 2002.

student script-writers and dramaturges, as was the imagining of processions and festivals indicated in only the sketchiest ways by the original sources. Most events took place in classrooms, corridors and courtyards.

The obsequies of the Apis bull has been perhaps our most challenging project to date. A class consisting of two tutorial groups divided the labour between the embalming and the funeral procession. The group in charge of the procession built a painted bier on wheels and choreographed a two-kilometre procession ending at the lake, where the tomb, a life-size replica of an Apis sarcophagus, was erected with a hieroglyphic stela in front. This operation combined the navigation of Osiris with the actual burial procession in a way that made use of the campus topography. The directors of the funeral choreographed a procession that made a number of stops for dancing, music and recitations from the *Book of the Dead*. An ethnomusicology major provided dance movements, percussion instruments and a musical score based on traditional Egyptian rhythms. Another student provided all the class members with appropriate costumes, including the rough linen shifts worn by the mourners.

Things did not go so smoothly for the other group. Since mummifying an actual bull was out of the question, they had to devise a substitute. After much discussion, the students set about creating a recumbent bull image out of wood, cloth and papier-mâché. The immediacy of the situation was heightened when vandals 'killed' the first bull, leading to general distress, if not mourning. As a result the reconstructed life-size model had

143

to be embalmed in a much shorter period than seventy days. After the Seth-masked slitter made the first cut, the bull's entrails, consisting of stuffed cloth shapes, were jammed into jars and he was taken to the wrapping room. Here, with the application of much oil, the forelegs were enclosed in painted bandages as per the embalming ritual. As Apis was wrapped, the lector priest read out the appropriate sections of the Standard Embalming Ritual. The day before the funeral, the rites of the 69th day where performed indoors, at it was snowing heavily. A version of the sailing on the lake was enacted with a model boat and figures. The lamentations of Isis and Nepthys from the Bremner-Rhind Papyrus were performed by two students with the names of the goddess written on their arms, both then and at the funeral. Luckily the weather improved the next day and the funeral was able to take place, although the long, cold route precluded any real outside audience.

What can be learned from these kinds of projects?

As noted above, a number of pedagogical benefits can be obtained from these activities. These include the building of critical thinking around writing, reading and comprehension. They are particularly useful in helping students to read and understand difficult texts that first appear to lack both recognizable form and content. They also engage students on a number of levels, allowing the less academically inclined among them ways of accessing such material. However, it can also be argued that from a scholarly perspective these student performances provide some valuable insights into the texts and the performances they record. These insights are both general and particular.

For example, the mummification of the Apis bull image demonstrated in a very concrete way the practicality of Vos' interpretation of the Vienna Papyrus, that natron was introduced into the body cavity in cloth bags (1993, 197). It is the only way that the large body cavity could be efficiently filled up and desiccated from the inside. Furthermore, this technique is the most efficient way of removing and recycling natron that has become saturated with moisture, an operation that Salima Ikram's experiments have shown to be essential to successful desiccation (2000). On another topic, while it is true that our students experienced practical problems in constructing and watering the moulds of barley and sand for the Osiris mystery and failed to get any of them to germinate, it must also be noted that the actual Osiris 'bricks', or mummies, examined by Angela Tooley had apparently not been intended to do so (1996, 179). Lastly, when papier-mâché masks were worn by the actors in the Triumph of Horus, they quickly discovered that they could not make themselves heard, and additional holes had to be made in the necks in order to solve the problem. These masks, which were modelled on theriomorphic representations of

144

Egyptian gods, once again raise the question of the status of masks in the ancient performances.

Other, more general observations can be made. Occasional failures of organization or difficulties working with other members of a team or the class as a whole illustrate the importance of an effective operating structure and interpersonal relationships for the success of such projects. They also illustrate the crucial role that advance planning played in an effective outcome. The mystery text at Dendara specifies that the barley for making the figures, as well as the flax from which came the linen to wrap them, was grown in a designated field the previous year (Chassinat 1968 (II), 511-27; Cauville 1997c, 11). While the students did not have that much forward time available to gather materials, it soon became apparent that early preparation was the key to successful completion of the assignment. Obviously the rituals and performances that actually took place in the temples or at public festivals were mostly likely to operate smoothly when a functioning organizational structure, well supplied with resources, was in place. The greatest difficulty that my students experienced was finding the time to complete the activities in a way that corresponded to the original directions. It is clear that for Egyptian priests and other temple functionaries in service in the prescribed rotation, their occupation was full-time, day and night. This clearly explains not only our students' difficulties, but also why the more elaborate performances could not be kept up without a fully professionalized temple staff.

As regards the most elaborate and secret operations, a most important observation can be made. While strictly speaking there is no permissible audience apart from those who take part in it at a secure location, it must be observed that their activities required large community support. There has to be provision for the singular materials and ancillary services required for their operations; someone has to make the water table for the Osiris figures in the mystery or provide the bed on which the substitute king sleeps for the rite of renewal of power at the New Year. In the case of the students, assistance was often provided by their friends and parents.

While it is true that large Egyptian temples were provided with many such services in-house, the people who provided them were also members of the larger community. Even the creation of the space in which the mystery of Osiris was celebrated at Dendara must have involved large numbers of builders and craftsmen who were not directly involved in the higher priesthood. Indeed, as we have seen in Chapter 4, the building of the 'secret' royal tombs of New Kingdom pharaohs gave rise to a long-lived and vibrant community whose rhythms of life and work were specifically geared to the king's Osirian transformation. Although such mysteries excluded wider direct participation, they also required community support to work at all. And while most of the actors in the performances we have discussed in the last two chapters would have been selected for their position in the priestly and wider social hierarchy, some owed their selection to their own unique qualities, like the twins of Memphis and Djeho the dwarf. In much the same way our students were self-selected for certain roles.

Other performance projects

Following a conference presentation about the Triumph of Horus, I encountered a number of Egyptological colleagues who had been facing pedagogical challenges similar to my own. There followed a number of discussions about the benefits and drawbacks of such activities in the classroom and how they may be modified or improved. Of particular interest is *The Victory of Horus*, an adaptation of this specific material prepared under the direction of Peter Piccione at the Charleston College in South Carolina (Piccione 2000). Piccione's approach was to allow the students total control of the production, which also entailed a public performance, and then graded them on the results. A video of the production reveals a very different outcome to both Fairman's and the York production. From a pedagogical perspective both approaches are equally effective, but with different results. Piccione regards this work as a pilot project which he would like to develop further in the future.

Performing the site

The rising level of interest in such classroom activities at a university level can be seen to reflect the 'urge to perform at the site' noted by Hodder (2002), where a variety of agents – archaeologists, performance artists, tourists, theatre companies and commercial film crews – have descended on archaeological sites as performance venues or have recreated them with actors and sets for the purposes of 'infotainment'. As noted above, this phenomenon is particularly prevalent in made-for-TV educational programming, where no evocation of ancient or even pre-twentieth-century life is complete without a costumed re-enactment. While this phenomenon is not without its problems from an educational view, despite the retention of specialists on such projects, there are other, more serious problems with on-site performance. Chief among these is the appropriation of such sites by affluent visitors and academic specialists from the developed world, or by oppressive political regimes for purposes that have little to do with the material or cultural needs of many in the local population. The resulting alienation is not of course just the result of a few overt performances, but it can have tragic outcomes (Gillam 2004), as may be seen at present in Iraq.

In the case of the developed world, a greater degree of intellectual empowerment and a more interactive style of performance may help solve this problem. However, the overarching self-disconnect that comes from a notion of performance rooted in a specular medium has unexpected conse-

6. Learning about Past Performances in the Present

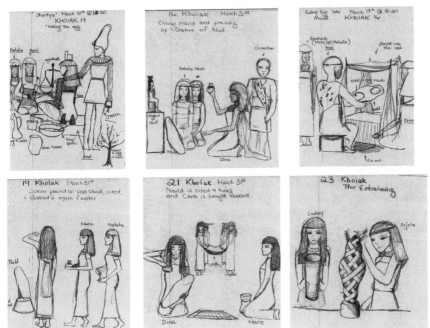

Fig. 12. Student's storyboard for making the egg and mummy of Sokar for the Mystery of Osiris in the month of Khoiak, York University, March 2004.

quences. Some of our most successful student performances arose out of the need to document the proceedings on video. Thus the Mystery of Osiris was coordinated not a by an Overseer of the Mystery, but by a movie director. One student acting in this capacity actually storyboarded the event.

Another unexpected outcome of this situation is the tendency of the participants to act against their roles instead of with them, a habit ingrained, if not suggested by, the practices of *Survivor* and other reality TV shows. (A similar process undermined the good intentions of the Channel 4 series *The Edwardian Country House*.) Although opening up the performance of the past could be an educational and broadening experience, it is difficult to shed the baggage of a century of mass-mediated interpretation. As for the mass-mediated form, it seems to be an inescapable part of who we are, whether there is a live audience or not.

While such problems are not absent from the developing world, other issues arise with regard to cultural, especially religious practices. Especially in the Middle East, Judaism, Christianity and Islam see themselves as superseding and in opposition to earlier beliefs and practices. Given these issues, acceptable on-site performance, especially as an educational tool for secondary school and university students, could involve creation of

147

soundscapes rather than use of the human body. The soundscape, which was developed by archaeologists in Europe, has been used to recreate past ecologies (as by prehistorians) (Mills 2000) or the more recent sacred landscape of sixteenth-century Slovenia, articulated by church bells (Mlekuz 2002). In Egypt, for example, sites suitable for such projects might be those with well-preserved settlement structures that are not so subject to intensive tourist traffic, but if such projects proved a success it might be possible to extend their range. The production of soundscapes need not involve expensive field equipment, although data from GIS surveys is highly desirable. As well as research it entails exploration of the area for appropriate sounds and allows its practitioners to explore a wider range of performances and space than we have done here. Along with more conventional performances and their documentation, such innovations as soundscape can extend both the educational and practical reach of archaeological research, raising new issues for the study of ancient cultures.

Conclusion

What Can Be Said about Egyptian Performances?

In the past six chapters we have examined evidence for performance activities in pharaonic Egypt. Although performance may be defined as any structured human activity taking place before witnesses, this study has tended to focus on 'dramatic' events that involve a measure of interaction between performer(s) and/or an audience. Such activities that we have some kind of record of are almost all embedded in holistic events called 'festivals', where they could be associated with other kinds of performances like music, dance or 'sports'. As almost all these records are products of an elite culture, the view these give of Egyptian performance is limited. Nevertheless, a number of observations may be made.

The performativity of performance

In my introductory remarks I noted the relationship of ideas about performance to the theory of performatives, or speech-acts. Thinkers interested in these issues have focussed on their use in the formation of authority structures in contemporary societies. While this approach certainly has some value in the analysis of Egyptian material, its most interesting application is to magic or 'effective' utterance, a category of speech-act of little or no interest to present-day theorists, but of central importance in Egyptian cultic and other religious activities. The role of magic in these activities reveals the fundamental connection between performance and performatives. A performance is always a re-presentation of something else that in some way makes it happen again. Sometimes the relationship between one and the other is less obvious than it could be. While the swearing-in of a president or a prime minister has a self-evident meaning, the relationship of a *pas de deux* in classical western ballet to sexual intercourse is not and may require some special knowledge of that particular performance tradition and the culture that produced it. In Egyptian sources, on the other hand, the meanings and purposes of these re-presentations may have been somewhat more subtle than they now appear from our detached, diachronic perspective.

There seems, however, to be little doubt that graphic and inscriptional re-presentations found on the walls of temples and tombs do have a performative character and were intended to generate as needed the activities recorded, in perpetuity. The necessarily idealizing nature of these materials makes their relationship to actual contingent performances problematic. Scripts in papyrus books may be of more assistance in imagining the performances, although they too are general in nature in that they generally function as guides to an activity rather than a detailed set of instructions. However, it must be remembered that most of the activities so recorded were specifically designed to be performative – they are ritual rather than theatre.

The tropes of performance: recombinant culture

In order better to understand the special character of Egyptian performances, we should step back from their stated or implied 'meanings', and regard them from a purely formal perspective. Some interesting patterns emerge in material from all periods, but they are most strongly marked in the later sources.

A basic motif is that of the inside and the outside, the public and the secret. This pattern can be discerned in the layout of the earliest ceremonial enclosures, the appearance of the king at the coronation or Sed Festival, the courtyard of Amenhotep III at the Luxor temple, and many other permutations such as the announcement of the divine birth or the sacred falcon at special shrines in Ptolemaic temples. The earlier method of revelation involved a public circuit of the structure from which the king appeared and gives rise to another basic unit in the vocabulary, circumambulation. This 'circuit of the walls' is first found in ceremonies connected with the king, Apis and Sokar, but is widely adapted in other contexts. The circuit may have given rise to the journey of a god out and to other temples and back, leading to the development of 'sailing' festivals and elaborate processions that required their own specially constructed sacred ways. On the other hand, a more static kind of appearance led to development of the 'viewing place', which can be understood as both an enclosed space surrounded by colonnades and a raised, shaded platform where the king or god does the viewing. Indeed, the act of seeing is of fundamental importance in Egyptian religion. Particularly during the New Kingdom, the pious left many records of their desire to see their god now and for all eternity. The god was supposed to notice the monuments left by particular kings on their processional ways and in the temples and respond to petitioners with oracular requests. In the most secret part of the cult, the officiant saw the face of the god when he uncovered it. These performances are specular, but the gaze travels in both directions.

Secret activities like the cult were also influenced by basic functioning of rituals. The cult of the god, which consisted of the ensoulment of an image and its revelation to the officiant, took place inside the innermost room of the temple, where the shrine containing the image was opened. The god could also be taken on procession within the temple in a circuit around the sanctuary itself, the 'mysterious corridor' of the later temples or up to and around the roof, as at the Dendara temple. The actual cult centred on the offering of various significant things to the image. While these could be food and drink that reverted to the priests themselves, they could also be objects of a significant transformative character, such as the eye of Horus or Maat, who embodied the cosmic order. The giving and receiving of these objects was not only the locus of the performative power of the ritual but re-presented a peculiarly Egyptian take on human sociability that encapsulated the most important of human relationships – those of parent and child, king and subject, on which those of the living and the ancestors and the human and the divine are modelled. Central to this particular performance is the concept that the givers give what they wish to receive themselves.

This play of reciprocity is based on a very clear notion of role-playing in which the officiants re-present gods or sometimes the king. In earlier documents like the Ramesseum Papyrus, the roles are taken by high-ranking men attached to the royal court. In later ones they are the preserve of different types of priest like the lector, the *sem* or the *fekety*. These assignments show that the roles are allocated first on the basis of social status, and second on expertise – in fact, one generally presupposes the other. Later documents also suggest that certain innate physical qualities, seen in the case of the Memphis twins and the dwarf Djeho, qualified certain individuals. The fact that women or girls playing the part of Isis and Nepthys had their character's name written on their arm emphasizes not only the performative character of their acts but also the highly self-conscious nature of the role-playing exercise. Apart from playing a particular role, the lector priest ('bearer of the festival-book' in Egyptian) or the Scribe of the God's Book often played the role of coordinator of activities. They not only directed a particular performance but recited or chanted the hymns or other utterances that accompanied an activity apart from 'lines' spoken by the actors.

The Ramesseum Dramatic Papyrus, as well as late texts like the rituals for the conservation of life, the Mystery of Osiris in the month of Khoiak and the confirmation of power in the New Year, also indicates the use of special objects or props in the performances. Sometimes they merely indicate their use but sometimes give very specific instructions about their manufacture and deployment. The Ramesseum Dramatic Papyrus tells us that an ox and a goose are to sacrificed to re-present the destruction of enemies, while the mystery text at Dendara gives precise measurements and materials for a canopied bedchamber for the mummy of Sokar. Such props are also deployed in special places like the House of Gold or the House of the God where the ancestors are buried at Esna. However, these places are not so much geographical as symbolic, as is the case in modern theatre.

In contrast to these symbolic, almost abstract qualities, later Egyptian

151

performances in particular place great emphasis on their concrete realization. The funeral of the Apis bull was made more vivid by the participation of freaks of nature such as the twins who re-presented the divine sisters Isis and Nepthys, and Djeho, the dwarf, whose dance demonstrated the rebirth of the divine child. Both the Confirmation of Royal Power in the New Year and the Enthronement of the Sacred Falcon involved the shedding of tears by a live falcon that re-presented Horus, thus manifesting the eye of Horus, the most powerful of protective amulets and signifier of sacred reciprocity. At Esna the potter's wheel of Khnum took an actual physical form and played a central role in performances of the mystery of the divine birth and the transmission of creative power to female beings. At Edfu the drama of Horus' triumph over his enemies ended with a live goose that embodied the hieroglyphic writing of the name of Geb, the heir of the gods. While such devices could be seen as a way of making a story more vivid to the audience, it must be remembered that at this period the audience might not always be present. This strategy of concrete visualization may have had a magical or performative function as well.

The same is also often true for the use of repetition, a fundamental characteristic of Egyptian performance. The Sed Festival is in itself a repetition of the coronation, to the point that it is often difficult to tell them apart. Individual performances are also marked by repetition and reduplication. The temple cult and Rite of the Opening of the Mouth consist largely of the constant offering of gifts to the statue accompanied by similar explanations of each act. *The Triumph of Horus* repeated the harpooning of the hippopotamus ten times and presented two different forms of the god. Many texts specify that an utterance be repeated a number of times for emphasis and/or effectiveness. The execration ritual at Mirgissa ensured its effectiveness through the smashing and immolation of hundreds of inscribed bowls and figures as well as the killing of a human being. But while repetition is integral to the performative act, it is also a structural necessity in processional performance because the stationary spectator cannot see what the actors are doing for the whole length of their route. Thus the bearers of the barque of Sokar repeated the cry 'Victory, victory, O Sovereign!' over and over again. We might also suppose that dancers and musicians who accompanied the Opet procession reprised their movements and routines over the course of the procession.

The repetition of many motifs or figures such as the tear of the falcon, the king's run, the raising of the Djed pillar, the making of model mummies, the Rite of the Opening of the Mouth or the execration of enemies, which can be seen in widely differing performance scripts from a number of periods, also suggests repetition attached not so much to the content or meaning of the activities but functioned as a vocabulary of performance, where acts are deployed and expanded beyond their original meaning and application. For example, the hourly watch over the Osiris mummies was perhaps grounded in the vigils over the dead mentioned in the Middle

Kingdom Coffin Texts. Such practices bring us from large-scale official performances to small-scale community celebrations.

As we have seen, there is little concrete evidence for such activities in Pharaonic Egypt, but they must have existed and no doubt represent the origin of many official performances. Music-making and dance, which played an important role in the large-scale festival, can be documented from the Predynastic Period, and professional musicians and dancers are known from the Old Kingdom onwards. Sometimes they are attached to royal or temple institutions and at other times to large private households. Sometimes they are described as masters ('stars' in Egyptian), implying skilled freelance professionals. The Middle Kingdom version of the myth of the divine birth has the three goddesses Isis, Nepthys and Heket masquerading as travelling musicians and midwives, suggesting that this was a normal configuration of occupations (Lichtheim, 1973, 220-1). Such persons may have played the part of the kites in private funerals or perhaps members of the deceased's household. Papyri from the Faiyum of the second century CE document a troupe of castanet dancers who could be hired to perform at weddings or other private celebrations (Westermann 1924).

Since the villagers at Deir el-Medina ran their own village cults, they also must have undertaken the appropriate rites and performances, like the ancestor ritual around their patron, King Amenhotep I. Indeed, the papyrus recording this ritual was found in the village. Other kinds of small-scale performances possibly connected with magic took place in private homes, as shown by the masks found at Kahun and Deir el-Medina, although how exactly they were used is unknown. From Deir el-Medina we also have evidence for less formal performances like the political demonstrations connected with the workmen's strikes during the 20th Dynasty. Such villages lacked obvious public spaces apart from the gates and forecourts of their small temples, but this role might have been filled by the riverbank, a place of social economic exchange alluded to in documents from Deir el-Medina (McDowell, 1999, 84). The Egyptian word for village court or assembly is *qenbet,* which means corner or crossroads (Erman and Grapow 1931, 53.5-54.17). Perhaps this was the venue for public storytelling, the existence of which is strongly implied by the existence of narratives that show many of the characteristics of oral literature. It may be that by the Graeco-Roman Period these performances had combined with Hellenistic mime to create a new, popular theatre. This theatre would have been influenced by Greek drama, which was generously subsidized by the Ptolemies, as were some large native temples.

Sports like running, archery or using a ball which featured in large-scale festivals no doubt existed on an informal level, and the enigmatic 'foreigner game' shown in Old Kingdom tombs might be a children's pastime, but then again, maybe not (Decker and Harb 1994, 628-9, pl. 249). The main character does wear a lion mask. The elaborate funeral ceremonies, brought to their highest pitch for the Apis bull, were also no doubt ultimately based on simple rites of passage for the non-elite which probably continued in a simpler form right through the life of Egyptian culture.

Drama and content

Victor Turner (1974) has suggested that social drama reflects a sequence of four actions: breach, crisis, corrective action and reintegration. This schema can be applied to both life situations and their re-presentation and is found in most aesthetic drama. It certainly forms the 'plot' of most Egyptian performances, although their dramatic character is often denied.

Both the daily cult ritual and the Rite of the Opening of the Mouth relate to the myth of Osiris and his son Horus, who performs his funeral rites and claims his inheritance. When the *sem* priest role-playing Horus cries out to his father in the Opening of the Mouth (see above, Chapter 4), it is an undoubtedly poignant moment, even for those of us who are not deeply aware of their story. The variant found in the Salt Papyrus, in the ritual for the preservation of life, which has Shu first murdering his son and then preserving and resurrecting his remains, is also a powerful scenario.

Although a convincing historical argument can be made for the origin of the Osiris myth in the royal funeral and mortuary cult (Griffiths 1980), it is surely the deep structure of the story that led to its widespread and effective use as a vehicle of performance and ritual. The Osiris myth was not, however, the only narrative that supplied this satisfying dramatic structure. At Esna we find a version of the myth of the destruction of humanity in which the creator runs and hides from the forces of chaos, which have to be defeated by his son Shu, who also ends by claiming his inheritance. This myth was vividly re-presented when, to represent these chaotic forces, a group of men surrounded the temple where the creator god's statue was hidden; an all-male night vigil was followed by a battle on a lake between the forces of chaos and order. It is not always certain who participated in such rites but classical sources suggest they did so enthusiastically, sometimes over-enthusiastically.

Audience and intention

The status and function of the audience remain a problem in any attempt to conceptualize, let alone recreate, Egyptian performances. Of course, in a ritual performance the audience and the actors can be one and the same. In the case of the cults in large temples of the New Kingdom and later periods, the main protagonists were joined by choirs of singers and musicians as well as servitors who moved the offerings. It has been suggested that there were also dancers (Spencer 2003), but they seem to have been confined largely to processional festivals or to the worship of Hathor in the forecourts or at the doors of the birth-house shrines. While processional festivals existed during the Old and Middle Kingdoms, they seem to have been greatly augmented after the beginning of the 18th Dynasty, when the acquisition of wealth through empire and trade created large urban centres where larger audiences came into being. Apart from development of 'public portals' to the gods like that at east Karnak, the importance of the temples to economic life would have ensured that many community members would have some connection with them. Even if the secret rites and performances that became increasingly popular in the later period were highly exclusive, their successful execution required the support of the whole community. Even if the mummies of Osiris were made in secret, many people must have been aware of, if not exactly privy to, what was going on. Participation by the elite in events like the Sed Festival or the New Kingdom processional feasts where they carried the barque of the god was not a totally open situation, but neither was admission to the viewing place of Dionysus in Athens. As noted above, it may be assumed that most large-scale festivals had small-scale equivalents. Documentary and archaeological evidence suggest that Graeco-Roman Egypt was filled with village shrines and temples run by local communities and that they were staging festivals long after the great temples had closed down.

*

There can be no doubt that performances existed in Ancient Egypt. Most of them are documented in the context of festivals or other religious events, not because of ideological coercion or 'belief' but because this way of thinking provided both a conceptual framework and an operating system for people who lived there, in much the same way as free-market capitalism does for us. By the same token, there was not really a market for performances, and some strategies for creating new performances seem to have failed – such as Akhenaten's experiment with abstract monotheism and a centralized ruler cult in the late 18th Dynasty. What is clear is that performances, both formal and informal, both social and magical, occupied a central position in Egyptian culture and society for the duration of its existence.

Bibliography

Adams, Barbara, 1974, *Ancient Hierakonpolis* (Warminster: Aris and Phillips).
———, 1987, *The Fort Cemetery at Hierakonpolis* (London: Kegan Paul).
———, 1995, *Ancient Nekhen: Garstang in the City of Hierakonpolis* (New Malden, Surrey: Sia).
———, 1999, 'Unprecedented Discoveries at Hierakonpolis', *Egyptian Archaeology* 15, pp. 29-31.
Aldred, Cyril, 1980, *Egyptian Art* (London: Thames and Hudson).
Allen, James P. 1988. *Genesis in Egypt: The Philosophy of Ancient Egyptian Creation Accounts* (New Haven: Yale Egyptological Seminar).
———, 1994, 'Reading a Pyramid' in C. Berger, G. Clerc and N. Grimal (eds), *Hommages à Jean Leclant* (Cairo: Institut Français d'archéologie orientale), pp. 5-28.
———, 2000, *Middle Egyptian: An Introduction to the Language and Culture of Hieroglyphs* (Cambridge: Cambridge University Press).
Alliot, M., 1954, *Le culte d'Horus à Edfou au tempes des Ptolémées* (Cairo: Institut Français d'archéologie orientale).
Alston, R., 2002, *The City in Roman and Byzantine Egypt* (London: Routledge).
Altenmüller, Hartwig, 1972, 'Djedpfeiler' in W. Helck and E. Otto (eds), *Lexikon der Ägyptologie* I (Wiesbaden: Harrassowitz), pp. 1100-5.
———, 1972, *Die Texte zum Begrabnisritual in den Pyramiden des Alten Reiches* (Wiesbaden: Harrassowitz).
———, 1977, 'Feste' in W. Helck and E. Otto (eds), *Lexikon der Ägyptologie* II (Wiesbaden: Harrassowitz), pp. 171-92.
———, 1978, 'Zur Bedeutung der Harfenlieder des alten Reiches', *Studien zur altägyptischen Kultur* 6, pp. 1-24.
Althusser, L., 1971, 'Ideology and Ideological State Apparatuses (Notes towards an Investigation)' in *Lenin and Philosophy and Other Essays*, trans. B. Brewster (London: New Left Books).
Angelo, T. and P. Cross, 1993, *Classroom Assessment Techniques: A Handbook for College Teachers*, 2nd ed (San Francisco: Bass).
Appleby, G.A., 2002, 'Roman Re-enactment: Fact and Fiction, the "Tunic Wars" ', pres. Annual Conference of the Theoretical Archaeology Group, Manchester, UK.
Arnold, D., 1974, *Der Tempel der Königs Mentuhotep von Deir el-Bahari* I (Mainz: Von Zabern).
———, 1979, *The Temple of Mentuhotep at Deir el-Bahari* (New York: Metropolitan Museum of Art).
———, 1981, *Der Tempel der Königs Mentuhotep von Deir el-Bahari* III (Mainz: Von Zabern).
———, 1999, *Temples of the Last Pharaohs* (New York: Oxford University Press).
Artaud, A., 1958, *Theatre and Its Double*, trans. M.C. Richards (New York: Grove Press).

Ashmore, Wendy and A. Bernard Knapp (eds), 1999, *Archaeologies of Landscape: Contemporary Perspectives* (Oxford: Blackwell).

Aubourg, E., and S. Cauville, 1998, 'En ce matin du 28 Décembre 47 ...' in H. Willems, W. Clarysse and A. Schoors (eds), *Egyptian Religion: The Last Thousand Years* (Leuven: Peeters), pp. 767-72.

Austin, J.L., 1962, *How to Do Things with Words: The William James Lectures Delivered at Harvard University in 1955* (Cambridge, MA: Harvard University Press).

Bagnall, R.S., 1993, *Egypt in Late Antiquity* (Princeton: Princeton University Press).

Baines, John, 1983, 'Literacy and Ancient Egyptian Society', *Man* NS 18, pp. 572-99.

——, 1985, 'Egyptian Twins', *Orientalia* 54, pp. 461-82.

——, 1988, 'Literacy, Social Organization and the Archaeological Record: The Case of Early Egypt' in B. Bender, J. Gledhill and M.T. Larsen (eds), *State and Society: The Emergence and Development of Social Hierarchy and Political Centralization* (London: Unwin Hyman), pp. 192-209.

——, 1989, 'Communication and Display: The Integration of Early Egyptian Art and Writing', *Antiquity* 63, pp. 471-82.

——, 1992, 'Merit by Proxy: The Biographies of the Dwarf Djeho and his Patron Tjaiharpta', *Journal of Egyptian Archeology* 78, pp. 241-57.

——, 1995, 'Origins of Egyptian Kingship' in D. O'Connor and D.P. Silverman (eds), *Ancient Egyptian Kingship* (Leiden: Brill Academic Publishers).

Baines, John, and J. Málek, 1980, *Atlas of Ancient Egypt* (New York: Facts on File).

Baines, John, and C.J. Eyre, 1983, 'Four Notes on Literacy', *Göttinger Miszellen* 61, pp. 65-96.

Bannerji, H., 1991, 'But Who Speaks for Us? Experience and Agency in Conventional Feminist Paradigms' in H. Bannerji, L. Carty, K. Dehli, S. Heald and K. McKenna, *Unsettling Relations: The University as a Site of Feminist Struggles* (Toronto: Women's Press), pp. 67-107.

Bard, Kathryn, 1994, *From Farmers to Pharaohs: Mortuary Evidence for the Rise of Complex Society in Ancient Egypt* (Sheffield: Sheffield Academic Press).

Barguet, P., 1962, *Le Papyrus N. 3176 (S) du Musée du Louvre* (Cairo: Institut Français d'archéologie orientale).

——, 1962a, *Le Temple d'Amon-Rê à Karnak* (Cairo: Institut Français d'archéologie orientale).

Barrett, John C., 2001, 'Agency, Duality of Structure and the Problem of the Archaeological Record' in I. Hodder (ed.), *Archaeological Theory Today* (Cambridge: Polity Press), pp. 141-61.

Barta, W., 1976, 'Der dramatische Ramesseumpapyrus als festrolle beim Hebsed-Ritual', *Studien zur altägyptischen Kultur* 4, pp. 31-43.

——, 1980, 'Köningskrönung' in W. Helck and E. Otto (eds), *Lexikon der Ägyptologie* IV (Wiesbaden: Harrassowitz), pp. 531-3.

——, 1981, *Die Bedeutung der Pyramidentexte für den verstorbenen König* (Berlin: MÄS 39).

Bell, Lanny, 1985, 'Luxor Temple and the Cult of the Royal *KA*', *Journal of Near Eastern Studies* 44, pp. 251-94.

Bender, Barbara, J. Gledhill and M.T. Larsen, 1988, *State and Society: The Emergence and Development of Social Hierarchy and Political Centralization* (London: Unwin Hyman).

Bibliography

Bennett, T., 1988, 'Museums and the People' in R. Lumley (ed.), *The Museum Time Machine: Putting Cultures on Display* (London: Routledge), pp. 63-85.

Berger, C., G. Clerc and N. Grimal (eds), 1994, *Hommages à Jean Leclant* (Cairo: Institut Français d'archéologie orientale).

Berlandini, Jocelyne, 1980, 'Meret' in W. Helck and E. Otto (eds), *Lexikon der Ägyptologie* IV (Wiesbaden: Harrassowitz), pp. 80-8.

Bieber, M., 1961, *The History of Greek and Roman Theater* (Princeton: Princeton University Press).

Blackman, A.M., and Michael Apted, 1953, *The Rock Tombs of Meir* V (London: Egypt Exploration Society).

Blackman, A.M., and H.W. Fairman, 1942, 'The Myth of Horus at Edfu II', *Journal of Egyptian Archaeology* 28, pp. 32-38.

———, 1944, 'The Myth of Horus at Edfu III', *Journal of Egyptian Archaeology* 30 pp. 5-22.

Blasius, A., and B.V. Schipper (eds), 2002, *Apokalyptik und Ägypten: Eine kritische Analyse der releventen Texte aus dem griechisch-romischen Ägypten* (Louvain: Peeters).

Bleeker, C.J., 1967, *Egyptian Festivals: Enactments of Religious Renewal* (Leiden: Brill Academic Publishers).

Borghouts, J.F., 1980, 'The "Hot One" in Ostracon Deir el Medina 1265', *Göttinger Miszellen* 38, pp. 21-6.

Bosse-Griffiths, Kate, 1977, 'A Beset Amulet from the Amarna Period', *Journal of Egyptian Archaeology* 63, pp. 98-106.

Bourdieu, Pierre, 1970, 'The Berber House or the World Reversed', *Social Science Information* 9, pp. 151-70; repr. in J. Thomas (ed.), *Interpretive Archaeology: A Reader* (London: Leicester University Press, 2000), pp. 493-509.

———, 1990, *The Logic of Practice*, trans. R. Nice (Stanford: Stanford University Press).

Bowman, A.K., 1986, *Egypt after the Pharaohs* (Berkeley: University of California Press).

Breasted, J.H., 1901, 'The Theology of a Memphite Priest', *Zeitschrift für Ägyptische Sprache* 39 pp. 39-54; pls I-II.

Brecht, B., 1964, *Brecht on Theatre* ed. J. Willett (New York: Hill and Wang).

Brugsch, H., 1884, 'Der Apis-Kreis aus der Zeiten der Ptolemäer nach den hieroglyphischen und demotischen Weihinschriften des Serapeums von Memphis', *Zeitschrift für Ägyptische Sprache* 22, pp. 110-39.

Brunner, H., 1964, *Die Geburt des Göttkönigs* (Wiesbaden: Harrassowitz).

Brunton, Guy, 1927-8, *Qau and Badari* I-II (London: British School of Archaeology in Egypt).

Budge, E.A.W., 1929, *The Rosetta Stone in the British Museum* (London: Religious Tract Society).

Burgh, T., 2002, 'Determining Minimum Performance Space in Ancient Cultic Performance', pres. Symposium of Performance Archaeology Annual Meeting, Society of American Archaeology, Denver, CO.

Burkert, W., 1985, *Greek Religion*, trans. J. Raffan (Cambridge, MA: Harvard University Press).

Butler, J., 1991, *Gender Trouble: Feminism and the Subversion of Identity* (New York: Routledge).

———, 1993, *Bodies That Matter* (New York: Routledge).

———, 1997, *Excitable Speech: A Politics of the Performative* (New York: Routledge).

Butzer, Karl W., 1976, *Early Hydraulic Civilization in Egypt* (Chicago: University of Chicago Press).
Cabrol, A., 2001, *Les voies processionnelles de Thèbes* (Leuven: Peeters).
Caminos, R., 1958, *The Chronicle of Prince Osorkon* (Rome: Pontificum Institutum Biblicum).
——, 1974, *Late Egyptian Miscellanies* (Oxford: Cumberledge).
Caso, David S., and Sarah L. Finkelberg, 1999, 'Psychoeducational Drama: An Improvisational Approach to Outreach', *Journal of College Student Development* 40(1), pp. 89-91.
Cauville, S., 1987, *Essai sur la théologie du Temple d'Horus à Edfou* (Cairo: Institut Français d'archéologie orientale).
——, 1988, 'Les mystères d'Osiris à Dendara: Interpretation des chapelles osiriennes', *Bulletin de la Société française d'égyptologie* 112, pp. 23-36.
——, 1990, *Le Temple de Dendara: Guide archéologique* (Cairo: Institut Français d'archéologie orientale).
——, 1997a, *Le zodiaque d'Osiris* (Louvain: Peeters).
——, 1997b, *Le temple de Dendara: Les chapelles osiriennes (Dendara X)* (Cairo: Institut Français d'archéologie orientale).
——, 1997c, *Dendara: Les chapelles osiriennes. Transcription et traduction* (Cairo: Institut Français d'archéologie orientale).
——, 1997d, *Dendara: Les chapelles osiriennes. Commentaire* (Cairo: Institut Français d'archéologie orientale).
Černý, J., 1927, 'Le culte d'Amenophis Ier chez les ouvriers de la nécropole Thébaine', *Bulletin de l'Institut Français d'archéologie orientale du Caire* 27, pp. 159-203.
——, 1949, *Répertoire onomastique de Deir el-Médineh* (Cairo: Institut Français d'archéologie orientale).
——, 1962, 'Egyptian Oracles' in R. Parker, *A Saite Oracle Papyrus from Thebes in the Brooklyn Museum (Papyrus Brooklyn 47.218.3)* (Providence: Brown University Press), pp. 35-48.
Certeau, Michel de, 1984, *The Practice of Everyday Life*, trans. S. Rendall (Berkeley: University of California Press).
Chassinat, É., 1901, 'Texts provenant du Sérapéum de Memphis', *Recueil de traveaux relatifs à l'archéologie égyptiennes et assyriennes* 23, pp. 70-90.
——, 1934, *Le Temple d'Edfou* XIII (Cairo: Institut Français d'archéologie orientale).
——, 1966, *Le Mystère d'Osiris au mois de Khoiak* (Cairo: Institut Français d'archéologie orientale).
Chomsky, N., 1968, *Language and the Mind* (New York: Jovanovich).
Clarysse, W., A. Schoors and H. Willems (eds), 1998, *Egyptian Religion: The Last Thousand Years. Studies Dedicated to the Memory of Jan Quaegebeur* (Louvain: Peeters).
Cohen, T., 2004, 'Contrafactual History Assignment', *CORE: York's Newsletter on University Teaching* 13(2), p. 7.
Corteggiani, J-P., 1979, 'Une stèle Héliopolitaine d'époque Saïte' in J. Vercoutter (ed.), *Hommages à la mémoire de Serge Sauneron* I (Cairo: Institut Français d'archéologie orientale).
Coulon, L., F. Leclère and S. Marchand, 1995, 'Catacombs osiriennes de Ptolémée IV à Karnak', *Cahiers de Karnak* 10, pp. 205-37.
Cumming, B., 1982, *Egyptian Historical Records of the Late Eighteenth Dynasty* I (Warminster: Aris and Phillips).

Bibliography

D'Amato, Rik Carl, and Raymond E. Dean, 1988, 'Psychodrama Research – Therapy and Theory: A Critical Analysis for an Arrested Modality', *Psychology in the Schools* 25, pp. 305-14.

Daumas, M., 1968, 'Les propylées du temple d'Hathor à Philae de le culte de la déese', *Zeitschrift für Ägyptische Sprache* 95, pp. 1-17.

——, 1977, 'Geburtshaus' in W. Helck and E. Otto (eds), *Lexikon der Ägyptologie* II (Wiesbaden: Harrassowitz), pp. 462-76.

David, Rosalie, 1981, *A Guide to Religious Ritual at Abydos* (Warminster: Aris and Phillips).

——, 1991, 'Religious Practices in a Pyramid Workmen's Town of the Twelfth Dynasty', *Bulletin of the Australian Centre for Egyptology* 2, pp. 33-40.

Davies, Benedict, 1992, *Egyptian Historical Records of the Later Eighteenth Dynasty* IV (Warminster: Aris and Phillips).

——, 1994, *Egyptian Historical Records of the Later Eighteenth Dynasty* V (Warminster: Aris and Phillips).

Davies, N. de G., 1902, *The Rock Tombs of Deir el Gebrâwi* II (London: Egypt Exploration Fund).

——, 1905, *The Rock Tombs of El Amarna* II (London: Egypt Exploration Fund).

——, 1920, *The Tomb of Antefoker, Vizier of Sesostris I, and of his Wife Senet* (London: Egypt Exploration Society).

Davis, Whitney, 1992, *Masking the Blow: The Scene of Representation in Late Prehistoric Egyptian Art* (Berkeley: University of California Press).

Decker, W., 1992, *Sports and Games in Ancient Egypt*, trans. A. Guttman (New Haven: Yale University Press).

Decker, W., and M. Harb, 1994, *Bildatlas zum Sport im Alten Ägypten* (Leiden: Brill Academic Publishers).

Deleuze, G., and F. Guattari, 1983, *Anti-Oedipus: Capitalism and Schizophrenia*, trans. R. Hurley, M. Seem and H.R. Lane (Minneapolis: University of Minnesota Press).

Derchain, P., 1965, *Le papyrus Salt 825 (BM 10051): Rituel pour la conservation de la vie en Égypte* (Brussels: Académie royale de Belgie).

——, 1970, 'La reception de Sinouhé a la cour de Sésostris I', *Revue d'Égyptologie* 22, pp. 79-83.

——, 1981, 'Rituels Égytiens' in Yves Bonnefoy (ed.), *Dictionnaire des mythologies et des religions des sociétés traditionelles et du monde antique* (Paris: Flammarion).

——, 1989, 'Á propos de performativité: Pensers anciens et articles récents', *Göttinger Miszellen* 110, pp. 13-18.

Docker, J., 1994, *Postmodernism and Popular Culture* (Cambridge: Cambridge University Press).

Dodson, A., 1995, 'Of Bulls and Princes: The Early Years of the Serapeum at Sakkara', *KMT: A Modern Journal of Ancient Egypt* 6(1), pp. 18-32.

Dreyer, Günter, 1998, *Umm-el-Qaab I: Das prädynastische Königsgrab U-j und seine frühen Schriftzeugnisse* (Mainz: Phillip von Zabern).

Drioton, Étienne, 1957, 'Le théâtre égyptien', *Pages d'Égyptologie* (Cairo: Revue du Caire).

Duplessis, Jean M. and L.M. Lochner, 1981, 'The Effects of Group Psychotherapy on the Adjustment of Four 12-Year-Old Boys with Learning and Behaviour Problems', *Journal of Learning Disabilities* 14(4), pp. 209-12.

DuQuesne, T., 1995, 'Openers of the Paths: Canid Psychopomps', *Journal of Ancient Civilizations* 10, pp. 41-53.

Eaton-Krauß, Marianne, 1984, *Representations of Statuary in Private Tombs of the Old Kingdom* (Wiesbaden: Harrassowitz).

Edel, E., 1970, *Das Akazienhaus und sein Rolle in den Begräbnisriten* (Berlin: Hessling).

Edgerton, W.F., 1951, 'The Strikes in Ramses III's Twenty-ninth Year', *Journal of Near Eastern Studies* 10, pp. 137-45.

Eide, T., T. Hägg, R.H. Pierce and L. Török, 1994, *Fontes Historiae Nubiorum* I (Bergen: University of Bergen Press).

Emery, Walter B., 1938, *The Tomb of Hemaka* (Cairo: Government Press).

———, 1958, *Great Tombs of the First Dynasty* III (London: Egypt Exploration Society).

———, 1961, *Archaic Egypt* (Harmondsworth, UK: Penguin).

———, 1962, *A Funerary Repast in an Egyptian Tomb of the Archaic Period* (Leiden: Nederlands Instituut voor het Nabije Oosten).

Epigraphic Survey, 1940, *Festival Scenes of Ramses III: Medinet Habu* IV (Chicago: Oriental Institute).

———, 1980, *The Tomb of Kheruef* (Chicago: Oriental Institute).

———, 1994, *The Festival Procession of Opet in the Colonnade Hall: Reliefs and Inscriptions at Luxor Temple* I (Chicago: Oriental Institute).

Erichsen, W., and S. Schott, 1954, *Fragmente memphitischer Theologie in demotischer Schrift. (Pap. demot. Berlin 13603)* in *Akademie der Wissenchaften und der Literatur: Abhandlung der Geistes und Sozialwissenschaftlichen Klasse* 7 (Wiesbaden: Steiner).

Erman, Adolf, 1911, 'Ein Denkmal memphitischer Theologie'; repr. in A. Burkardt and W.F. Reineke (eds), *Adolf Erman: Akademieschriften (1880-1928)* II (Leipzig: Zentralantiquariat DDR, 1986), pp. 1-35.

Erman, Adolf, and Hermann Grapow (eds), 1955, *Wörterbuch der Aegyptischen Sprache* I-V (Berlin: Akademie Verlag).

Eyre, C.J., 2002, *The Cannibal Hymn: A Cultural and Literary Study* (Liverpool: Liverpool University Press).

Fairman, H.W., 1935, 'The Myth of Horus at Edfu I', *Journal of Egyptian Archaeology* 21, pp. 26-36.

———, 1973, *The Triumph of Horus* (London: Batsford).

Faulkner, R.O., 1936, 'The Bremner-Rhind Papyrus I', *Journal of Egyptian Archaeology* 22, pp. 121-32.

———, 1938, 'The Bremner-Rhind Papyrus II', *Journal of Egyptian Archaeology* 23, pp. 10-14.

———, 1938a, 'The Bremner-Rhind Papyrus III', *Journal of Egyptian Archaeology* 23, pp. 166-75.

———, 1939, 'The Bremner-Rhind Papyrus IV', *Journal of Egyptian Archaeology* 25, pp. 41-53.

———, 1969, *The Ancient Egyptian Pyramid Texts* (Oxford: Clarendon).

———, 1973, *The Ancient Egyptian Coffin Texts* I (Warminster: Aris and Phillips).

Felber, H., 2002, 'Die demotische Chronik' in A. Blasius and B.V. Schipper (eds), *Apokalyptik und Ägypten: Eine kritische Analyse der relevanten Texte aus dem griechisch-romischen Ägypten* (Louvain: Peeters), pp. 65-111.

Fischer, H.G., 1959, 'An Example of Memphite Influence in a Theban Stela of the 11th Dynasty', *Artibus Asiae* 22, pp. 240-52.

———, 1968, *Dendara in the Third Millennium BC* (Locust Valley, NY: J.J. Augustin).

Bibliography

Fischer-Elfert, H.W., 1998, *Die Vision von der Statue in Stein* (Heidelberg: Winter).

Fiske, J., 1989, *Understanding Popular Culture* (Boston: Unwin Hyman).

Foucault, M., 1977, *Discipline and Punish: The Birth of the Prison* (London: Allen Lane).

Frandsen, P., 1990, 'Editing Reality: The Turin Strike Papyrus', in S. Groll (ed.), *Studies in Egyptology Presented to Miriam Lichtheim* I (Jerusalem: Hebrew University).

Frankfort, Henri, 1948, *Kingship and the Gods* (Chicago: Oriental Institute).

Frankfurter, D., 1998, *Religion in Roman Egypt* (Princeton: Princeton University Press).

Freed, R., Y. Markowitz and S. D'Auria (eds), 1999, *Pharaohs of the Sun* (Boston: Museum of Fine Arts).

Friedman, Florence, 1995, 'The Underground Relief Panels of King Djoser at the Step Pyramid Complex', *Journal of the American Research Center in Egypt* 32, pp. 1-42.

Friedman, Renée, 1996, 'The Ceremonial Centre at Hierakonpolis Locality 29A' in Jeffrey Spencer (ed.), *Aspects of Early Egypt* (London: British Museum Publications), pp. 16-35.

Friedman, Renée, and Barbara Adams (eds), 1992, *The Followers of Horus: Studies Dedicated to Michael Allen Hoffman* (Oxford: Oxbow Books).

Gaballa, G.A. and K.A Kitchen, 1969, 'The Festival of Sokar', *Orientalia* 38, pp. 1-76.

Galvin, Marianne, 1984, 'The Hereditary Status of the Titles of the Cult of Hathor', *Journal of Egyptian Archaeology* 70, pp. 42-9.

Gardiner, Alan H., 1915, *The Tomb of Amenemhet* (London: Egypt Exploration Fund).

———, 1935, *Hieratic Papyri in the British Museum, Third Series: Chester Beatty Gift* (London: British Museum).

———, 1938, 'The House of Life', *Journal of Egyptian Archeology* 24, pp. 157-79.

———, 1944, 'Horus the Behdetite', *Journal of Egyptian Archaeology* 30, pp. 23-63.

———, 1947, *Ancient Egyptian Onomastica* I-II (Oxford: Oxford University Press).

———, 1953, 'The Coronation of King Haremhab', *Journal of Egyptian Archaeology* 39, pp. 13-31.

———, 1955, 'A Unique Funerary Liturgy', *Journal of Egyptian Archaeology* 41, pp. 9-17.

———, 1957, *Egyptian Grammar*, 3rd ed. (Oxford: Griffith Institute).

Garfinkel, Y., 2001, 'Dancing or Fighting: A Recently Discovered Predynastic Scene from Abydos, Egypt', *Cambridge Archaeological Journal* 11, pp. 241-54.

Gaudard, F., 1999, 'A New Dramatic Version of the Horus and Seth Myth', pres. Annual Meeting of the American Research Center in Egypt, Chicago, IL.

Geertz, C., 1983, 'Blurred Genres: The Refiguration of Social Thought', in *Local Knowledge: Further Essays in Interpretive Anthropology* (New York: Basic Books).

Geßler-Löhr, B., 1983, *Die heiligen Seen ägyptischer Tempel: ein Beitrag zur Deutung sakraler Baukunst im alten Ägypten* (Hildesheim: Gerstenberg).

Gillam, R., 1994, 'Past Performances: Actors in Museums Teach Us Something about Ourselves', *Theatrum* 37 (February/March), pp. 19-24.

———, 1995, 'Priestesses of Hathor: Their Function, Decline and Disappearance', *Journal of the American Research Center in Egypt* 32, pp. 211-37.

————, 2000, 'Re-staging the Triumph of Horus: Hunting the Hippo in Toronto', *KMT: A Modern Journal of Ancient Egypt* 11(1), pp. 72-83.

————, 2002, 'Presentation and Re-presentation: The Site of Drama or Performance?', *Archaeology and Performance* http://traumwerk.stanford.edu:3455/ArchaeologyPerformance/19

————, 2002a, 'The Mysteries of Osiris', *Positive Pedagogy* 2(2) http://www.mcmaster.ca/ cll/postped/index.htm.

————, 2004, 'Site Specific Texts: Embodied Performances in the Written Record of the Late Period in Egypt in the Past and the Present', TAG 2002, Papers, Archaeology and Performance, Stanford University http://traumwerk.stanford.edu:3455/ArchaeologyPerformance/19

Gitton, M., 1984, *Les divines épouses de la 18e dynastie* (Paris: Université de Bescançon).

Gitton, M. and J. Leclant, 1977, 'Gottesgemahlin' in W. Helck and E. Otto (eds), *Lexikon der Ägyptologie* II (Wiesbaden: Harrassowitz), pp. 792-812.

Goelet, O., 2001, 'The Anaphoric Style in Egyptian Hymnody', *Journal of the Society for the Study of Egyptian Antiquities* 28, pp. 75-89.

Gohary, J., 1992, *Akhenaten's Sed-festival at Karnak* (London: Kegan Paul).

Goldwasser, O., 1995, *From Icon to Metaphor: Studies in the Semiotics of Hieroglyphs* (Fribourg: Vandenhoek and Göttingen).

Gomaà, F., 1973, *Chaemwese: Sohn Ramses II und Hoherpriester von Memphis* (Wiesbaden: Harrassowitz).

Goody, Jack, 1975, *Literature in Traditional Societies* (Cambridge: Cambridge University Press).

Goyon, Jean-Claude, 1972, *Rituels funéraires de l'ancienne Égypte* (Paris: Éditions du Cerf).

————, 1972a, *Confirmation du pouvoir royal au nouvel an* (Cairo: Institut Français d'archéologie orientale).

Grapow, H., 1936, *Sprachliche und schriftliche Formung ägyptischer Texte* (Glückstadt: J.J. Augustin).

Grdseloff, Bernhard, 1941, *Das Ägyptische Reingungszelt* (Cairo: Institut Français d'archéologie orientale).

Grieshammer, R., 1972, 'Atfih' in W. Helck and E. Otto (eds), *Lexikon der Ägyptologie* I (Wiesbaden: Harrassowitz), p. 519.

Griffiths, J. Gwyn, 1970, *Plutarch's De Iside et Osiride* (Cambridge: University of Wales Press).

————, 1977, 'Hakerfest' in W. Helck and E. Otto (eds), *Lexikon der Ägyptologie* II (Wiesbaden: Harrassowitz), pp. 929-30.

————, 1980, *The Origins of Osiris and His Cult* (Leiden: Brill Academic Publishers).

Gülden, S.A., 2001, *Die hieratischen Texte des P. Berlin 3049* (Wiesbaden: Harrassowitz).

Habachi, Labib, 1963, 'King Nebheptere Mentuhotep: His Monuments, Place in History, Deification and Unusual Representations in the Form of Gods', *Mitteilungen des Deutschen archäologisches Instituts Abteilung Kairo* 19, pp. 16-52.

Hamiliakas, Y., M. Pluciennik and Sarah Tarlow (eds), 2002, *Thinking Through the Body: Archaeologies of Corporality* (New York: Kluwer/Plenum).

————, 2002, 'Thinking Through the Body' in Y. Hamiliakas, M. Pluciennik and S. Tarlow (eds), *Thinking Through the Body: Archaeologies of Corporality* (New York: Kluwer/Plenum), pp. 1-21.

Bibliography

Harpur, Yvonne, 1987, *Decoration in Egyptian Tombs of the Old Kingdom* (London: Kegan Paul).

Hayes, W.C., 1951, 'Inscriptions from the Palace of Amenhotep III', *Journal of Near Eastern Studies* 10, pp. 35-40, 82-104, 156-83, 321-42.

———, 1953, *The Scepter of Egypt* I (New York: Metropolitan Museum of Art).

———, 1973, 'Egypt: Internal Affairs from Tuthmosis I to the Death of Amenophis III' in I.E.S. Edwards, C.J. Gadd, N.G.L. Hammond and E. Sollberger (eds), *Cambridge Ancient History*, 3rd edn, vol. II, part 1: *History of the Middle East and Aegean Region c. 1800-1380 BC* (Cambridge: Cambridge University Press).

Hazzard, R., 2000, *Imagination of a Monarchy: Studies in Ptolemaic Propaganda* (Toronto: University of Toronto Press).

Helck, W., 1950, '$R^c pt$ auf dem Thron des *Gb*', *Orientalia* 19, pp. 416-34.

———, 1954, *Untersuchungen zu den Beamtentiteln des Ägyptischen alten Reiches* (Glückstadt: J.J. Augustin).

———, 1985, 'Tekenu' in W. Helck and W. Westendorf (eds), *Lexikon der Ägyptologie* (Wiesbaden: Harrassowitz), pp. 308-9.

———, 1987, *Untersuchungen zur Thinitenzeit* (Wiesbaden: Harrassowitz).

Hodder, I., 1991, 'Archaeological Theory in Contemporary European Societies: The Emergence of Contemporary Traditions' in *Archaeological Theory in Europe: The Last Three Decades* (London: Routledge), pp. 1-24.

———, 1992, *Theory and Practice in Archaeology* (London: Routledge).

——— (ed.), 2001, *Archaeological Theory Today* (Cambridge: Polity Press).

———, 2002, 'Performances at Archaeological Sites', *Archaeology and Performance* http://traumwerk.stanford.edu:3455/ArchaeologyPerformance/19

Hoffman, Michael A., 1979, *Egypt before the Pharaohs* (New York: Knopf).

Hoffman, Valerie, 1995, *Sufism, Mystics and Saints in Modern Egypt* (Columbia: University of South Carolina).

Hölscher, U., 1934, *The Excavation of Medinet Habu* I: *General Plans and Views* (Chicago: Oriental Institute).

———, 1941, *The Excavation at Medinet Habu* I: *The Mortuary Temple of Ramses III*, trans. Mrs K. Seele (Chicago: Oriental Institute).

Huß, W., 2001, *Ägypten in hellenistischer Zeit* (Munich: Beck).

Ikram, Salima and Aidan Dodson, 1998, *The Mummy in Ancient Egypt* (London: Thames and Hudson).

Ikram, Salima, 2000, 'Animal Mummies and Experimental Archaeology', pres. Annual Meeting of the American Research Center in Egypt, Berkeley, CA.

Ingold, T., 1993, 'The Temporality of Landscape', *World Archaeology* 25, pp. 152-74; repr. in J. Thomas (ed.), *Interpretive Archaeology: A Reader* (London: Leicester University Press, 2000), pp. 510-30.

Jameson, F., 1983, 'Pleasure: A Political Issue', repr. in *The Ideologies of Theory: Essays 1971-1986* II (Minneapolis: University of Minnesota Press, 1988).

Jasen, P., 1989, 'In Pursuit of Human Values (or Laugh When You Say That): The Student Crtique of the Arts Curriculum in the 1960s' in P. Axelrod and J.G. Reid (eds), *Youth, University and Canadian Society* (Kingston: McGill-Queens University Press), pp. 217-47.

Johnson, J., 1998, 'Women, Wealth and Work in Egyptian Society in the Ptolemaic Period' in W. Clarysse, A. Schoors and H. Willems (eds), *Egyptian Religion: The Last Thousand Years. Studies Dedicated to the Memory of Jan Quaegebeur* (Louvain: Peeters), pp. 1393-1421.

Jones, M., and A. Milward Jones, 1982, 'The Apis House Project at Mit Rahinah:

First Season, 1982', *Journal of the American Research Center in Egypt* 19, pp. 51-8.

——, 1983, 'The Apis House Project at Mit Rahinah: Preliminary Report of the Second and Third Seasons, 1982-1983', *Journal of the American Research Center in Egypt* 20, pp. 33-45.

——, 1988, 'The Apis House Project at Mit Rahinah: Preliminary Report on the Sixth Season, 1986', *Journal of the American Research Center in Egypt* 25, pp. 105-16.

Junge, F., 1973, 'Zur Felhdatierung des sog. Denkmal memphitischer Theologie', *Mitteilungen des Deutschen archäologisches Instituts Abteilung Kairo* 29, pp. 195-204.

Junker, H., 1911, *Die Stundenwachen in den Osirismysterien* (Vienna: Hölder).

——, 1941, *Die Politische Lehre von Memphis* (Berlin: Akademie der Wissenschaften).

——, 1947, *Grabungen auf dem Friedhof des alten Reiches bei den Pyramiden von Gîza* VIII (Vienna: Hölder-Pichler-Tempslof).

——, 1949, 'Zu den Titeln des *Wr-nww*', *Annales du Service des Service des Antiquités d'Égypte* 49, pp. 207-15.

Kaiser, Werner, 1969, 'Zu den Königlichen Talbezirken der 1 und 2 Dynastie in Abydos und zur Baugeschichte des Djoser-Grabmals', *Mitteilungen des Deutschen archäologisches Instituts Abteilung Kairo* 25, pp. 1-21.

——, 1971, 'Die kleine Hebseddarstellung im Sonnenheiligtum des Neuserre', *Aufsätze zum 70. Geburtstag von Herbert Ricke. Beiträge zur ägyptischen Bauforschung und Altertumskunde* XII (Wiesbaden: Steiner), pp. 87-105.

Kákosy, L., 1980a, 'Ischedbaum' in W. Helck and E. Otto (eds), *Lexikon der Ägyptologie* III (Wiesbaden: Harrassowitz), pp. 182-3.

——, 1980b, 'Mnevis' in W. Helck and E. Otto (eds), *Lexikon der Ägyptologie* IV (Wiesbaden: Harrassowitz), pp. 165-7.

Kanawati, N., 1977, *The Egyptian Administration in the Old Kingdom: Evidence for its Economic Decline* (Warminster: Aris and Phillips).

Kaplony, P., 1963, *Die Inschriften der ägyptischen Frühzeit* (Wiesbaden: Harrassowitz).

Kemp, Barry, 1972, 'Abydos' in W. Helck and E. Otto (eds), *Lexikon der Ägyptologie* I (Wiesbaden: Harrassowitz), pp. 28-41.

——, 1976, 'The Window of Appearance at el Amarna and the Basic Structure of the City', *Journal of Egyptian Archaeology* 62, pp. 81-99.

——, 1989, *Ancient Egypt: Anatomy of a Civilization* (London: Routledge).

Kessler, D., 1985, 'Tierkult' in W. Helck and W. Westendorf (eds), *Lexikon der Ägyptologie* VI (Wiesbaden: Harrassowitz), pp. 571-87.

Kitchen, K.A., 1973, *The Third Intermediate Period in Egypt (1100-650 BC)* (Warminster: Aris and Phillips).

Koenig, Yvan, 1990, 'Les textes d'envoûtement de Mirgissa', *Revue d'Égyptologie* 41, pp. 101-25.

Königliche Museen zu Berlin, general Verwaltung, 1901, *Hieratische Papyrus auf den Königlichen Museen zu Berlin* I (Leipzig: Hinrichs).

Kozloff, A., B. Bryan and L. Berman, 1992, *Egypt's Dazzling Sun: Amenhotep III and his World* (Cleveland: Cleveland Museum of Art).

Kruchten, J-M., 1986, *Le grand texte oraculaire de Djéhutimose, intendant du domaine d'Amon sous le pontificat de Pinedjem II* (Bruxelles: Fondation reine Elisabeth).

Bibliography

Lacovara, P., 1999, 'The City of Amarna' in R. Freed, Y. Markowitz and S. D'Auria (eds), *Pharaohs of the Sun* (Boston: Museum of Fine Arts), pp. 61-71.

Lauer, J-P., 1936, *La pyramide à degrés: L'architecture* I (Cairo: Institut Français d'archéologie orientale).

———, 1962, *Histoire monumentale d'Égypte* I: *Les pyramides à degrés (IIIe Dynastie)* (Cairo: Institut Français d'archéologie orientale).

———, 1999, 'The Step Pyramid Precinct of King Djoser' in John P. O'Neill (ed.), *Egyptian Art in the Age of the Pyramids* (New York: Metropolitan Museum of Art) pp. 13-19.

Lauer, J-P., and C. Picard, 1955, *Les statues ptolémaïques du Serapieion de Memphis* (Paris: Presses Universitaires).

Leahy, Anthony, 1977, 'The Osiris "Bed" Reconsidered', *Orientalia* NS 46, pp. 424-34.

———, 1989, 'A Protective Measure at Abydos in the Thirteenth Dynasty', *Journal of Egyptian Archaeology* 75, pp. 41-60.

Leclant, J., 1965, *Recherches sur les monuments Thébains de la XXVe Dynastie dite éthiopienne* (Cairo: Institut Français d'archéologie orientale).

———, 1977, 'Gottesgemahlin' in W. Helck and E. Otto (eds), *Lexikon der Ägyptologie* II (Wiesbaden: Harrassowitz), pp. 792-812.

Lehner, Mark, 1985, *The Pyramid Tomb of Hetep-heres and the Satellite Pyramid of Khufu* (Mainz: Von Zabern).

———, 1997, *The Complete Pyramids* (London: Thames and Hudson).

Leprohon, R.J., 1978, 'The Personnel of the Middle Kingdom Funerary Stelae', *Journal of the American Research Center in Egypt* 15, pp. 33-8.

———, forthcoming, 'Ritual Drama in Ancient Egypt' in M. Miller and E. Csapo (eds), *The Origins of Theatre in Ancient Greece and Beyond: From Ritual to Drama* (Cambridge: Cambridge University Press).

Lesko, L, 1991, 'Ancient Egyptian Cosmogonies and Cosmology' in Byron Shafer (ed.), *Religion in Ancient Egypt* (Ithaca, NY: Cornell University Press), pp. 88-122.

Letellier, B., 1977, 'Gründungsbeigabe' in W. Helck and E Otto (eds), *Lexikon der Ägyptologie* II (Wiesbaden: Harrassowitz), pp. 906-12.

Lichtheim, Miriam, 1945, 'The Songs of the Harpers', *Journal of Near Eastern Studies* 4, pp. 178-212.

———, 1973, *Ancient Egyptian Literature* I: *The Old and Middle Kingdoms* (Berkeley: University of California Press).

———, 1976, *Ancient Egyptian Literature* II: *The New Kingdom* (Berkeley: University of California Press).

———, 1980, *Ancient Egyptian Literature* III: *The New Kingdom* (Berkeley: University of California Press).

———, 1988, *Ancient Egyptian Autobiographies Chiefly of the Middle Kingdom* (Freiburg: Universitatsverlag; Göttingen: Vandenhoeck und Ruprecht).

Lucas, A. and J.R. Harris, 1962, *Ancient Egyptian Materials and Industries* (London: Edward Arnold).

Manniche, L., 1991, *Music and Musicians in Ancient Egypt* (London: British Museum).

Manuelian, P. Der, 1994, *Living in the Past: Studies in Archaism of the Egyptian Twenty-Sixth Dynasty* (London: Kegan Paul).

Marshall, K. (ed.), 1993, *Rediscovering the Muses: Women's Musical Traditions* (Boston: Northeastern University Press).

Martin, K., 1984, 'Sedfest' in W. Helck and W. Westendorf (eds), *Lexikon der Ägyptologie* V (Wiesbaden: Harrassowitz), pp. 782-90.

McDowell, A.G., 1999, *Village Life in Ancient Egypt: Laundry Lists and Love Songs* (Oxford: Oxford University Press).

McLuhan, M., 1966, *Understanding Media: The Extensions of Man* (New York: McGraw-Hill).

Meeks, Dimitri, and Christine Favard-Meeks, 1997, *Daily Life of the Egyptian Gods,* trans. G.M. Goshgarian (London: John Murray).

Meskell, L., 1999, *Archaeologies of Social Life* (Oxford: Blackwell).

Mills, S., 2000, 'An Approach for Integrating Multisensory Data: The Examples of Sesklo and the Teleorman Valley' in C. Buck et al. (eds), *UK Chapter of Computer Applications and Quantitative Methods in Archaeology: Proceedings of the Fourth Meeting, Cardiff University, 27 and 28 February 1999* (Oxford: British Archaeological Reports), pp. 27-37.

Mlekuz, D., 2002, 'Listening to the Landscapes: Modelling Past Soundscapes within GIS', pres. Annual Conference of the Theoretical Archaeology Group, Manchester, UK.

Mond, R. and O. Myers, 1934a, *The Bucheum* I (London: Egypt Exploration Society).

———, 1934b, *The Bucheum* II (London: Egypt Exploration Society).

———, 1934c, *The Bucheum* III (London: Egypt Exploration Society).

Montet, P., 1964, 'Le rituel de fondation des temples Égyptiens', *Kêmi* 17, pp. 74-100.

Moreno, J.L., 1963, *Introduction to Psychodrama* (New York: Beacon House).

Moret, A., 1902, *Le rituel du culte divine journalier en Égypte* (Genève: Slatkine, repr. 1988).

Morkot, R.G., 2000, *The Black Pharaohs: Egypt's Nubian Rulers* (London: Rubicon).

Murnane, W., 1980, 'Opetfest' in W. Helck and E. Otto (eds), *Lexikon der Ägyptologie* IV (Wiesbaden: Harrassowitz), pp. 574-9.

Myśliwiec, C., 2000, *The Twilight of Ancient Egypt,* trans. D. Lorton (Ithaca, NY: Cornell University Press).

Naguib, Saphinaz-Amal, 1990, *Le clergé féminin d'Amon Thébain à la 21e Dynastie* (Louvain: Peeters).

———, 1990a, 'The Festivals of Opet and Abul Haggag. Survival of an Ancient Tradition?', *Temenos* 26, pp. 67-84.

Nagy, G., 1996, *Homeric Questions* (Austin: University of Texas Press).

Naville, E., 1892, *The Festival Hall of Osorkon II in the Great Temple of Bubastis* (London: Egypt Exploration Fund).

Nelson, Harold H., 1949a, 'Certain Reliefs at Karnak and Medinet Habu and the Ritual of Amenophis I', *Journal of Near Eastern Studies* 8, pp. 201-32, 310-45.

———, 1949b, 'The Rite of "Bringing the Foot" as portrayed in Temple Reliefs', *Journal of Egyptian Archeology* 35, pp. 82-6.

Ockinga, B., 1984, *Die Gottebenbildlichkeit im alten Ägypten und im alten Testament* (Wiesbaden: Harrassowitz).

O'Connor, David, 1985, 'The "Cenotaphs" of the Middle Kingdom at Abydos' in *Mélanges Gamal Eddin Mokhtar* II (Cairo: Institut Français d'archéologie orientale), pp. 161-77.

———, 1989, 'New Funerary Enclosures (*Talbezirke*) of the Early Dynastic Period at Abydos', *Journal of the American Research Center in Egypt* 26, pp. 51-86.

———, 1992, 'The Status of Early Temples' in Renée Friedman and Barbara

Bibliography

Adams (eds), *The Followers of Horus: Studies Dedicated to Michael Allen Hoffman* (Oxford: Oxbow Books).

———, 1995, 'The Earliest Royal Boat Graves', *Egyptian Archaeology* 6 pp. 3-7.

O'Connor, David and David P. Silverman (eds), 1995, *Ancient Egyptian Kingship* (New York, Leiden and Köln: Brill Academic Publishers).

Oldfather, C.H., 1933, *Diodorus of Sicily* I (London: Heinemann).

O'Neill, John P. (ed.), 1999, *Egyptian Art in the Age of the Pyramids* (New York: Metropolitan Museum of Art).

Onstine, Suzanne, 2000, 'The Role of the Chantress (ŠMcYT) in Ancient Egypt', PhD diss. (unpub.), University of Toronto.

Otto, Eberhard, 1960, *Das Ägyptische Mundöffnungsritual* (Wiesbaden: Harrassowitz).

———, 1966, *Osiris und Amun: Kult und heilige Stätten* (Munich: Hirmer).

Parker, Richard. A., 1962, *A Saite Oracle Papyrus from Thebes in the Brooklyn Museum (Papyrus Brooklyn 47.218.3)* (Providence: Brown University Press).

Parker, Richard A., J. Leclant and J-C. Goyon, 1979, *The Edifice of Taharqa by the Sacred Lake of Karnak* (Providence: Brown University Press).

Parker Pearson, M., and Ramilisonina, 1998, 'Stonehenge for the Ancestors: The Stones Pass on the Message', *Antiquity* 72, pp. 308-26.

Parkinson, R.B., 2000, '*Sinuhe* Speaks Again', *Egyptian Archaeology* 16, p. 44.

———, 2002, *Poetry and Culture in Middle Kingdom Egypt: A Dark Side to Perfection* (London: Continuum International).

———, 2003, 'Textes ou poèmes? Quelques perspectives nouvelles sur les textes littéraires du Moyen Empire', *Egypte Afrique & Orient* 31, pp. 41-52.

Pearson, Mike and Michael Shanks, 2001, *Theatre/Archaeology* (London: Routledge).

Peet, E.T., 1930, *The Great Tomb Robberies of the Twentieth Egyptian Dynasty* (Oxford: Clarendon Press).

Petrie, W.M.F., 1890, *Kahun, Gurob and Hawara* (London: Kegan Paul, Trench, Trübner).

———, 1902, *Abydos* I (London: Egypt Exploration Fund).

———, 1915, *Heliopolis, Kafr Ammar and Shurafa* (London: Quaritch).

Piccione, Peter, 2000, *The Victory of Horus: A Sacred Drama of Ancient Egypt* http://www.cofc.edu /~piccione/hist270/horus/horus.html.

Pickard-Cambridge, A., 1968, *The Dramatic Festivals of Athens*, 2nd rev. edn, J. Gould and D.M. Lewis (eds) (Oxford: Clarendon Press).

Pietschmann, R., 1894, 'Apis' in G. Wissowa (ed.), *Paulys Real-Encyclopädie der Classischen Altertumswissenschaft* I (Stuttgart: Metzlerscher Verlag).

Pinch, Geraldine, 1993, *Votive Offerings to Hathor* (Oxford: Griffith Institute).

Poethke. G., 1972, 'Epagomenen' in W. Helck and E. Otto (eds), *Lexikon der Ägyptologie* I (Wiesbaden: Harrassowitz), pp. 1231-2.

Porten, B., 1996, *The Elephantine Papyri in English* (Leiden: Brill Academic Publishers).

Posener, G., 1956, *Littérature et politique dans l'Égypte de la XIIᵉ dynastie* (Paris: Champion).

Posener-Kriéger, P., 1976, *Les archives du temple funéraire de Néferirkare-Kakai, les papyrus d'Abousir: Traduction et Commentaire* (Cairo: Institut Français d'archéologie orientale).

Postman, N., 1985, *Amusing Ourselves to Death: Public Discourse in the Age of Show Business* (New York: Viking Books).

Pouls-Wegner, Mary-Ann, 2002, 'The Cult of Osiris in Abydos: An Archaeological

Investigation of the Development of an Ancient Egyptian Sacred Center during the Eighteenth Dynasty', PhD diss., University of Pennsylvania.

Pusch, E.B., 1984, 'Senet' in W. Helck and W. Westndorf (eds), *Lexikon der Ägyptologie* V (Wiesbaden: Harrassowitz), pp. 851-5.

Quack, J.F., 1994, *Die Lehres des Ani: Ein neuägyptischer Wiesheitext in seinem Kulturellen Umfeld* (Göttingen: Vandenhoeck und Ruprecht).

Quaegebeur, J., 1987, *Le roman démotique et gréco-égyptien* (Liège: Université de Liège).

Quibell, J.E., 1898, *The Ramesseum and the Tomb of Ptah-hetep* (London: Quaritch).

———, 1900, *Hierakonpolis* I (London: Egyptian Research Account).

Quibell, J.E. and F.W. Green, 1902, *Hierakonpolis* II (London: Egyptian Research Account).

Quirke, Stephen, 1991, ' "Townsmen" in the Middle Kingdom', *Zeitschrift für Ägyptische Sprache* 118, pp. 141-9.

——— (ed.), 1997, *The Temple in Ancient Egypt: New Discoveries and Recent Research* (London: British Museum).

Ramsay, G.G. (trans.), 1928, *Juvenal and Persius* (London: Heinemann).

Randall-McIver, D. and A. Mace, 1902, *El Amrah and Abydos* (London: Egypt Exploration Fund).

Raven, M., 1978-9, 'Papyrus Sheaths and Ptah-Sokar-Osiris Figures', *Oudheidkundige Medede e uit het Rijksmuseum van Oudheden te Leiden* 59-60, pp. 252-96.

———, 1982, 'Corn-mummies', *Oudheidkundige Medede e uit het Rijksmuseum van Oudheden te Leiden* 63, pp. 7-38.

Ray, J.D., 1972, 'The House of Osarapis' in P. Ucko, R. Tringham and G.W. Dimbleby (eds), *Man, Settlement and Urbanism* (Cambridge, MA: Schenkman).

———, 1976, *The Archive of Hor* (London: Egypt Exploration Society).

Redford, Donald B., 1984, *Akhenaten: The Heretic King* (Princeton: Princeton University Press).

———, 1986, *Pharaonic King-Lists, Annals and Day Books* (Toronto: Benben Publications).

———, 1992, *Egypt, Canaan and Israel in Ancient Times* (Princeton: Princeton University Press).

———, 1999, 'The Beginning of the Heresy' in R. Freed, Y. Markowitz and S. D'Auria (eds), *Pharaohs of the Sun* (Boston: Museum of Fine Arts), pp. 50-9.

Reeves, N., 1990, *The Complete Tutankhamun* (London: Thames and Hudson).

———, 2000, *Ancient Egypt: The Great Discoveries* (London: Thames and Hudson).

Reymond, E.A.E., 1981, *From the Records of a Priestly Family from Memphis* (Wiesbaden: Harrassowitz).

Rice, E.E., 1983, *The Grand Procession of Ptolemy Philadelphus* (Oxford: Oxford University Press).

Richards, C., 1993, 'Monumental Choreography: Architecture and Spatial Representation in Late Neolithic Orkney' in C. Tilley (ed.), *Interpretive Archaeology* (London: Berg), pp. 143-78.

Richards, Janet E., 1999, 'Conceptual Landscapes in the Egyptian Nile Valley' in Wendy Ashmore and A. Bernard Knapp (eds), *Archaeologies of Landscape: Contemporary Perspectives* (Oxford: Blackwell), pp. 83-100.

Ricke, Herbert, 1935, 'Der "Hohe Sand" in Heliopolis', *Zeitschrift für Ägyptische Sprache* 71, pp. 107-11.

———, 1944, *Beiträge zur Ägyptischen Bauforschung und Altertumskunde* IV:

Bibliography

Bemerkungen zur Ägyptischen Baukunst des Alten Reiches I (Zurich: Borchardt Institut).

Riesman, D., 1969, *The Lonely Crowd* (New Haven: Yale University Press).

Ritner, Robert K., 1993, *The Mechanics of Ancient Egyptian Magical Practice* (Chicago: Oriental Institute).

Robbins, D., 1991, *The Work of Pierre Bourdieu: Recognizing Society* (Boulder, CO: Westview Press).

Roberts, Alison, 1995, *Hathor Rising: The Serpent Power in Ancient Egypt* (Totnes, UK: Northgate).

Ross, A., 1989, *No Respect: Intellectuals and Popular Culture* (New York: Routledge).

Roth, Ann Macy, 1991, *Egyptian Phyles in the Old Kingdom: The Evolution of a System of Social Organization* (Chicago: Oriental Institute).

———, 1993, 'Social Change in the Fourth Dynasty: The Spatial Organization of Pyramids, Tombs and Cemeteries', *Journal of the American Research Center in Egypt* 30, pp. 35-55.

Sadek, A.I., 1987, *Popular Religion in Egypt during the New Kingdom* (Hildesheim: Gerstenberg).

Salih, S., 2002, *Judith Butler* (London: Routledge).

Sandison, A.T., 1972, 'Balsamierung' in W. Helck and E. Otto (eds), *Lexikon der Ägyptologie* I (Wiesbaden: Harrassowitz), pp. 610-14.

Sauneron, S., 1952, *Rituel d'embaument* (Cairo: Imprimerie nationale).

———, 1962, *Les fêtes religieuses d'Esna aux derniers siècles du paganisme* (Cairo: Institut Français d'archéologie orientale).

———, 2000, *The Priests of Ancient Egypt*, trans. D. Lorton (Ithaca, NY: Cornell University Press).

Scandone-Matthiae, G., 1985, 'La dea e il gioiello: simbologia religiosa nella famiglia reale femminile della XII Dinastia', *La parola del passato* 224, pp. 321-37.

Schäfer, H., 1902, 'Ein Bruchstück altägyptischer Annalen', *Abhandlung der Preußischen Akademie der Wissenschaften* (Berlin: Königlich Akademie der Wissenschaften).

———, 1964, *Die Mysterien des Osiris in Abydos unter König Sesostris III* (Hildesheim: Olms).

———, 1986, *Principles of Egyptian Art*, trans. J. Baines (Oxford: Griffith Institute).

Schechner, Richard, 1988, *Performance Theory*, rev. ed. (New York: Routledge).

Schlögl, H.A., 1980, *Der Gott Tatenen* (Göttingen: Vandenhoeck und Ruprecht).

Schott, S., 1952, *Das schöne Fest von Wüstentale* (Wiesbaden: Akademie der Wissenschaften der Literatur).

Sélincourt, A. de (trans.), 1972, *Herodotus: The Histories*, rev. ed. J. Marincola (ed.) (London: Penguin Classics).

Serrano, Alejandro Jiménez, 2002, *Royal Festivals in the Late Predynastic Period and the First Dynasty* (Oxford: British Archaeological Reports).

Sethe, Kurt, 1928, *Dramatische Texte zu Altägyptischen Mysterienspielen* (Leipzig: Hinrichs).

Settgast, Jürgen, 1963, *Untersuchungen zu altägyptischen Bestattungsdarstellungen* (Glückstadt: J.J. Augustin).

Shafer, Byron, (ed), 1991, *Religion in Ancient Egypt* (Ithaca, NY: Cornell University Press).

Shanks, M., and C. Tilley, 1987, *Re-constructing Archaeology* (Cambridge: Cambridge University Press).

Simpson, W.K., 1974, *The Terrace of the Great God at Abydos* (New Haven: Peabody Museum).

——, 1976, *The Mastabas of Qar and Idu* (Boston: Museum of Fine Arts).

——, 1984, 'Sinuhe' in W. Helck and E. Otto (eds), *Lexikon der Ägyptologie* V (Wiesbaden: Harrassowitz), pp. 950-6.

Smith, H.S., 1974, *A Visit to Ancient Egypt* (Warminster: Aris and Phillips).

——, 1984, 'Saqqara, Late Period' in W. Helck and E. Otto (eds), *Lexikon der Ägyptologie* V (Wiesbaden: Harrassowitz), pp. 412-28.

Smith, W. Stevenson, 1981, *The Art and Architecture of Ancient Egypt*, rev. edn W.K. Simpson (ed.) (Harmondsworth, UK: Penguin).

Spalinger, A.J., 1996, *The Private Feast Lists of Ancient Egypt* (Wiesbaden: Harrassowitz).

Spencer, Jeffrey (ed.), 1996, *Aspects of Early Egypt* (London: British Museum).

Spencer, P., 1984, *The Egyptian Temple: A Lexicographical Study* (London: Kegan Paul).

——, 2003, 'Dance in Ancient Egypt', *Near Eastern Archaeology* 68(3), pp. 111-21.

Spiegel, J., 1960, *Das Auferstehungritual der Unas Pyramid* (Wiesbaden: Harrassowitz).

Stadelmann, R., 1997, 'The Development of the Pyramid Temple in the 4th Dynasty' in Stephen Quirke (ed.), *The Temple in Ancient Egypt: New Discoveries and Recent Research* (London: British Museum), pp. 1-18.

Strudwick, Nigel, 1985, *The Administration of Egypt in the Old Kingdom* (London: Kegan Paul).

Szpakowska, Kasia, 2003, *Behind Closed Eyes: Dreams and Nightmares in Ancient Egypt* (Swansea: Classical Press of Wales).

Teeter, E., 1993, 'Female Musicians in Pharaonic Egypt' in K. Marshall, *Rediscovering the Muses: Women's Musical Traditions* (Boston: Northeastern University Press), pp. 68-91.

Te Velde, H., 1967, *Seth, God of Confusion* (Leiden: Brill Academic Publishers).

Thomas, J. (ed.), 2000, *Interpretive Archaeology: A Reader* (London: Leicester University Press).

——, 2000a, 'The Polarities of Post-Processual Archaeology' in *Interpretive Archaeology: A Reader* (London: Leicester University Press), pp. 1-18.

Thompson, D.J., 1988, *Memphis under the Ptolemies* (Princeton: Princeton University Press).

Tooley, Angela J., 1996, 'Osiris Bricks', *Journal of Egyptian Archaeology* 82, pp. 167-79.

Trigger, B.G., B.J. Kemp, David O'Connor and A.B. Lloyd, 1983, *Social History of Egypt* (Cambridge: Cambridge University Press).

Turner, V., 1974, *Dramas, Fields and Metaphors* (Ithaca, NY: Cornell University Press).

Ucko, P., R. Tringham and G.W. Dimbleby (eds), 1972, *Man, Settlement and Urbanism* (Cambridge, MA: Schenkman).

Vandier, J., 1936, *La famine dans l'Égypt ancienne* (Cairo: Institut Français d'archéologie orientale).

——, 1952, *Manuel d'archéologie Égyptienne* I: *Les Époques de formation: Les premières Dynasties* (Paris: Picard).

Bibliography

——, 1964, *Manuel d'archéologie Égyptienne* IV: *Bas-reliefs et peintures: Scènes de la vie quotidienne* (Paris: Picard).

Vercoutter, J., 1962, *Texts biographiques du Sérapéum de Memphis* (Paris: Champion).

——, 1972, 'Apis' in W. Helck and E. Otto (eds), *Lexikon der Ägyptologie* I (Wiesbaden: Harrassowitz), pp. 338-50.

Varille, A., 1942, 'L'autel de Ptolémée III à Médamoud', *Bulletin de l'Institut Français d'archéologie orientale du Caire* 41, pp. 39-42.

Vila, André, 1963, 'Un dépot de textes d'envoutement au Moyen Empire', *Journal des Savants* pp. 135-60.

Vinson, S., 2000, 'Tragedy, Comedy and Reconciliation in the First Tale of Setne Khamwas?' pres. at Annual Meeting of the American Research Center in Egypt, Berkeley, CA.

Von Bissing, F.W., 1923, *Das Re-Heiligtum des Königs Ne-user-Re* II: *Die kleine Festdarstellung* (Leipzig: Hinrichs).

——, 1928, *Das Re-Heiligtum des Königs Ne-user-Re* III: *Die große Festdarstellung* (Leipzig: Hinrichs).

Vos, R.L., 1993, *The Apis Embalming Ritual* (Louvain: Peeters).

Walker, Susan and Peter Higgs, 2001, *Cleopatra of Egypt: From History to Myth* (Princeton: Princeton University Press).

Watterson, Barbara, 1998, *The House of Horus at Edfu* (Stroud, UK: Tempus).

Wendorf, Fred, and Romauld Schild, 1980, *Prehistory of the Eastern Sahara* (New York: Academic Press).

Westermann, W.L., 1924, 'The Castanet Dancers of Arsinoe', *Journal of Egyptian Archaeology* 10, pp. 134-44.

Wilkinson, Toby A.H., 1996, *State Formation in Egypt: Chronology and Society* (Oxford: British Archaeological Reports).

——, 1999, *Early Dynastic Egypt* (London: Routledge).

——, 2003, *Genesis of the Pharaohs* (London: Thames and Hudson).

Witt, R.E., 1971, *Isis in the Graeco-Roman World* (London: Thames and Hudson).

Wobst, H.M., 1978, 'The Archaeo-ethnology of Hunter-gatherers or the Tyranny of the Ethnographic Record in Archaeology', *American Antiquity* 113, pp. 303-9.

Wolinsky, A., 1986, 'Ancient Egyptian Ceremonial Masks', *Discussions in Egyptology* 6, pp. 47-53.

Index

Abbott Papyrus, 92
Abul Haggag, 134
Abusir Papyri, 78
Abydos, 38; festivals at, 29, 55-9; Mystery of Osiris at, 55-9, 78, 79, 100, 102; Osiris complex at, 20, 104; royal tombs at, 18, 31; temples at, 33, 36, 41, 56, 75
Abydos formula, 56, 58
acacias, 39-40
actors, 45; children as, 125; costumes of, 70, 131-2, 140; in Greek theatre, 128; physically unusual, 112, 113-14, 145-6, 151, 152; in Sed Festival, 34, 85; at York University, 147. *See also specific roles and events*
agon, 128
Akhenaten (Amenhotep IV), 81-2, 90; cultic acts under, 17, 21, 76-7; and Sed Festival, 86-7
Akhetaten, 87
Akh-menu temple, 102
Alexander of Macedon, 23, 93, 128
Alexandria, 129
Alliot, Maurice, 115
altars, 130-1
Altenmüller, Hartwig, 43
Althusser, Louis, 9, 12
Amarna, 77, 90
Amarna Period, 73
Amenemhet I, 50, 84
Amenhotep I, 74, 91, 153
Amenhotep III, 89-90, 118; and Sed Festival, 84-6; structures erected by, 77, 81, 83, 84, 86
Amenhotep IV. *See* Akhenaten
Amenhotep (son of Hapu), 84, 85
Amenmose, 85
Amesysia, 131
Amun: cult of, 68, 73-4, 75-6; God's Wife of, 76, 93, 123; kiosk of, 102; in Opet Festival, 80-2; oracle of, 82, 84, 123-4; processional festivals of, 77, 78-9, 80-3. *See also* Amun, temple of
Amun, temple of (Karnak), 21, 88, 93, 108, 123; rituals at, 22, 23, 104; staff of, 76, 145; structures of, 83, 124
Amun-Re, 117, 123
ancestor rituals, 73, 74-7, 153
Ani, Wisdom of, 82

animals: cults of, 22-3, 126; embalming of, 109-12, 126. *See also specific animals*
Antefoker, 63
anthropology, 5, 14-15
Antinoopolis, 129
Antinous, 130
Antiochus IV, 127
Anubis, 52, 62, 101, 133
Apep, 89, 104, 112, 116
Apis: as oracle, 109, 124; popularity of, 108, 113; tomb of (Memphis), 108, 109. *See also* Apis Bull
Apis Bull, Running of the, 27, 29, 35, 103
Apis Bull cult (Memphis), 22, 27, 32, 108-14, 126; embalming ritual, 23, 109-12; funeral, 109-13, 131, 152, 154; mourners at, 109-10, 111, 112; in York University re-presentation, 143-4
Apophis. *See* Apep
Appearance of the King of Upper and Lower Egypt, 26-7, 35
archaeology, 3-4, 5-6, 9-10; performance and, 1-2, 10, 146
Archaic Period, 18, 101; labels from, 26, 29, 31, 43; Sed Festival in, 31, 65
archery, 90
Arnold, Dieter, 36
Artaud, Antonin, 6
Arts de faire (de Certeau), 7-8
asceticism, 109-10
Assyrians, 22, 93
Aten, 76-7, 86-7
Atfih, 126
Athena, 128
Athens, 127-8
Atum, 55
audience, 2, 131, 136; in Egypt, 52, 61, 77, 137, 154-5; at Mystery of Osiris, 103; at Opet Festival, 81; at processional festivals, 80, 83, 84; at Sed Festival, 87; for sports, 90; at York University, 142. *See also rekhyt*
Austin, J.L., 8-9

baboons, 29, 30, 32, 126
Bacchae (Euripides), 129
Baines, John, 12-13
barques. *See* boats

174

179

Index

Salt Papyrus 825, 99-100, 106, 107, 108, 132, 154
Sankhkare, 58
Saqqara, 29-33, 39, 41-2, 44
Sat-Hathor, 55
Sat-Hathor-Iunet, 55
satyrs, 128
Sauneron, Serge, 121, 125, 132
Saussure, Ferdinand de, 8
Schama, Simon, 1, 2, 10
Schechner, Richard, 30, 31-2, 33, 44, 52, 78
Scorpion macehead, 32
Scott, Ridley, 4
Scribe of the God's Book, 103, 151
Sed, 28, 56
Sed Festival, 27-35, 44, 84-8; actors in, 34, 85; in Archaic Period, 31, 65; audience of, 31, 32; boats in, 86; changes to, 87-8; dancers at, 89; Djed pillar in, 51, 85-6; elite participation in, 28, 31, 32, 44, 85; as funerary ceremony, 34-5; in later periods, 122-3; in New Kingdom, 51, 84-8; New Year rites in, 99; Opening of the Mouth rite compared to, 72; Ramesseum Dramatic Papyrus compared to, 51, 86; repetition in, 152; re-presentation of, 30-1; royal participation in, 86-8; sports at, 85; structures for, 29-30, 31-3, 34-5
semeru. See friends
Sefkhet Abwy, 88
sekhenu ankh, 50
Sekhmet, 98, 99, 119, 120, 121
self-regeneration, 41, 43, 106
sem priest, 64, 133, 154; in Mystery of Osiris, 57, 106, 107; in Opening of the Mouth rite, 58, 69, 70-2
senet, 41, 43
Senet (wife of Antefoker), 63-4
sen netcheru, 43
Senwosret I, 50, 52, 53, 58, 63, 78
Senwosret II, 62
Senwosret III, 76
Serapis, 109, 133
serdab, 41
Serrano, Alejandro J., 35
servitors, 99, 154
Seth, 50, 121; festival of, 127; Horus and, 89, 95-6, 114-15; and Osiris, 105, 111, 120-1
Sethe, Kurt, 48-9, 95, 137
Seti I, 69
Setne Khamwas cycle, 127
Settgast, Jurgen, 65-6
Setting Up of the Potter's Wheel, Festival of (Esna), 119-20, 125, 132-3
Shabaka, 93, 97, 98
Shabaka Stone, 47-8, 95-8, 135
shabtis, 73

shemayt, 76, 89, 91
Shanks, Michael, 10
Shenty(t), 106
shrines, 33-4, 64-5, 73, 102, 117; as birth houses, 118-19; carriers of (*pastaphoroi*), 126; local, 155. *See also* kiosks; *per wer*
Shu, 120, 132, 154
Simpson, William Kelly, 58
singers, 76, 80, 89, 99, 154. *See also* hymns
Sinuhe, 50, 53-4, 55, 63-4
sistrum, 54, 64, 76, 77, 119
sites, 11; ceremonial, 22-3, 51, 151; for performance, 127-8, 145, 153; performing of, 146-8; public, 90, 124; of ritual, 41-2; sacred, 64-5, 73, 93
Skansen, 3
skene, 127, 128
Smashing the Red Pots rite, 52, 60
Sneferu, 45
social science, 5, 11-12
Sokar: Bringing In of, 104; figures of, 105-6, 107-8; house of, 102; procession of, 102, 105, 107, 133, 136, 142, 152. *See also* Sokar Festival; Sokar-Osiris
Sokar Festival (Memphis), 26, 35, 77-80, 86, 133; Osiris in, 79, 86, 100, 101
Sokar-Osiris, 79, 101-2, 105-6, 107-8
solar court. *See maru*
'Songs of Isis and Nepthys', 104
soundscapes, 148
southern Opet temple, 77, 80-3, 102, 118, 134. *See also* Opet Festival
space (performance), 10, 145. *See also* sites; structures
speech, 6-7, 8-9. *See also* language; speech acts
speech acts, 9-10, 149; as effective utterances, 40, 43, 149, 152; performative, 2, 8-9
sphinxes, 83, 124
sports, 85, 89-90, 130, 153; as ritual, 88-9, 122
Stadelmann, Rainer, 36
'stars,' 45
statues: funerary (of deceased), 37, 41, 44; Tekenu, 64, 65. *See also* cultic ritual; Mystery of Osiris; Opening of the Mouth rite
Step Pyramid complex (Saqqara), 29-33, 39, 41-2, 44
stick-fighting, 89
Striking of the Ball rite, 88-9, 122
structures, 11; for festivals, 44, 123; in funerary complexes, 36-7, 43-4; for Sed Festival, 29-30, 31-3, 34-5. *See also specific structures*
students, 138-9, 140-1, 147
Swarney, Paul, 138, 139